Pedro de Castañeda, et al.

The JOURNEY OF CORONADO

TRANSLATED AND EDITED BY
George Parker Winship
INTRODUCTION AND ADDITIONAL NOTES
by Frederick Webb Hodge

DOVER PUBLICATIONS, INC.
New York

Published in Canada by General Publishing Company, Ltd., 30 Lesmill Road, Don Mills, Toronto, Ontario.

Published in the United Kingdom by Constable and Company, Ltd., 10 Orange Street, London WC2H 7EG.

This Dover edition, first published in 1990, is an unabridged republication of the work published in an edition of 550 copies by The Grabhorn Press, San Francisco, in 1933 under the title *The Journey of Francisco Vazquez De Coronado 1540–1542*. For the 1933 edition, the decorative initials were drawn by Fred Glauser and the illustrations by Arvilla Parker. Initials, typographic ornaments and occasional paragraphs of text which were printed in orange in the 1933 edition are printed here in black.

Manufactured in the United States of America
Dover Publications, Inc.
31 East 2nd Street
Mineola, N.Y. 11501

Library of Congress Cataloging-in-Publication Data

The journey of Coronado / Pedro de Casteñeda, et al; translated and edited by George Parker Winship ; introduction and additional notes by Frederick Webb Hodge.
     p.   cm.
    Reprint. Originally published: San Francisco : The Grabhorn Press, 1933.
    ISBN 0-486-26308-8
    1. Southwest, New—Description and travel. 2. Southwest, New—Discovery and
exploration. 3. Vázquez de Coronado, Francisco, 1510-1549—Journeys—Southwest, New. I. Castañeda de Nágera, Pedro de, 16th cent. II. Winship, George   Parker,
1871–1952.
  E125.V3J68   1990
  917.904′1—dc20   90-32798
                                                     CIP

TRANSLATOR'S PREFACE
by George Parker Winship

HE narratives printed in the present volume tell the story of one of the most remarkable explorations recorded in the annals of American history. Seventy-five years before the English succeeded in establishing themselves on the northeastern coast of North America, a band of Spaniards, starting from what was already a populous and flourishing colony at the City of Mexico, penetrated the opposite extreme of the continent, and explored thoroughly a region as extensive as the coast line of the United States from Maine to Georgia.

The accounts of their experiences printed herewith were all written by members of the expedition. With two exceptions they were written during the journey, and were the official reports prepared by the general and sent to the viceroy in Mexico or the emperor-king in Spain, or by the lieutenants in charge of special explorations. The first and principal narrative was written for the purpose of providing a history of the expedition, by one of the common soldiers some time after his return to Mexico, when he apparently felt there was danger that posterity would forget the deeds of those with whom he had toiled and suffered in the vain search for something which would reward their costly undertaking. All that is known of the author, Pedro Castañeda, beyond what he relates in this narrative, is that he was a native of the Biscayan town of Najera in northern Spain, who had established himself in the Spanish outpost at Culiacan, in northwestern Mexico, at the time Coronado organized his expedition, and that he was the father of eight surviving children, who, with their mother, presented in 1554 a claim against the Mexican treasury, on account of the father's exploits. The Spanish text of Castañeda's history is preserved in the Lenox Library, now absorbed into the New York Public Library. It is printed, together with the translations reprinted herewith, in the Fourteenth Annual Report of the United States Bureau of Ethnology, Washington, D. C., 1896, a volume which has long been out of print. In the present book many passages in these translations have been revised and corrected. The editor is under obligations to Mr. F. W. Hodge of the

Smithsonian Institution, Mr. W. M. Tipton of Santa Fé, Mr. Charles F. Lummis of Los Angeles, and Mr. Ripley Hitchcock and Mr. F. S. Dellenbaugh of New York, for suggestions and assistance in regard to these improvements in the text.

In February, 1540, the army whose fortunes are recounted in these narratives assembled at Compostela, on the Pacific Coast west of Mexico City. When it passed in review before the viceroy Mendoza, who had provided the funds and equipment, the general in command, Francisco Vazquez de Coronado, rode at the head of some two hundred and fifty horsemen and seventy Spanish foot soldiers armed with crossbows and harquebuses. Besides these there were three hundred or more native allies, and upward of a thousand negro and Indian servants and followers, to lead the spare hoses, drive the pack mules, carry the extra luggage, and herd the droves of oxen and cows, sheep and swine.

The expedition started on February 23d, and a month later, on Easter day, it entered Culiacan, then the northwestern out-post of European civilization, half way up the mainland coast of the Gulf of California. Here Coronado reorganized his force and, toward the end of April, he started northward into the unknown country with a picked force of two hundred men equipped for rapid marching, leaving the rest to follow at the slower pace of the pack trains and the four-footed food supplies. Following the river courses up stream, the advance party was soon deep in the mountains. For two long months they persistently pushed ahead, the inhospitable country steadily growing worse. Eventually other streams showed them the way out on to a level district crossed by well-worn trails which led them toward the "Seven Cities of Cibola." These were the goal of whose fame they had heard from the Franciscan friar, Marcos de Niza, who had viewed them from a distant hilltop two years previously, and who now accompanied the expedition as guide and chaplain.

It was perhaps on July 4th, 1540, that Coronado drew up his force in front of the first of the "Seven Cities," and after a sharp fight forced his way into the stronghold, the stone and adobe-built pueblo of Hawikuh, whose ruins can still be traced on a low hillock a few miles southwest of the village now occupied by the New Mexican Zuñi Indians. Here the Europeans camped for several weeks, seeking rest, refreshment, and news of the land. A small party was sent off toward the northwest, where another group of seven villages was found in the region still occupied by the descen-

dants of the people whom the Spaniards visited, the Moqui tribes of
Tusayan. As a result of the information secured here, another party journeyed westward until its progress was stopped by the Grand Cañon of the
Colorado, then seen for the first time by Europeans. Explorations were also
made toward the east, where the river villages along the Rio Grande were
found to be larger and better stocked with food supplies than the settlements at Cíbola-Zuñi. Coronado therefore moved his headquarters to the
largest of these river towns, Tiguex, near the modern Bernalillo, a short distance north of Albuquerque. Here, as the winter of 1540-41 was setting
in, he was rejoined by the main body of the army, which had laboriously
followed the trail of its general through the mountains and across the desert.

In one of the river villages Coronado found an Indian slave who said he
was a native of Quivira, which he described as a rich and populous place far
away in the east. Acting upon this information, with the Indian as a guide,
Coronado started on April 23d, 1541, with his whole army to march to
Quivira. From Cicuye or Pecos, whose ruins can still be seen by the travel-
ler from the Atchison, Topeka and Santa Fé trains, the guide seems to have
led the white men down the Pecos River until they were out of the mountains, and on to the vast plains where they soon met the countless herds of
bison or "humpbacked oxen." For five weeks the Europeans plodded on-
ward across what is now known as the "Staked Plains," following a generally easterly direction.

They had probably crossed the upper branches of the Colorado River of
Texas and reached the head waters of the Nueces, when Coronado became
convinced that his guide was endeavoring to lose him in this limitless
expanse of rolling prairie. The food supplies were beginning to run low,
and so the army was ordered to return to the villages on the Rio Grande.
Some of the natives of the plains, met with on the march, had answered
the questions about Quivira by pointing toward the north. That no chance
might be left untried, the general selected thirty of the freshest and best-
mounted of his men to accompany him in a search in that direction. For
forty-two days they followed the compass needle, whose variation probably
took them about three degrees west of a true northward course. At last
their guides told them that they had reached Quivira, when they were not
far from Great Bend on the Arkansas River, whose course they had followed
from the neighborhood of Dodge City. It was a village of Wichita Indian
tepees.

Coronado spent a month in exploring the surrounding country, moving his camp to a larger village further north, and sending out messengers and reconnoitering parties in all directions. Having assured himself that there was nothing to reward his search, he returned to the main body of his army, the Quiviran guides leading him by a much shorter route, along the line of the famous Santa Fé trail, to the Rio Grande. Every clew which promised anything of value to the Spaniards had been followed to its utmost, without revealing anything which they desired. In the spring of 1542 Coronado started back with his men to Cíbola-Zuñi, through the rough mountain passages to the Gulf of California, and so on down to the City of Mexico, where he arrived in the early autumn, "very sad and very weary, completely worn out and shame-faced." He had failed to find any of the things for which he went in search. But he had added to the world as known to Europeans an extent of country bounded on the west by the Colorado River from its mouth to the Grand Cañon, on the east by the boundless prairies, and stretching northward to the upper waters of the Rio Grande and the southern boundary of Nebraska.

GEORGE PARKER WINSHIP.

New York, 1904.

CONTENTS

INTRODUCTION
by Frederick Webb Hodge

PARADOXICAL though it may seem, the so-called Seven Cities of Cíbola, which became the lure of the expedition of Francisco Vásquez de Coronado in 1540-42, had their origin in a myth of eight centuries earlier. In brief, the story runs thus:

In 1474 the Florentine cosmographer Toscanelli mentioned in a letter to a friend in the service of the king of Portugal, "the island Antillia, which you call the seven cities," a statement repeated on the Behaim globe of 1492, on which is appended a long inscription to the effect that in the year 734, when Spain had been won by the Moors, the island of "Antilia," called "Septe citate," was inhabited by an archbishop from Porto in Portugal, with six other bishops and other Christians, men and women, who with their cattle and belongings had sailed thence from Spain; that in the year 1414 a Spanish ship neared it without danger. Again, Ferdinand Columbus (1488-1539), son of Christopher, wrote that some Portuguese cartographers had located "Antilla" not more than two hundred leagues due west from the Canaries and Azores, "which they conclude to be certainly the island of the seven cities, peopled by the Portuguese at the time that Spain was conquered by the Moors in the year 714," when the seven bishops with their people sailed to this island, where each of them built a city, and that their people might not think of returning to Spain, they burned the ships and everything else necessary for sailing. A concomitant tale is to the effect that about the year 1430 a Portuguese ship was driven by storm to the island Antilla, but found its way back to Portugal after it was learned that the sand gathered on the island for the cook-room was a third part pure gold! With such a background of legend and mystery, whatever the grain of fact in which it may have had its origin, the Island of the Seven Cities became identified with some supposed patch of land far out in the Atlantic, sometimes with the Island of Brazil, more often with Antilia; hence there is little wonder that, as they were not found in the Antilles, the Seven Cities were given place on the maps of mainland America soon after the discovery and were shifted about according to the fancy and the uncertainty of the cartographers of the period, their insular location, however, not being neglected in the meantime. Finally the name disappeared from the maps toward the close of the sixteenth century by reason of the discoveries of Fray Marcos de Niza in 1539, and today it survives alone in the valley and the village of the Sete Cidades on the Island of San Miguel in the Azores group.

The legend of the Seven Cities, probably often related at family firesides, had no doubt become a part of the lore of the time before the first Spanish explorers approached the Indian country of our present Southwest. Indeed the legend had not wholly died out at the beginning of the eighteenth century, for in 1716 Padre Luis Velarde referred to the northern provinces of New Spain as being placed by some writers "close to the seven caves or cities, whence came the Mexican nation, although most of this legend," adds the discerning father, "seems to me to be guesswork, and so judge also the learned and intelligent." The reference to the seven caves has allusion to the ancient Nahua or Aztec tale of Chicomoztoc, or the "Seven Caves," and its supposed effect on the belief of the Spaniards in Mexico with respect to the existence of seven cities in the north, a tale well adapted, as Bandelier asserted, to fit the European legend of the Seven Cities.

The notorious Nuño de Guzmán, who had become president of the Audiencia and governor of New Spain in 1528, had in his possession an Indian called Tejo, the son of a trader in the valley of Oxitipar, who had died. This Indian said that when a little boy he had accompanied his father once or twice on journeys into the interior to trade fine feathers for ornaments, and had brought back a large quantity of gold and silver. While with his father, Tejo said, he had seen seven towns so large that they could be compared in size to Mexico and its suburbs, and that in them were whole streets occupied by silversmiths. He informed Nuño de Guzmán that these settlements could be reached by traveling northward between the two seas and crossing a grassy desert for forty days. These were the first rumors, exaggerated in the extreme, concerning the Pueblo Indian villages in the unexplored country of our Southwest, hazy knowledge that had been passed from tribe to tribe over hundreds of leagues and during a long period of time.

Acting on this information, Guzmán assembled an army of four hundred Spaniards and twenty thousand friendly Indians of New Spain, and in December, 1529, the expedition set out toward the northwest, following the Pacific coast. In the course of this journey during the next two years the Seven Cities, by which name the country had already become known, eluded the Spaniards. The post of Culiacan in Sinaloa was established by Guzmán before his return to Mexico in October, 1531, as a base for slave-raids in Sinaloa and Sonora, and it became an important point in subsequent expeditions. The Indian guide Tejo died about this time, according to Castañeda, "and thus the name of these Seven Cities and the search for them remains until now, since they have not been discovered."

It cannot be known to what extent the Indian Tejo's story was the result of leading questions on the part of his inquisitors, but it is certain that his tale of the finding of quantities of precious metals in the northern country was mere fabrication, and indeed the entire account bears little semblance of truth. It is characteristic of Indians generally to afford the kind of information they believe their questioners desire.

Don Antonio de Mendoza became the first viceroy of New Spain in 1535, arriving in Mexico in October. In the following year Nuño de Guzmán was deprived of his *residencia* and imprisoned for two years, thus ending any prospect he may have had of resuming search of the northern regions and its supposed wealth. In July, 1536, there appeared in Mexico the forlorn survivors of the Florida expedition of Pánfilo de Narváez in 1527-28: Alvar Nuñez Cabeza de Vaca, Andrés Dorantes de Carranza, Alonso del Castillo Maldonado, and the Barbary negro Estevan, or Estevanico, slave of Dorantes. These gave the viceroy an account of "some large and powerful villages, four and five stories high, of which they had heard a great deal in the countries they had crossed" from coast to coast. These doubtless were the towns of the Pueblo Indians of New Mexico, which then extended along the Rio Grande from the northern border of the Jornada del Muerto to Taos. It should be noted that the Spaniards had not seen these settlements, but merely spoke of them from hearsay.

The viceroy made various attempts to follow the lead made clear by Cabeza de Vaca, but to no immediate avail, for the Spanish survivors of the ill-fated Narváez expedition evidently had enough of the northern wilds after their eight years of slavery and wandering to last them the rest of their lives. In 1538, however, Fray Juan de la Asunción and Fray Pedro Nadal were dispatched by the provincial of the Franciscans in New Spain on a mission beyond Nueva Galicia "to convert new people." Little is known of this journey and its results, save that the friars traveled nearly eight hundred miles and were told of a country where the people were clothed in cotton and wool, wore shoes, had many turquoises, and dwelt on the shore of a great river in enclosed villages composed of many-storied houses built of "sod," and that beyond the river were larger and wealthier villages. It is probable that the friars penetrated as far as the lower Gila and possibly to the lower Colorado in southern Arizona. In any event their journey and report kept afresh the hope and prospects of important discoveries in the north.

At this time the vice-commissary general of the Franciscan order in New Spain was Fray Marcos de Niza, a native of Nice in the duchy of Savoy, as the name by which he is commonly known indicates. He went to the island of Santo Domingo in 1531, and to Peru in the year following. After remaining some years in the provinces of Peru and Quito, he proceeded afoot to Mexico, probably with Pedro de Alvarado. His first missionary labors in New Spain seem to have been in Jalisco, but he soon assumed a position of such prominence that in 1539 he became vice-commissary of his order, and in the following year was elected provincial. Fray Marcos had already written three reports on the Indians of Peru and Quito, the accuracy of which was strongly impugned by Cortés, who however was then claiming as discoveries of his own, the countries which Fray Marcos had visited in North America.

The veracity of Fray Marcos will probably never be settled to the satisfaction of all. Bandelier, ever a staunch advocate of the friar, regarded him as the worst slandered man in history; he was "a shrewd and very able man, of no ordinary attainments for the period in which he lived, and wholly devoted to duty." The same authority calls repeated attention to the things which the friar states that he saw and those of which he had only heard from the Indians. But the Spaniards at that time doubtless had visions of treasure such as had been looted by Cortés in Mexico and by Pizarro in Peru, and their frame of mind was not such as to enable them to discriminate these niceties. Among the milder critics of Fray Marcos was Castañeda, whose narration forms the basic text of the present volume. Bandelier takes Castañeda especially to task as a traducer of the friar, stating that he "is usually reliable in regard to matters touching the Indians and on geographical topics, but he is also very partial, and often slanderous in regard to the actions and motives of his countrymen." As a matter of fact, Castañeda merely reflects the attitude of the members of the expedition, especially Coronado himself, unjustifiably holding the friar responsible, so far as known. Rather than admit that Fray Marcos returned from Cíbola to Mexico because he was no longer safe with the army, Bandelier says that the obvious reason for his return was "the feeble health of the friar. Hardships and physical suffering had nearly paralyzed the body of the already aged man. He never regained his vigor, and died in Mexico after having in vain sought relief in the delightful climate of Jalapa, in the year 1558"—eighteen years later.

With this digression let us return to the year 1539, when Fray Marcos, in order to satisfy himself of the truth of what Juan de la Asunción had reported, determined to suffer any exposure to take the lead before any others could conclude to do so. Said to have been influenced by his friend Fray Bartolomé de las Casas, the viceroy Mendoza selected Fray Marcos to carry out his new policy of northwestern acquisition. Besides Fray Marcos the party consisted of Fray Onorato, Estevan the negro (who had become a slave of Mendoza, but was known as Estevan de Dorantes, after his former master), and a number of Piman Indians who had followed Cabeza de Vaca to Mexico and had there been Christianized and trained as interpreters. Provided with detailed instructions from the viceroy, the friar left Culiacan on March 7, 1539, the little party having been accompanied thither by Francisco Vásquez de Coronado, governor of Nueva Galicia. Proceeding to the Rio Petatlan, the present Fuerte, Fray Onorato became ill and remained behind; but the party was greatly augmented by native followers from the villages along the route.

Fray Marcos was received with the greatest friendliness wherever he went. While journeying through the land of the Pimas Bajos, or Nevome, of Sonora, the Indians told him that four or five days' journey inland there were settlements of people who wore cotton garments, had vessels and ornaments of gold, and used golden sweat-scrapers. Instead of pursuing this phantom, he followed his instructions by keeping as near the coast as possible, finally reaching a settlement called Vacapa, said to have been forty leagues from the coast, and which has been identified with Mátape, or Mátapa, a village of the Eudeve division of the Opata in central Sonora.

Deciding to remain at Vacapa until Easter, Fray Marcos dispatched Estevan toward the north fifty or sixty leagues to observe and report on the character of the land. If the negro found or heard of any great or rich country, he was to stop and send a message by the Indians in the form of a white cross. If the discovery was of moderate importance, he was to send a cross of one span in length; if important, the cross was to be two spans long; and if more important than New Spain, he was to send a large cross.

Departing on Passion Sunday, in four days Estevan's messengers returned with a cross as tall as a man and word that Fray Marcos should follow forthwith, for he had gained information of the greatest thing in the world, as the friar would be told by one of the Indian messengers, who had been there. This Indian said that from where Estevan then was it was thirty days' march to this land of promise, which was called Cíbola, and consisted of seven very large cities, all under one "lord," with houses of stone and lime, the smallest ones having two stories and with a flat roof, and others of three and four stories, and that of the lord with five, all placed together in order; and on the door-sills and lintels of the principal houses were many figures of turquoises, of which there was great abundance; and the people were very well clothed.

With the elusive "Seven Cities" seemingly within reach, there is little wonder that Fray Marcos exclaimed, "I give thanks to Our Lord!" The legendary Seven Cities of the bishops of ancient times had now become translated and localized into the "Seven Cities of Cíbola."

While awaiting the return of some Indians whom he had dispatched to the coast, and expecting the negro to follow instructions by tarrying until overtaken, the friar was visited at Vacapa by three Indians of the tribe whom he called Pintados, evidently the extinct Sobaipuri, who were called by the Pima *Rsársavina,* meaning "spotted." These Indians gave information regarding the Seven Cities, almost in the same manner as the messenger dispatched by Estevan. Fray Marcos continued his journey from Vacapa two days after Easter, following the route of the negro, from whom he received new messengers, who bore a cross of the bigness of the first. It is believed that he now was traveling up the valley of the Rio Sonora. In three days he reached the village, probably Babiacora, where Estevan had learned the first news of Cíbola, and where the friar was told that the Seven Cities were thirty days' off, as he had before been informed. These Opata of the Teguima division also said that Cíbola was the name of only the first town of the provinces, or "kingdoms," called evidently in their garbled manner Marata, Acus, and Totonteac. They knew this Cíbola province well, because they traded there for turquoises and buffalo-skins, giving of their services as farmers in exchange; and they described the turquoise ornaments of the Cíbola people, and their cotton garments, and showed the friar buffalo-hides which had been obtained from them.

Thenceforward for seven days Fray Marcos passed from one settlement to another, following the trail of his negro guide, who, contrary to instructions, still hastily continued his journey, but almost daily sent back crosses as tokens of the encouraging news he learned as he proceeded. On the seventh day the friar reached the last village, which may have been Arizpe, the "Arispa" of Castañeda and the "Ispa" of Jaramillo, for Coronado followed the friar's route in the following year. A desert stretch of eighty miles from the headwaters of the Rio Sonora to the source of the San Pedro was now crossed to the land of the Pintados—a journey of four days.

Among the Pintados Fray Marcos observed many turquoise ornaments worn, and he remarked that "Cibola was as well known here as Mexico City is in New Spain or Cuzco in Peru." These natives told him very much the same story as the Opata.

We shall not discuss in detail the statement made by Fray Marcos that from this point he made a journey to the gulf coast and back, a distance of more than four hundred miles, which has proved very puzzling to every student of the route and gave Coronado ground for severely criticizing the friar, who, he said, claimed to have covered the journey in five days.

The friar now continued down the San Pedro for five days, passing various small settlements. The people knew Cíbola from having been there; indeed Fray Marcos here met an aged native of Cíbola who informed him that the "lord" of these seven cities lived in one of them called Ahacus; that Cíbola (evidently "Ahacus") was a big city in which there were many people, streets, and squares, that in some parts there were houses eleven stories high, that the entrances and fronts of the principal buildings were of turquoises, and other fantasies.

Reaching the end of the Sobaipuri settlements, Marcos was now at the mouth of the San Pedro or on the Gila nearby in southern Arizona. Before him lay a stretch of totally uninhabited country which Coronado's chroniclers later described as the *despoblado*. This was the region between the Gila and the Cíbola pueblos.

Fray Marcos entered the wilderness on May 9, accompanied by many Sobaipuri who supplied him with abundance of game and who "expected to return wealthy." But tragedy was in the air. At the end of twelve days, when within two or three days' journey of Cíbola, the friar was met by one of the Indians who had gone forward with Estevan and who now brought tidings that the negro had reached Cíbola but that the people of that place had killed him, with many of his escort, and that the survivors were in flight. The reason for the killing of this first foreigner to set foot on the soil of our Southwest belongs to another story which need not concern us here. His own life threatened, Fray Marcos was able to assuage the anger and grief of Estevan's surviving companions by dividing the last of his gifts and in persuading them to accompany him to a small hill within sight of the first of Cíbola's pueblos. This village was found to be situated in a plain on the slope of a round height. "It was a very fine appearance for a village," the friar wrote; "the best that I have seen in these parts. The houses, as the Indians had told me, are all of stone, built in stories, and with flat roofs. Judging by what I could see from the height where I placed myself to observe it, the settlement is larger than the City of Mexico. I was somewhat tempted to go thither, knowing that I did not risk more than my life . . . but finally I feared . . . that if I should die, there would be no knowledge of this land, which, in my estimation, is the largest and best of all yet discovered." Whereupon Fray Marcos raised a pile of stones, on which he placed a wooden cross, and naming the country the New Kingdom of Saint Francis (the first name to be given to the region of New Mexico and Arizona), the friar commenced his long return journey "with far more fright than food."

The pueblo seen by Fray Marcos de Niza, and the one at which Estevan was killed a few days before, was the "Ahacus" of which the friar had previously heard—the Zuñi pueblo of Hawikuh in western New Mexico, one of the "Cities of Cíbola" which became the goal of the Coronado expedition in the following year.

That Fray Marcos was received in Mexico City with open arms there is every indication. The viceroy Mendoza wrote of him in laudatory terms to the king, his praises resounded from the pulpits, and he was soon appointed to fill a vacancy in the office of father provincial of the Order of St. Francis. Moreover, "the country was so stirred up by the news which the friar had brought from the Seven Cities," wrote Juan Suarez de Peralta half a century later, "that nothing else was thought about." For Fray Marcos is alleged to have said that the city of Cíbola was "big enough to have contained two Sevilles and over, . . . & that the houses were very fine edifices, four stories high . . . He exaggerated things so much that everybody was for going there and leaving Mexico depopulated." As to the truth of this and of other statements, comparison should be made with the moderate official report presented by Fray Marcos on his return to Mexico. The fact that he was perfectly willing to guide an expedition to the new-found land should have tended to quell more or less of the criticism that afterward arose and which proved to be the friar's undoing in the eyes of Coronado and his followers.

The enthusiasm with which the report of Fray Marcos was received by the Spaniards of Mexico was such that great rivalry arose among the leaders of the time to continue the exploration of the northern region which was believed to offer such brilliant prospects. Among these were Cortés, Hernando de Soto, Nuño de Guzmán, and Pedro de Alvarado; but the choice of Mendoza fell to Francisco Vásquez de Coronado. The proposed expedition was planned not alone to follow up the observations made and the information gained by Marcos, but as a means of ridding Mexico and the viceroy of the host of influential but worthless young gentlemen who had been sent from Spain to keep them from further mischief at home.

The gathering place of the expedition was Compostela, in the present state of Guadalajara, whither Mendoza went about the middle of February, 1540, and on the 22nd held a grand review of the assembled army. According to the conflicting statements the force was composed of 250 to 300 horsemen, 70 to 200 footmen, and from 300 to more than a thousand friendly Indian servants. Arms, horses, and supplies were provided in abundance. Some of the men were arrayed in coats of mail, others wore iron helmets or visored headpieces of rawhide; the horsemen were equipped with lances and other weapons, while the footmen carried crossbows and harquebuses, and some were armed with sword and shield. When the army started on its long northward journey on the following day, the servants and followers led the spare horses, drove the pack-animals, bore the extra baggage of their masters, and herded the droves of oxen and cows, sheep, and perhaps swine, which had been collected to provide food for the army. There were more than a thousand horses, besides the mules, packed with camp supplies and provisions, and carrying half a dozen swivel guns. Altogether it was the most pretentious and spectacular exploratory expedition that has ever set foot within the limits of the United States. It was destined

to give to the tribes of the Southwest and as far as Kansas their first knowledge of domestic animals, except the dog and the turkey, and ultimately
to exert a far-reaching influence on the Indians generally.

As mentioned above, the army was guided by Fray Marcos, who led it
over practically the same course he had pursued the year before. The force
proceeded to Chiametla and to Culiacan, where it was hoped to communicate with Alarcón, who was skirting the coast with his ships; but the plan
proved abortive and the extra supplies which Alarcón carried were never
available for their intended purpose. Selecting seventy-five or eighty horsemen, twenty-five or thirty foot-soldiers, and four friars (including Fray
Marcos), Coronado went in advance of the main army. Crossing the
streams mentioned in the report of the friar—the Fuerte, the Mayo, and
the Yaqui,—the march was continued to the valley of the Rio Sonora with
its Opata inhabitants, and was followed to its source beyond the town of
Arizpe. The desert stretch to the headwaters of the San Pedro, or "Nexpa,"
of Arizona was crossed in about four days, and the latter was followed
downstream for two days, when it was left, the Spaniards "going toward
the right to the foot of the mountain chain in two days' journey." Here
they heard of the ruin of Chichilticalli, the "Red House," apparently similar to the present Casa Grande in the Gila valley, northwest of where Coronado then was. Crossing the mountains, evidently the Pinaleño range,
after a couple of days' rest they proceeded by way of Railroad Pass and San
Simeon valley to the Gila, the "deep and reedy river," probably in the
vicinity of the present Solomonville.

Fording the Gila, they entered the *despoblado* mentioned by Fray
Marcos and soon encountered the Gila sierra and then range after range of
rugged masses until well within the drainage of the Colorado Chiquito—
"a worse way through mountains and more dangerous passes than we had
experienced previously," wrote Coronado to Mendoza. Crossing the San
Juan (probably the Gila Bonito), in two or three days the Rio de las Balsas
was reached and overcome by means of rafts, whence its name; this seemingly was Salt River. Continuing northeastwardly for two short days, a
stream flowing in a *barranca* in the White Mountains was crossed, then in
another day's journey they came to the Rio Frio, evidently the Colorado
Chiquito. Visiting a piney mountain in another day, in two days more,
traveling less toward the northeast, the advance guard reached another
stream which they called Rio Vermejo, on account of its reddish waters;

this was the Zuñi River, which the Spaniards found at a point about eight leagues below the first town of Cíbola, or about fifteen miles below where the present New Mexico-Arizona boundary intersects that stream. In another day's journey they advanced to within two leagues of the first Cíbola village.

On the day following that on which the force had left the wilderness, García Lopez de Cárdenas, the army-master, was sent forward with fifteen men to prepare the way, as the food was about exhausted and such of the horses as had not already succumbed were jaded. After the first day's march four Indians came peacefully and with words of welcome, saying that on the next day their tribe would provide the whole force with food. Cárdenas gave them a cross, telling them to inform their people that they need have no fear, because the Spaniards were coming to help them.

Two of the Indians remained with Cárdenas until Coronado arrived. He gave them some paternosters and little cloaks, repeating the message that Cárdenas had given respecting the peaceful intentions of the strangers. But notwithstanding the pacific attitude of these emissaries from Cíbola, Coronado sent the army-master forward again to learn if there were any dangerous passages, a precaution well taken, for that night the Indians assaulted the Spaniards who had taken possession of a very bad place, but fled before inflicting any damage. The next day the general started off again, his Spanish companions and Indians almost starved.

Coming within sight of the pueblo, Cárdenas was sent with two friars, Ferrando Vermizzo, and some horsemen, a little way ahead to inform the Indians that the Spaniards intended no harm, but had come to defend them in the name of the king; but the Indians were little affected by these overtures—the Spaniards being few in number, there would be no difficulty in conquering them. An arrow pierced the gown of Fray Luis de Ubeda, Coronado meanwhile arriving and finding on the plains a large body of Indians who began to shoot with their arrows. The Indians became bolder, seeing that Coronado would not permit his men to attack; but finally he felt compelled to charge, whereupon the natives took to flight, some toward the pueblo, others scattering to the plain. A number were killed (one chronicler says "more than twenty"). As the village was where the food was, Coronado assembled his entire force and began the assault, during which he was knocked to the ground by stones thrown from the terraced houses above; but for the protection of his gilded armor with a good headpiece, which was bedecked with a plume, and the help given by Cárdenas who rushed to his rescue, the wounded Coronado would have fared more seriously. The Indians finally surrendered and the hunger of the invaders was appeased by the stores of corn, beans, turkeys, and salt, which were found. Aside from Coronado four others were slightly wounded, and others suffered bruises. The warriors fled from the pueblo the following night.

Such was the battle of Hawikuh on July 7, 1540, the first of the "Cities of Cíbola," as reported by Coronado to Mendoza in a letter written at Hawikuh (called Granada by Coronado in honor of the viceroy) on August 3. Confirmatory information is given by other members of the expedition, including Castañeda, but the latter wrote of the fight from hearsay, as he was with the main army that had not yet arrived.

In less than a fortnight Coronado had recovered sufficiently from his bruises and from an arrow wound in his foot to enable him to go four leagues from Hawikuh to see a "rock," which is readily identified as Corn Mountain, on Tówayálane, a great sandstone mesa about three miles from present Zuñi, on which the Indians had fortified themselves, as they did when serious trouble arose in after years.

There is no longer any question regarding the identity of the "Cities of Cíbola" with the Zuñi pueblos of the sixteenth century. Some of the evidences of the identification are:

1. The line of travel by the Spaniards led undeniably, according to all the narratives of the period directly to the Zuñi villages in western central New Mexico.

2. The former pueblo of Hawikuh accords in every respect with the description of the situation of the first of the Cíbola towns as described by Fray Marcos de Niza and by the chroniclers of the Coronado expedition. Hawikuh is the only pueblo that could have been first reached in traveling northeastward up the Zuñi River (Rio Vermejo); it is the only one that could have been seen by Fray Marcos, and the only one, according to the confirmatory accounts of the approach to it by Coronado, that could have been stormed and captured by him.

3. Castañeda mentions the Cíbolan pueblo of Maçaque, which was reached by Coronado in one day from Hawikuh on his way to A'coma. This settlement was unquestionably the Zuñi pueblo of Mátsaki, near the northwestern base of Corn Mountain above referred to, which was on the road to A'coma.

4. Coronado's account mentions that from Granada (Hawikuh) "very good grass is found a league away, where there is pasturage for our horses as well as mowing for hay." This is exactly true of the little Ojo Caliente valley, with its abundant springs, a league southeast of Hawikuh.

5. Coronado also notes that the Cíbola Indians "have very good salt in crystals which they bring from a lake a day's journey distant." Melchior Díaz, from information given by Indians far to the southward, stated that the Cíbola natives "have salt from a marshy lake which is two days from the province of Cíbola." This is without doubt the noted Zuñi Salt Lake, thirty miles south by east from Hawikuh, which aroused the wonderment of the Spaniards under Oñate who visited it in 1598.

6. Castañeda states that the Cíbola people "have priests whom they call *papas*. These are the elders." *Pápa* in the Zuñi language means "elder brother," and is employed to denote both consanguineal and ceremonial relationship.

7. Important physiographical evidence is afforded by Captain Juan Jaramillo of Coronado's army. He says that "all the waterways we found as far as this one at Cibola—and I do not know but what for a day or two beyond—the rivers and streams run into the South [Pacific] Sea, and those from here on into the North [Atlantic] Sea." This is a perfect description of the drainage of the Zuñi country, for the Zuñi River, rising on the west side of the Zuñi mountains, which form the continental divide, flows into the Little Colorado, which drains into the Colorado and the Gulf of California, whereas east of the mountains the drainage is into the Rio Grande and the Gulf of Mexico.

8. Castañeda records the highly important fact that when Coronado and his army passed through Cíbola on their return to Mexico in 1542, they "rested before starting across the wilderness, because this [Coronado's Granada] was the last settlement in that country . . . Several of our Indian allies remained there." The Cíbola people followed the army and "carried off several people besides those who had remained of their own accord, among whom good interpreters could be found today." The significance of Castañeda's statement assumes great importance in the light of the chroniclers of the Espejo expedition of 1583. Traveling westward from Ácoma twenty-four leagues, wrote Espejo, "we found a province comprising six pueblos, which they call Amí [an obvious misprint of Cuni, or Zuñi], or by another name Cibola . . . We learned that Francisco Vazquez

Coronado and some of the captains he had with him had been there. In this province near the pueblos we found crosses erected; and here we found three Christian Indians, who said their names were Andrés of Cuyuacan, Gaspar of Mexico, and Anton of Guadalajara, and stated that they had come with the said governor Francisco Vazquez. We instructed them again in the Mexican tongue, which they had almost forgotten. From them we learned that the said Francisco Vazquez Coronado and his captains had been there." Confirmatory of this is the entry of the diarist of the Espejo expedition, Diego Pérez de Luxán, who wrote: "We halted at the first pueblo of the province of Zuñi [they were traveling westward from Ácoma] which they called Málaque [Mátsaki] . . . . The people of this province, which comprised six pueblos, one of which is called Mazaque . . . We found very well built crosses †† in all these pueblos, because Coronado had been in this land . . . Here we found Mexican Indians and also some from Guadalajara, of those that Coronado had brought. We could understand them, but they spoke with difficulty. Here we found a book and a small old trunk left by Coronado." From this pueblo, presumably Mátsaki, the Espejo party went to another, "called Aguico [Hawikuh], which is four leagues from the first one in the province."—the exact distance that Coronado traveled in going from Granada [Hawikuh] to Corn Mountain at the base of which Mátsaki was situated.

Without presenting other evidence it would be difficult to imagine, in the light of such incontrovertible testimony, how by any possibility the province of Cíbola could have been other than the Zuñi pueblos of the sixteenth century.

The various narrations regarding the province of Cíbola, aside from that of Castañeda, agree that it contained seven pueblos, with the exception of Jaramillo, who wrote: "From here we came in two days' journey to the said village [Granada-Hawikuh], the first of Cibola. The houses have flat roofs and walls of stone and mud, and this was where they killed Steve [Estevan] ... In this province of Cibola there are *five* little villages besides this ... These villages are about a league or more apart from each other, within a circuit of perhaps six leagues."

The statements of the other chroniclers of the expedition to the effect that Cíbola consisted of seven villages must be taken with allowance for the reason that (1) the tales of the existence of Seven Cities somewhere or other, over a period of eight centuries, doubtless caused the Spaniards to presuppose that Cíbola contained that number; (2) forty years later the narrators of the Chamuscado and Espejo expeditions of 1581 and 1583, respectively, specifically mention six, and the contemporary accounts of the Oñate expedition of 1598 do the same; (3) there is no archeological evidence, and no evidence that can be based on Zuñi tradition, that more than six pueblos were occupied at any one time during the historic period. The six Zuñi-Cíbola pueblos as known to the Spaniards after the Coronado expedition and the ruins of which are well known today are: Hawikuh, Kechipauan or Kyanawa, Kwakina, Halona, Kiakima, and Mátsaki.

While at Hawikuh-Granada, Coronado dispatched Pedro de Tovar and Fray Juan de Padilla to the province of Tusayan, the Hopi country of northern Arizona, where they learned of a great gash in the earth. To explore this Coronado sent García López de Cárdenas, who discovered the Grand Cañon of the Colorado. Hernando de Alvarado was ordered toward the east by way of Ácoma on a journey of exploration which took him as far as the buffalo plains.

After the arrival of the main army at Hawikuh in September, the force moved on to the Rio Grande and established winter quarters in one of the Tigua pueblos, called Tiguex by the Spaniards, near the present Bernalillo. Of the cruel treatment of the natives there Castañeda gives a circumstantial account. In the spring of 1541 the entire army started for the province of Quivira under the guidance of "the Turk," a Pawnee Indian who told the Spaniards wonderful tales of the wealth of that country; but after the force had traveled a month or more, the lying informant confessed that his aim was to lose the Spaniards on the boundless plains. This necessitated the return of most of the army to the Rio Grande and resulted in the execution of the false Indian guide. Coronado continued northward with thirty horsemen from this place of separation in Texas, and after traveling forty-two days by the needle, reached a stream that flowed northeastward. This they followed for a week, when they reached the beginning of the Quivira settlements; but instead of wealth the Spaniards found only a semi-agricultural people which lived in grass houses. These were the Wichita Indians of the Arkansas valley in central Kansas.

Coronado remained in Quivira twenty-five days, sending his aides to explore the land wherever prospects of treasure seemed promising, but no El Dorado was found. The region everywhere was as barren of riches as the hundreds of leagues over which the army had traveled. Nothing therefore remained but to return to New Mexico, there to join the main army at Tiguex in October. In this journey the Spaniards did not follow their long outward course, but traversed a well-worn road—that path of native commerce which in later times, taken over by venturesome American traders, became renowned as the Santa Fé Trail.

The expedition of Coronado was of far-reaching importance from a geographical point of view, for it combined with the journey of De Soto in revealing to the world an insight into the vast interior of the North American continent and formed the basis of the cartography of that region. It was the means of making known the sedentary Pueblo Indians of the Southwest and the hunting tribes of the Great Plains, the Grand Cañon of the Colorado and the lower reaches of that stream, and the teeming herds of bison and the absolute dependence on them by the hunting Indians for every want in life; and although the remarkable journey was wellnigh forgotten for a time, it proved to be the first step toward the ultimate colonization of the great Province of New Mexico in 1598.

As before mentioned, there are several narratives of the Coronado expedition, all of which were translated by Mr. George Parker Winship and first published in 1896 in the *Fourteenth Annual Report of the Bureau of Ethnology;* but the most extended and important, by reason of its detailed and comprehensive character, is that of Pedro de Castañeda, a translation of which, also by Mr. Winship, forms the chief text of the present volume.

Our author was born at Nájera, in the province of Logroño, in Old Castile, probably between 1510 and 1518; but as he was but a common soldier under Coronado, little is known of him. He was one of the colonists of San Miguel Culiacan, founded by Nuño de Guzmán in 1531, where, in all probability, he lived when the expedition reached that point in its northward journey to Cíbola, and where, more than twenty years later, he wrote his narrative. It is possible that Pedro may have been related to one Alonso de Castañeda, a resident of Compostela, son of Juan Rodríguez and Teresa Hernández Castañeda, who came to the New World with Pánfilo de Narváez bound for Florida, "where he was and remained until the fleet was destroyed." Thence he went to New Spain and was with Nuño de Guzmán "in the conquest of the terrible Chichimecas;" here he remained and served as occasion offered with his arms and horses. He was married, had a home established, and Indians in *encomienda,* from which he derived scant benefit (*Historical Documents relating to Nueva Vis-*

caya, etc., I, 35, Washington, 1923). In 1554, according to a document published in the *Colección de Documentos Inéditos del Archivo de Indias* (XIV, 206), his wife, María de Acosta, with her four sons and four daughters, filed a claim against the treasury for the services the husband and father rendered in behalf of the crown.

The original transcript from which Mr. Winship's translation was made was copied in Seville in 1596 and is now in the Lenox Collection of the New York Public Library; it bears the title "Relacion de la jornada de Cibola compuesta por Pedro de Castañeda de Naçera donde se trata de todos aquellos poblados y ritos, y costumbres, la cual fue el año de 1540." It was faultily translated into French and published, together with other documents relating to the expedition, under the title "Relation du voyage de Cibola entrepris en 1540 . . ." by Henri Ternaux-Compans, in his *Voyages,* tome IX, Paris, 1838.

The Winship translation of the narrative of Castañeda and related chronicles were reprinted as a volume of *The Trail Makers Series* under the title "The Journey of Coronado 1540-1542 from the City of Mexico to the Grand Cañon of the Colorado and the Buffalo Plains of Texas, Kansas, and Nebraska as told by Himself and His Followers. Translated and Edited, with an Introduction by George Parker Winship." New York: A. S. Barnes & Company, 1904.

In 1907 the translation of Castañeda was again reprinted in the series *Original Narratives of Early American History,* edited by Dr. J. Franklin Jameson, with the title "The Narrative of the Expedition of Coronado, by Pedro de Castañeda." Edited (with an Introduction) by Frederick W. Hodge, New York: Charles Scribner's Sons.

Southwest Museum
   Los Angeles
   September, 1933

The JOURNEY
OF CORONADO

CASTAÑEDA'S NARRATIVE

❡ Account of the expedition to Cibola which took place in the year 1540, in which all those settlements, their ceremonies & customs, are described. ❡ Written by Pedro de Castañeda, of Najara.

PREFACE

TO ME it seems very certain, my very noble lord, that it is a worthy ambition for great men to desire to know and wish to preserve for posterity correct information concerning the things that have happened in distant parts, about which little is known. I do not blame those inquisitive persons who, perchance with good intentions, have many times troubled me not a little with their requests that I clear up for them some doubts which they have had about different things that have been commonly related concerning the events and occurrences that took place during the expedition to Cibola, or the New Land, which the good viceroy —may he be with God in His glory[1]—Don Antonio de Mendoza, ordered and arranged, and on which he sent Francisco Vazquez de Coronado as captain-general.

In truth, they have reason for wishing to know the truth, because most people very often make things of which they have heard, and about which they have perchance no knowledge, appear either greater or less than they are. They make nothing of those things that amount to something, and those that do not they make so remarkable that they appear to be something impossible to believe. This may very well have been caused by the fact that, as that country was not permanently occupied, there has not been anyone who was willing to spend his time in writing about its peculiarities, because all knowledge was lost of that which it was not the pleasure of God—He alone knows the reason—that they should enjoy.

In truth, he who wishes to employ himself thus in writing out the things that happened on the expedition, and the things that were seen in those lands, and the ceremonies and customs of the natives, will have matter enough to test his judgment, & I believe that the result can not fail to be an account which, describing only the truth, will be so remarkable that it will seem incredible.

And besides, I think that the twenty years and more since that expedition took place have been the cause of some stories which are related. For example, some make it an uninhabitable country, others have it bordering on Florida, and still others on Greater India, which does not appear to be a slight difference. They are unable to give any basis upon which to found their statements. There are those who tell about some very peculiar animals, who are contradicted by others who were on the expedition, declaring that there was nothing of the sort seen. Others differ as to the limits of the provinces and even in regard to the ceremonies and customs, attributing what pertains to one people to others. All this has had a large part, my very noble lord, in making me wish to give now, although somewhat late, a short general account for all those who pride themselves on this noble curiosity, and to save myself the time taken up by these solicitations. Things enough will certainly be found here which are hard to believe. All or most of these were seen with my own eyes, and the rest is from reliable information obtained by inquiry of the natives themselves.

Understanding as I do that this little work would be nothing in itself, lacking authority, unless it were favored and protected by a person whose authority would protect it from the boldness of those who, without reverence, give their murmuring tongues liberty, and knowing as I do how great are the obligations under which I have always been, & am, to Your Grace, I humbly beg to submit this little work to your protection. May it be received as from a faithful retainer and servant.

It will be divided into three parts, that it may be better understood. The first will tell of the discovery and armament or army that was made ready, and of the whole journey, with the captains who were there; the second, of the villages and provinces which were found, their limits, and ceremonies and customs, the animals, fruits, vegetation, and in what parts of the country these are; the third, of the return of the army and the reasons for abandoning the country, although these were insufficient, because this is the best place there is for discoveries—the marrow of the land in these western parts, as will be seen. And after this has been made plain, some remarkable things which were seen will be described at the end, and the way by which one might more easily return to discover that better land which we did not see, since it would be no small advantage to enter the country through the land which the Marquis of the Valley, Don Fernando Cortes, went in search of under the Western Star, and which cost him no small sea armament.

May it please our lord to so favor me that with my slight knowledge and small abilities I may be able, by relating the truth, to make my little work pleasing to the learned and wise readers, when it has been accepted by Your Grace. For my intention is not to gain the fame of a good composer or rhetorician, but I desire to give a faithful account and to do this slight service to Your Grace, who will, I hope, receive it as from a faithful servant and soldier who took part in it. Although not in a polished style, I write that which happened—that which I heard, experienced, saw, and did.

I always notice, and it is a fact, that for the most part when we have something valuable in our hands, and deal with it without hindrance, we do not value or prize it as highly as if we understood how much we would miss it after we had lost it, and the longer we continue to have it the less we value it; but after we have lost it and miss the advantages of it, we have a great pain in the heart, and we are all the time imagining and trying to find ways and means by which to get it back again. It seems to me that this has happened to all or most of those who went on the expedition which, in the year of our Savior Jesus Christ 1540, Francisco Vazquez de Coronado led in search of the Seven Cities.

Granted that they did not find the riches of which they had been told, they found a place in which to search for them and the beginning of a good country to settle in, so as to go on farther from there. Since they came back from the country which they conquered and abandoned, time has given them a chance to understand the direction and locality in which they were, and the borders of the good country they had in their hands, and their hearts weep for having lost so favorable an opportunity. Just as men see more at the bullfight when they are upon the seats than when they are around in the ring, now when they know and understand the direction and situation in which they were, and see, indeed, that they can not enjoy it nor recover it, now when it is too late they enjoy telling about what they saw, and even of what they realize that they lost, especially those who are now as poor as when they went there. They have never ceased their labors and have spent their time to no advantage. I say this because I have known several of those who came back from there who amuse themselves now by talking of how it would be to go back and proceed to recover that which is lost, while others enjoy trying to find the reason why it was discovered at all. And now I will proceed to relate all that happened from the beginning.

CHAPTER I. ⊂ Which treats of the way we first came to know about the Seven Cities, and how Nuño de Guzman made an expedition to discover them.

IN THE year 1530, Nuño de Guzman, who was President of New Spain, had in his possession an Indian, a native of the valley or valleys of Oxitipar, who was called Tejo by the Spaniards. This Indian said he was the son of a trader who was dead but that when he was a little boy his father had gone into the back country with fine feathers to trade for ornaments, and that when he came back he brought a large amount of gold and silver, of which there is a good deal in that country. He went with him once or twice, and saw some very large villages, which he compared to Mexico and its environs. He had seen seven very large towns which had streets of silver workers. It took forty days to go there from his country, through a wilderness in which nothing grew, except some very small plants about a span high. The way they went was up through the country between the two seas, following the northern direction. Acting on this information, Nuño de Guzman got together nearly 400 Spaniards and 20,000 friendly Indians of New Spain, and as he happened to be in Mexico, he crossed Tarasca, which is in the province of Michoacan, so as to get into the region which the Indian said was to be crossed toward the North sea, in this way getting to the country which they were looking for, which was already named "The Seven Cities." He thought, from the forty days of which the Tejo had spoken, that it would be found to be about 200 leagues, and that they would easily be able to cross the country.

Omitting several things that occurred on this journey, as soon as they had reached the province of Culiacan, where his government ended and where the New Kingdom of Galicia is now, they tried to cross the country, but found the difficulties very great, because the mountain chains which are near that sea are so rough that it was impossible, after great labor, to find a passageway in that region. His whole army had to stay in the district of Culiacan for so long on this account that some rich men who were with him, who had possessions in Mexico, changed their minds, and every day became more anxious to return. Besides this, Nuño de Guzman received word that the Marquis of the Valley, Don Fernando Cortes, had come from Spain with his new title,[1] and with great favors and estates, and as Nuño de Guzman had been a great rival of his at the time he was president,[2] and had done much damage to his property and to that of his friends, he feared that Don Fernando Cortes would want to pay him back in the same way, or worse. So he decided to establish the town of Culiacan there and to go back with the other men, without doing anything more.

After his return from this expedition, he founded Xalisco, where the city of Compostela is situated, and Tonala, which is called Guadalaxara,[3] and now this is the New Kingdom of Galicia. The guide they had, who was called Tejo, died about this time, and thus the names of these Seven Cities and the search for them remain until now, since they have not been discovered.[4]

CHAPTER II. ⌐ How Francisco Vazquez de Coronado came to be governor, and the second account which Cabeza de Vaca gave.

EIGHT years after Nuño de Guzman made this expedition, he was put in prison by a *juez de residencia*,[1] named the licentiate Diego de la Torre, who came from Spain with sufficient powers to do this.[2] After the death of the judge, who had also managed the government of that country himself, the good Don Antonio de Mendoza, viceroy of New Spain, appointed as governor of that province Francisco Vazquez de Coronado, a gentleman from Salamanca, who had married a lady in the City of Mexico, the daughter of Alonso de Estrada, the treasurer and at one time governor of Mexico, and the son, most people said, of His Catholic Majesty Don Ferdinand, and many stated it as certain. As I was saying, at the time Francisco Vazquez was appointed governor, he was traveling through New Spain as an official inspector, and in this way he gained the friendship of many worthy men who afterward went on his expedition with him.

It happened that just at this time three Spaniards, named Cabeza de Vaca, Dorantes, and Castillo Maldonado, and a negro, who had been lost on the expedition which Pamfilo de Narvaez led into Florida, reached Mexico. They came out through Culiacan, having crossed the country from sea to sea, as anyone who wishes may find out for himself by an account which this same Cabeza de Vaca wrote and dedicated to Prince Don Philip, who is now King of Spain and our sovereign.[3] They gave the good Don Antonio de Mendoza an extended account of some powerful villages, four and five stories high, of which they had heard a great deal in the countries they had crossed, and other things very different from what turned out to be the truth. The noble viceroy communicated this to the new governor, who gave up the visits he had in hand, on account of this, and hurried his departure for his government, taking with him the negro who had come [with Cabeza de Vaca] with three friars of the order of Saint Francis, one of whom was named Friar Marcos de Niza, a regular priest, and another Friar Daniel, a lay brother, and the other Friar Antonio de Santa Maria. When he reached the province of Culiacan he sent the friars just mentioned and the negro, who was named Stephen, off in search of that country, because Friar Marcos offered to go and see it, because he had been in Peru at the time Don Pedro de Alvarado went there overland.

It seems that, after the friars I have mentioned and the negro had started, the negro did not get on well with the friars, because he took the women that were given him and collected turquoises, and got together a stock of everything. Besides, the Indians in those places through which they went got along with the negro better, because they had seen him before. This was the reason he was sent on ahead to open up the way and pacify the Indians, so that when the others came along they had nothing to do except keep an account of the things for which they were looking.

CHAPTER III. ☙ Of how they killed the negro Stephen at Cibola, and Friar Marcos returned in flight.

AFTER Stephen had left the friars, he thought he could get all the reputation and honor himself, and that if he should discover those settlements with such famous high houses, alone, he would be considered bold and courageous. So he proceeded with the people who had followed him, and attempted to cross the wilderness which lies between the country he had passed through and Cibola. He was so far ahead of the friars that, when these reached Chichilticalli, which is on the edge of the wilderness, he was already at Cibola, which is 80 leagues beyond. It is 220 leagues from Culiacan to the edge of the wilderness, and 80 across the desert, which makes 300, or perhaps 10 more or less. As I said, Stephen reached Cibola laden with the large quantity of turquoises they had given him and some beautiful women whom the Indians who followed him and carried his things were taking with them and had given him. These had followed him from all the settlements he had passed, believing that under his protection they could traverse the whole world without any danger.

But as the people in this country were more intelligent than those who followed Stephen, they lodged him in a little hut they had outside their village, and the older men and the governors heard his story and took steps to find out the reason he had come to that country. For three days they made inquiries about him and held a council. The account which the negro gave them of two white men who were following him, sent by a great lord, who knew about the things in the sky, and how these were coming to instruct them in divine matters, made them think that he must be a spy or a guide from some nations who wished to come and conquer them, because it seemed to them unreasonable to say that the people were white in the country from which he came and that he was sent by them, he being black. Besides these other reasons, they thought it was hard of him to ask them for turquoises and women, and so they decided to kill him. They did this, but they did not kill any of those who went with him, although they kept some young fellows and let the others, about 60 persons, return freely to their own country. As these, who were badly scared, were returning in flight, they happened to come upon the friars in the desert 60 leagues from Cibola, and told them the sad news, which frightened them so much that they would not even trust these folks who had been with the negro, but opened the packs they were carrying and gave away everything they had except the holy vestments for saying mass. They returned from here by double marches, prepared for anything, without seeing any more of the country except what the Indians told them.

CHAPTER IV. ⟨ Of how noble Don Antonio de Mendoza made an expedition to discover Cibola.

AFTER Francisco Vazquez de Coronado had sent Friar Marcos de Niza and his party on the search already related, he was engaged in Culiacan about some business that related to his government, when he heard an account of a province called Topira,[1] which was to the north of the country of Culiacan. He started to explore this region with several of the conquerors and some friendly Indians, but he did not get very far, because the mountain chains which they had to cross were very difficult. He returned without finding the least signs of a good country, and when he got back, he found the friars who had just arrived, and who told such great things about what the negro Stephen had discovered and what they had heard from the Indians, and other things they had heard about the South Sea and islands and other riches, that, without stopping for anything, the governor set off at once for the City of Mexico, taking Friar Marcos with him, to tell the viceroy about it. He made the things seem more important by not talking about them to anyone except his particular friends, under promise of the greatest secrecy, until after he had reached Mexico and seen Don Antonio de Mendoza. Then it began to be noised abroad that the Seven Cities for which Nuño de Guzman had searched, had already been discovered, and a beginning was made in collecting an armed force and in bringing together people to go to conquer them.

The noble viceroy arranged with the friars of the order of Saint Francis so that Friar Marcos was made father provincial, as a result of which the pulpits of that order were filled with such accounts of marvels and wonders that more than 300 Spaniards and about 800 natives of New Spain collected in a few days. There were so many men of such high quality among the Spaniards, that such a noble body was never collected in the Indies, nor so many men of quality in such a small body, there being 300 men. Francisco Vazquez de Coronado, governor of New Galicia, was captain-general, because he had been the author of it all. The good viceroy Don Antonio did this because at this time Francisco Vazquez was his closest and most intimate friend, and because he considered him to be wise, skillful, and intelligent, besides being a gentleman. Had he paid more attention and regard to the position in which he was placed and the charge over which he was placed, and less to the estates he left behind in New Spain, or, at least more to the honor he had and might secure from having such gentlemen under his command, things would not have turned out as they did. When this narrative is ended, it will be seen that he did not know how to keep his position nor the government that he held.

CHAPTER V. ⊂ Concerning the captains who went to Cíbola.

WHEN the viceroy, Don Antonio de Mendoza, saw what a noble company had come together, and the spirit and good will with which they had all presented themselves, knowing the worth of these men, he would have liked very well to make every one of them captain of an army; but as the whole number was small he could not do as he would have liked, and so he issued the commissions & captaincies as he saw fit, because it seemed to him that if they were appointed by him, as he was so well obeyed and beloved, nobody would find fault with his arrangements. After everybody had heard who the general was, he made Don Pedro de Tovar ensign-general, a young gentleman who was the son of Don Fernando de Tovar, the guardian and lord high steward of the Queen Doña Juana, our demented mistress—may she be in glory—and Lope de Samaniego, the governor of the arsenal at Mexico,[1] a gentleman fully equal to the charge, army-master. The captains were Don Tristan de Arellano;[2] Don Pedro de Guevara, the son of Don Juan de Guevara and nephew of the Count of Oñate; Don Garcia Lopez de Cardenas; Don Rodrigo Maldonado, brother-in-law of the Duke of the Infantado; Diego Lopez, alderman of Seville,[3] and Diego Gutierres, for the cavalry.

All the other gentlemen were placed under the flag of the general, as being distinguished persons, and some of them became captains later, and their appointments were confirmed by order of the viceroy and by the general, Francisco Vazquez. To name some of them whom I happen to remember, there were Francisco de Barrionuevo, a gentleman from Granada; Juan de Saldivar, Francisco de Ovando, Juan Gallego, and Melchior Diaz—a captain who had been mayor of Culiacan, who, although he was not a gentleman, merited the position he held. The other gentlemen, who were prominent, were Don Alonso Manrique de Lara; Don Lope de Urrea, a gentleman from Aragon; Gomez Suarez de Figueroa, Luis Ramirez de Vargas, Juan de Sotomayor, Francisco Gorbalan, the commissioner Ribe-ros, and other gentlemen, men of high quality, whom I do not now recall. The infantry captain was Pablo de Melgosa of Burgos, and of the artillery, Hernando de Alvarado de Montañez.[4] As I say, since then I have forgotten the names of many gentlemen. It would be well if I could name some of them, so that it might be clearly seen what cause I had for saying that they had on this expedition the most brilliant company ever collected in the Indies to go in search of new lands. But they were unfortunate in having a captain who left in New Spain estates and a pretty wife, a noble and excel-lent lady, which were not the least causes for what was to happen.

CHAPTER VI. ⟨ Of how all the companies collected in Compostela and set off on the journey in good order.

WHEN the viceroy, Don Antonio de Mendoza, had fixed & arranged everything as we have related, and the companies and captaincies had been arranged, he advanced a part of their salaries from the chest of His Majesty to those in the army who were in greatest need. And as it seemed to him that it would be rather hard for the friendly Indians in the country if the army should start from Mexico, he ordered them to assemble at the city of Compostela, the chief city in the New Kingdom of Galicia, 110 leagues from Mexico, so that they could begin their journey there with everything in good order. There is nothing to tell about what happened on this trip, since they all finally assembled at Com-postela by shrove-tide, in the year [fifteen hundred and] forty-one.[1]

After the whole force had left Mexico, he ordered Don Pedro de Alarcon to set sail with two ships that were in the port of La Natividad on the South Sea coast, and go to the port of Xalisco to take the baggage which the sol-diers were unable to carry,[2] and thence to sail along the coast near the army, because he had understood from the reports that they would have to go through the country near the seacoast, & that we could find the harbors by means of the rivers, and that the ships could always get news of the army, which turned out afterward to be false, and so all this stuff was lost, or, rather, those who owned it lost it, as will be told farther on. After the viceroy had completed all his arrangements, he set off for Compostela, accompanied by many noble and rich men. He kept the New Year of [fifteen hundred and] forty-one at Pasquaro,[3] which is the chief place in the bishopric of Michoacan, and from there he crossed the whole of New Spain, taking much pleasure in enjoying the festivals and great receptions which were given him, till he reached Compostela, which is, as I have said, 110 leagues. There he found the whole company assembled, being well treated & entertained by Christobal de Oñate, who had the whole charge of that government for the time being. He had had the management of it and was in command of all that region when Francisco Vazquez was made governor.[4]

All were very glad when he arrived, and he made an examination of the company and found all those whom we have mentioned. He assigned the captains to their companies, and after this was done, on the next day, after they had all heard mass, captains and soldiers together, the viceroy made them a very eloquent short speech, telling them of the fidelity they owed to their general and showing them clearly the benefits which this expedition might afford, from the conversion of those peoples as well as in the profit of those who should conquer the territory, and the advantage to His Majesty & the claim which they would thus have on his favor and aid at all times. After he had finished, they all, both captains and soldiers, gave him their oaths upon the Gospels in a Missal that they would follow their general on this expedition and would obey him in everything he commanded them, which they faithfully performed, as will be seen. The next day after this was done, the army started off with its colors flying. The viceroy, Don Antonio, went with them for two days, and there he took leave of them, returning to New Spain with his friends.

CHAPTER VII. ☞ Of how the army reached Chiametla, the killing of the army-master, and the other things that happened up to the arrival at Culiacan.

AFTER the viceroy, Don Antonio, left them, the army continued its march. As each one was obliged to transport his own baggage and all did not know how to fasten the packs, and as the horses started off fat and plump, they had a good deal of difficulty and labor during the first few days, and many left many valuable things, giving them to anyone who wanted them, in order to get rid of carrying them. In the end necessity, which is all powerful, made them skillful, so that one could see many gentlemen become carriers, and anybody who despised this work was not considered a man.

With such labors, which they then thought severe, the army reached Chiametla, where it was obliged to delay several days to procure food. During this time the army-master, Lope de Samaniego, went off with some soldiers to find food, and at one village a crossbowman having entered it indiscreetly in pursuit of the enemies, they shot him through the eye and it passed through his brain, so that he died on the spot. They also shot five or six of his companions before Diego Lopez, the alderman from Seville, since the commander was dead, collected the men and sent word to the general. He put a guard in the village and over the provisions. There was great confusion in the army when this news became known. He was buried here. Several sorties were made, by which food was obtained and several of the natives taken prisoners. They hanged those who seemed to belong to the district where the army-master was killed.

It seems that when the general, Francisco Vazquez, left Culiacan with Friar Marcos to tell the viceroy, Don Antonio de Mendoza, the news, as already related, he left orders for Captain Melchior Diaz and Juan de Saldivar to start off with a dozen good men from Culiacan and verify what Friar Marcos had seen and heard. They started and went as far as Chichilticalli, which is where the wilderness begins, 220 leagues from Culiacan, & there they turned back, not finding anything important. They reached Chiametla just as the army was ready to leave, and reported to the general. Although they were kept secret, the bad news leaked out, and there were some reports which, although they were exaggerated, did not fail to give an indication of what the facts were.[1] Friar Marcos, noticing that some were feeling disturbed, cleared away these clouds, promising that what they would see should be good, and that he would place the army in a country where their hands would be filled, & in this way he quieted them so that they appeared well satisfied. From there the army marched to Culiacan, making some detours into the country to seize provisions. They were two leagues from the town of Culiacan at Easter vespers, when the inhabitants came out to welcome their governor and begged him not to enter the town till the day after Easter.

CHAPTER VIII. ⟨Of how the army entered the town of Culiacan and the reception it received, and other things which happened before the departure.

WHEN the day after Easter came, the army started in the morning to go to the town, and, as they approached, the inhabitants of the town came out on to an open plain with foot and horse drawn up in ranks as if for a battle, and having its seven bronze pieces of artillery in position, making a show of defending their town. Some of our soldiers were with them. Our army drew up in the same way and began a skirmish with them, and after the artillery on both sides had been fired they were driven back, just as if the town had been taken by force of arms, which was a pleasant demonstration of welcome, except for the artilleryman who lost a hand by a shot, from having ordered them to fire before he had finished drawing out the ramrod.

After the town was taken, the army was well lodged and entertained by the townspeople, who, as they were all very well-to-do people, took all the gentlemen and people of quality who were with the army into their own apartments, although they had lodgings prepared for them all just outside the town. Some of the townspeople were not ill repaid for this hospitality, because all had started with fine clothes and accoutrements, & as they had to carry provisions on their animals after this, they were obliged to leave their fine stuff, so that many preferred giving it to their hosts instead of risking it on the sea by putting it in the ship that had followed the army along the coast to take the extra baggage, as I have said. After they arrived and were being entertained in the town, the general, by order of the viceroy Don Antonio, left Fernandarias de Saabedra, uncle of Hernandarias de Saabedra, count of Castellar, formerly mayor of Seville, as his lieutenant and captain in this town. The army rested here several days, because the inhabitants had gathered a good stock of provisions that year and each one shared his stock very gladly with his guests from our army. They not only had plenty to eat here, but they also had plenty to take away with them, so that when the departure came they started off with more than six hundred loaded animals, besides the friendly Indians and the servants — more than a thousand persons. After a fortnight had passed, the general started ahead with about fifty horsemen and a few foot soldiers and most of the Indian allies, leaving the army, which was to follow him a fortnight later, with Don Tristan de Arellano in command as his lieutenant.

At this time, before his departure, a pretty sort of thing happened to the general, which I will tell for what it is worth. A young soldier named Trugillo (Truxillo) pretended that he had seen a vision while he was bathing in the river. Feigning that he did not want to, he was brought before the general, whom he gave to understand that the devil had told him that if he would kill the general, he could marry his wife, Doña Beatris, and would receive great wealth and other very fine things. Friar Marcos de Niza preached several sermons on this, laying it all to the fact that the devil was jealous of the good which must result from this journey and so wished to break it up in this way. It did not end here, but the friars who were in the expedition wrote to their monasteries about it, and this was the reason the pulpits of Mexico proclaimed strange rumors about this affair.

The general ordered Truxillo to stay in that town and not to go on the expedition, which was what he was after when he made up that falsehood, judging from what afterward appeared to be the truth. The general started off with the force already described to continue his journey, and the army followed him, as will be related.

CHAPTER IX. C Of how the army started from Culiacan and the arrival of the general at Cíbola and of the army at Señora and of other things that happened.

THE general, as has been said, started to continue his journey from the valley of Culiacan somewhat lightly equipped, taking with him the friars, since none of them wished to stay behind with the army. After they had gone three days, a regular friar who could say mass, named Friar Antonio Victoria, broke his leg, and they brought him back from the camp to have it doctored. He stayed with the army after this, which was no slight consolation for all. The general and his force crossed the country without trouble, as they found everything peaceful, because the Indians knew Friar Marcos and some of the others who had been with Melchior Diaz when he went with Juan de Saldivar to investigate.

After the general had crossed the inhabited region and came to Chichilticalli, where the wilderness begins, and saw nothing favorable, he could not help feeling somewhat downhearted, for, although the reports were very fine about what there was ahead, there was nobody who had seen it except the Indians who went with the negro, and these had already been caught in some lies. Besides all this, he was much affected by seeing that the fame of Chichilticalli was summed up in one tumble-down house without any roof, although it appeared to have been a strong place at some former time when it was inhabited, and it was very plain that it had been built by a civilized and warlike race of strangers who had come from a distance.[1] This building was made of red earth. From here they went on through the wilderness, and in fifteen days came to a river about eight leagues from Cibola, which they called Red River,[2] because its waters were muddy and reddish. In this river they found mullets like those of Spain. The first Indians from that country were seen here—two of them, who ran away to give the news. During the night following the next day, about two leagues from the village, some Indians in a safe place yelled so that, although the men were ready for anything, some were so excited that they put their saddles on hind-side before; but these were the new fellows. When the veterans had mounted and ridden round the camp, the Indians fled. None of them could be caught because they knew the country.

The next day they entered the settled country in good order, and when they saw the first village, which was Cibola, such were the curses that some hurled at Friar Marcos that I pray God may protect him from them.

It is a little, crowded village, looking as if it had been crumpled all up together. There are ranch houses in New Spain which make a better appearance at a distance.[3] It is a village of about 200 warriors, is three and four stories high, with the houses small and having only a few rooms, and without a courtyard. One yard serves for each section. The people of the whole district had collected here, for there are seven villages in the province, and some of the others are even larger and stronger than Cibola. These folk waited for the army, drawn up by divisions in front of the village. When they refused to have peace on the terms the interpreters extended to them, but appeared defiant, the Santiago[4] was given, and they were at once put to flight. The Spaniards then attacked the village, which was taken with not a little difficulty, since they held the narrow and crooked entrance. During the attack they knocked the general down with a large stone, and would have killed him but for Don Garcia Lopez de Cardenas and Hernando de Alvarado, who threw themselves above him and drew him away, receiving the blows of the stones, which were not few. But the first fury of the Spaniards could not be resisted, and in less than an hour they entered the village and captured it. They discovered food there, which was the thing they were most in need of.[5] After this the whole province was at peace.

The army which had stayed with Don Tristan de Arellano started to follow their general, all loaded with provisions, with lances on their shoulders, and all on foot, so as to have the horses loaded. With no slight labor from day to day, they reached a province which Cabeza de Vaca had named Corazones (Hearts), because the people here offered him many hearts of animals. He founded a town here and named it San Hieronimo de los Corazones (Saint Jerome of the Hearts). After it had been started, it was seen that it could not be kept up here, and so it was afterward transferred to a valley which had been called Señora. The Spaniards call it Señora, and so it will be known by this name.[6]

From here a force went down the river to the seacoast to find the harbor and to find out about the ships. Don Rodrigo Maldonado, who was captain of those who went in search of the ships, did not find them, but he brought back with him an Indian so large and tall that the best man in the army reached only to his chest.[7] It was said that other Indians were even taller on that coast. After the rains ceased the army went on to where the town of Señora was afterward located, because there were provisions in that region, so that they were able to wait there for orders from the general.

About the middle of the month of October[8] Captains Melchior Diaz and Juan Gallego came from Cibola, Juan Gallego on his way to New Spain and Melchior Diaz to stay in the new town of Hearts, in command of the men who remained there. He was to go along the coast in search of ships.

CHAPTER X. ℂ How the army started from Señora, & how it reached Cibola, & of what happened to Captain Melchior Diaz and how he discovered the Tison (Firebrand) River.

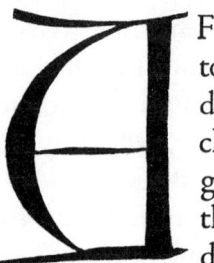

AFTER Melchior Diaz and Juan Gallego had arrived in the town of Señora, it was announced that the army was to depart for Cibola; that Melchior Diaz was to remain in charge of that town with 80 men; that Juan Gallego was going to New Spain with messages for the viceroy, and that Friar Marcos was going back with him, because he did not think it was safe for him to stay in Cibola, seeing that his report had turned out to be entirely false, because the kingdoms that he had told about had not been found, nor the populous cities, nor the wealth of gold, nor the precious stones which he had reported, nor the fine clothes, nor other things that had been proclaimed from the pulpits. When this had been announced, those who were to remain were selected and the rest loaded their provisions and set off in good order about the middle of September on the way to Cibola, following their general.

Don Tristan de Arellano stayed in this new town with the weakest men, and from this time on there was nothing but mutinies and strife, because after the army had gone Captain Melchior Diaz took 25 of the most efficient men, leaving in his place one Diego de Alcaraz, a man unfitted to have people under his command. He took guides and went toward the north & west in search of the seacoast. After going about 150 leagues, they came to a province of exceedingly tall and strong men—like giants. They are naked and live in large straw cabins built under ground like smoke houses, with only the straw roof over ground. They enter these at one end and come out at the other. More than a hundred persons, old and young, sleep in one cabin. When they carry anything, they can take a load of more than three or four hundred-weight on their heads. Once when our men wished to fetch a log for the fire, and six men were unable to carry it, one of these Indians is reported to have come and raised it in his arms, put it on his head alone, and carried it very easily.[1] They eat bread cooked in the ashes, as big as the large two-pound loaves of Castile. On account of the great cold, they carry a firebrand (*tison*) in the hand when they go from one place to another, with which they warm the other hand and the body as well, & in this way they keep shifting it every now and then.[2] On this account the large river which is in that country was called Rio del Tison (Firebrand River). It is a very great river and is more than two leagues wide at its mouth; here it is half a league across. Here the captain heard that there had been ships at a point three days down toward the sea. When he reached the place where the ships had been, which was more than fifteen leagues up the river from the mouth of the harbor, they found written on a tree: "Alarcon reached this place; there are letters at the foot of this tree." He dug up the letters and learned from them how long Alarcon had waited for news of the army and that he had gone back with the ships to New Spain, because he was unable to proceed farther, since this sea was a bay, which was formed by the Isle of the Marquis,[3] which is called California, and it was explained that California was not an island, but a point of the mainland forming the other side of that gulf.[4]

After he had seen this, the captain turned back to go up the river, without going down to the sea to find a ford by which to cross to the other side, so as to follow the other bank. After they had gone five or six days, it seemed to them as if they could cross on rafts. For this purpose they called together a large number of the natives, who were waiting for a favorable opportunity to make an attack on our men, and when they saw that the strangers wanted to cross, they helped make the rafts with all zeal & diligence, so as to catch them in this way on the water and drown them or else so divide them that they could not help one another. While the rafts were being made, a soldier who had been out around the camp saw a large number of armed men go across to a mountain, where they were waiting till the soldiers should cross the river. He reported this, and an Indian was quietly shut up, in order to find out the truth, and when they tortured him he told all the arrangements that had been made. These were, that when our men were crossing and part of them had got over and part were on the river and part were waiting to cross, those who were on the rafts should drown those they were taking across and the rest of their force should make an attack on both sides of the river. If they had had as much discretion and courage as they had strength and power, the attempt would have succeeded.

When he knew their plan, the captain had the Indian who had confessed the affair killed secretly, and that night he was thrown into the river with a weight, so that the Indians would not suspect that they were found out. The next day they noticed that our men suspected them, and so they made an attack, shooting showers of arrows, but when the horses began to catch up with them and the lances wounded them without mercy and the musketeers likewise made good shots, they had to leave the plain and take to the mountain, until not a man of them was to be seen. The force then came back and crossed all right, the Indian allies and the Spaniards going across on the rafts and the horses swimming alongside the rafts, where we will leave them to continue their journey.

To relate how the army that was on its way to Cibola got on: Everything went along in good shape, since the general had left everything peaceful, because he wished the people in that region to be contented and without fear and willing to do what they were ordered. In a province called Vacapan there was a large quantity of prickly pears, of which the natives make a great deal of preserves.[5] They gave this preserve away freely, and as the men of the army ate much of it, they all fell sick with a headache and fever, so that the natives might have done much harm to the force if they had wished. This lasted regularly twenty-four hours. After this they continued their march until they reached Chichilticalli. The men in the advance guard saw a flock of sheep one day after leaving this place. I myself saw and followed them. They had extremely large bodies and long wool; their horns were very thick and large, and when they run they throw back their heads and put their horns on the ridge of their back. They are used to the rough country, so that we could not catch them and had to leave them.

Three days after we entered the wilderness we found a horn on the bank of a river that flows in the bottom of a very steep, deep gully, which the general had noticed and left there for his army to see, for it was six feet long and as thick at the base as a man's thigh. It seemed to be more like the horn of a goat than of any other animal. It was something worth seeing. The army proceeded and was about a day's march from Cibola when a very cold tornado came up in the afternoon, followed by a great fall of snow, which was a bad combination for the carriers. The army went on till it reached some caves in a rocky ridge, late in the evening. The Indian allies who were from New Spain, and for the most part from warm countries, were in great danger. They felt the coldness of that day so much that it was hard work the next day taking care of them, for they suffered much pain and had to be carried on the horses, the soldiers walking. After this labor the army reached Cibola, where their general was waiting for them, with their quarters all ready, and here they were reunited, except some captains and men who had gone off to discover other provinces.

CHAPTER XI. ☾ How Don Pedro de Tovar discovered Tusayan or Tutahaco[1] and Don García Lopez de Cardenas saw the Firebrand River, and the other things that had happened.

HILE the things already described were taking place, Cibola being at peace, the General Francisco Vazquez found out from the people of the province about the provinces that lay around it, and got them to tell their friends and neighbors that Christians had come into the country, whose only desire was to be their friends, and to find out about good lands to live in, and for them to come to see the strangers and talk with them. They did this, since they know how to

communicate with one another in these regions, and they informed him about a province with seven villages of the same sort as theirs, although somewhat different. They had nothing to do with these people. This province is called Tusayan. It is twenty-five leagues from Cíbola. The villages are high and the people are warlike.

The general had sent Don Pedro de Tovar to these villages with seventeen horsemen and three or four foot-soldiers. Juan de Padilla, a Franciscan friar, who had been a fighting man in his youth, went with them. When they reached the region, they entered the country so quietly that nobody observed them, because there were no settlements or farms between one village and another and the people do not leave the villages except to go to their farms, especially at this time, when they had heard that Cíbola had been captured by very fierce people, who travelled on animals which ate people. This information was generally believed by those who had never seen horses, although it was so strange as to cause much wonder. Our men arrived after nightfall and were able to conceal themselves under the edge of the village, where they heard the natives talking in their houses. But in the morning they were discovered and drew up in regular order, while the natives came out to meet them, with bows, and shields, and wooden clubs, drawn up in lines without any confusion. The interpreter was given a chance to speak to them and give them due warning, for they were very intelligent people, but nevertheless they drew lines and insisted that our men should not go across these lines toward their village.[2]

While they were talking, some men acted as if they would cross the lines, and one of the natives lost control of himself and struck a horse a blow on the cheek of the bridle with his club. Friar Juan, fretted by the time that was being wasted in talking with them, said to the captain: "To tell the truth, I do not know why we came here." When the men heard this, they gave the Santiago so suddenly that they ran down many of the Indians and the others fled to the town in confusion. Some indeed did not have a chance to do this, so quickly did the people in the village come out with presents, asking for peace. The captain ordered his force to collect, and, as the natives did not do any more harm, he and those who were with him found a place to establish their headquarters near the village. They had dismounted here when the natives came peacefully, saying that they had come to give in the submission of the whole province and that they wanted him to be friends with them and to accept the presents which they gave him.[3] This was some cotton cloth, although not much, because they do not make it in that district.[4] They also gave him some dressed skins and corn-meal, and pine nuts and corn and birds of the country. Afterward they presented some turquoises, but not many. The people of the whole district came together that day and submitted themselves, and they allowed him to enter their villages freely to visit, buy, sell, and barter with them.

It is governed like Cibola, by an assembly of the oldest men. They have their governors and generals. This was where they obtained the information about a large river, and that several days down the river there were some people with very large bodies.[5]

As Don Pedro de Tovar was not commissioned to go farther, he returned from there and gave this information to the general, who dispatched Don Garcia Lopez de Cardenas with about twelve companions to go to see this river. He was well received when he reached Tusayan and was entertained by the natives who gave him guides for his journey. They started from here laden with provisions, for they had to go through a desert country before reaching the inhabited region, which the Indians said was more than 20 days' journey. After they had gone 20 days they came to the banks of the river. It seemed to be more than three or four leagues in an air line across to the other bank of the stream which flowed between them.[6]

This country was elevated and full of low twisted pines, very cold, and lying open toward the north, so that, this being the warm season, no one could live there on account of the cold. They spent three days on this bank looking for a passage down to the river, which looked from above as if the water was six feet across, although the Indians said it was half a league wide. It was impossible to descend, for after these three days Captain Melgosa & one Juan Galeras and another companion, who were the three lightest and most agile men, made an attempt to go down at the least difficult place, and went down until those who were above were unable to keep sight of them. They returned about four o'clock in the afternoon, not having succeeded in reaching the bottom on account of the great difficulties which they found, because what seemed to be easy from above was not so, but instead very hard and difficult. They said that they had been down about a third of the way and that the river seemed very large from the place which they reached, and that from what they saw they thought the Indians had given the width correctly. Those who stayed above had estimated that some huge rocks on the sides of the cliffs seemed to be about as tall as a man, but those who went down swore that when they reached these rocks they were bigger than the great tower of Seville. They did not go farther up the river, because they could not get water.

Before this they had had to go a league or two inland every day late in the evening in order to find water, and the guides said that if they should go four days farther it would not be possible to go on, because there was no water within three or four days, for when they travel across this region themselves they take with them women laden with water in gourds, and bury the gourds of water along the way, to use when they return, & besides this, they travel in one day over what it takes us two days to accomplish.

This was the Tison (Firebrand) River, much nearer its source than where Melchior Diaz and his company crossed it. These were the same kind of Indians, judging from what was afterward learned. They came back from this point & the expedition did not have any other result. On the way they saw some water falling over a rock and learned from the guides that some bunches of crystals which were hanging there were salt. They went and gathered a quantity of this & brought it back to Cibola, dividing it among those who were there. They gave the general a written account of what they had seen, because one Pedro de Sotomayor had gone with Don Garcia Lopez as chronicler for the army.[7] The villages of that province remained peaceful, since they were never visited again, nor was any attempt made to find other peoples in that direction.[8]

CHAPTER XII. ❰ How people came from Cicuye to Cibola to see the Christians, & Hernando de Alvarado went to see the cows.

HILE they were making these discoveries, some Indians came to Cibola from a village which was 70 leagues east of this province, called Cicuye.[1] Among them was a captain who was called Bigotes (Whiskers) by our men, because he wore a long mustache. He was a tall, well-built young fellow, with a fine figure. He told the general that they had come in response to the notice which had been given, to offer themselves as friends, and that if we wanted to go through their country they would consider us as their friends. They brought a present of tanned hides and shields and headpieces, which were very gladly received, and the general gave them some glass dishes and a number of pearls and little bells which they prized highly, because these were things they had never seen. They described cows which, from the picture that one of them had painted on his skin, seemed to be cows, although from the hides this did not seem possible, because the hair was woolly and snarled so that we could not tell what sort of skins they had. The general ordered Hernando de Alvarado to take twenty companions & go with them, & gave him a commission for eighty days, after which he should return to give an account of what he had found.[2]

Captain Alvarado started on this journey & in five days reached a village which was on a rock called Acuco,[3] having a population of about 200 men. These people were robbers, feared by the whole country round about. The village was very strong, because it was up on a rock out of reach, having steep sides in every direction, and so high that it was a very good musket that could throw a ball as high. There was only one entrance by a stairway built by hand, which began at the top of a slope which is around the foot of the rock. There was a broad stairway for about 200 steps, then a stretch of about 100 narrower steps, and at the top they had to go up about three times as high as a man by means of holes in the rock, in which they put the points of their feet, holding on at the same time by their hands. There was a wall of large and small stones at the top, which they could roll down without showing themselves, so that no army could possibly be strong enough to capture the village. On the top they had room to sow and store a large amount of corn, and cisterns to collect snow and water. These people came down to the plain ready to fight, and would not listen to any arguments. They drew lines on the ground and determined to prevent our men from crossing these, but when they saw that they would have to fight they offered to make peace before any harm had been done. They went through their forms of making peace, which is to touch the horses and take their sweat and rub themselves with it, and to make crosses with the fingers of the hands. But to make the most secure peace they put their hands across each other, and they keep this peace inviolably. They made a present of a large number of [turkey] cocks with very big wattles, much bread, tanned deerskins, pine [piñon] nuts, flour [corn meal], and corn.

From here they went to a province called Triguex,[4] three days distant. The people all came out peacefully, seeing that Whiskers was with them. These men are feared throughout all those provinces. Alvarado sent messengers back from here to advise the general to come and winter in this country. The general was not a little relieved to hear that the country was growing better. Five days from here he came to Cicuye, a very strong village four stories high. The people came out from the village with signs of joy to welcome Hernando de Alvarado and their captain, and brought them into the town with drums and pipes something like flutes, of which they have a great many. They made many presents of cloth and turquoises, of which there are quantities in that region. The Spaniards enjoyed themselves here for several days and talked with an Indian slave, a native of the country toward Florida, which is the region Don Fernando de Soto discovered. This fellow said that there were large settlements in the farther part of that country. Hernando de Alvarado took him to guide them to the cows; but he told them so many and such great things about the wealth of gold & silver in his country that they did not care about looking for cows, but returned after they had seen some few, to report the rich news to the general. They called the Indian "Turk," because he looked like one.[5]

Meanwhile the general had sent Don Garcia Lopez de Cardenas to Tiguex with men to get lodgings ready for the army, which had arrived from Señora about this time, before taking them there for the winter; and when Hernando de Alvarado reached Tiguex, on his way back from Cicuye, he found Don Garcia Lopez de Cardenas there, & so there was no need for him to go farther. As it was necessary that the natives should give the Spaniards lodging places, the people in one village had to abandon it and go to others belonging to their friends, and they took with them nothing but themselves and the clothes they had on. Information was obtained here about many towns up toward the north, and I believe that it would have been much better to follow this direction than that of the Turk, who was the cause of all the misfortunes which followed.

CHAPTER XIII.**C** How the general went toward Tutahaco with a few men & how Don Tristan took the army to Tiguex.

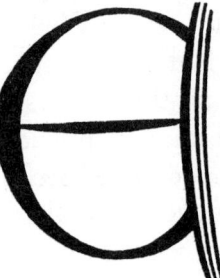VERYTHING already related had happened when Don Tristan de Arellano reached Cibola from Señora. Soon after he arrived, the general, who had received notice of a province containing eight villages, took thirty of the men who were most fully rested and went to see it, going from there directly to Tiguex with the skilled guides who conducted him. He left orders for Don Tristan de Arellano to

proceed to Tiguex by the direct road, after the men had rested twenty days. On this journey, between one day when they left the camping place and midday of the third day, when they saw some snow-covered mountains, toward which they went in search of water, neither the Spaniards nor the horses nor the servants drank anything. They were able to stand it because of the severe cold, although with great difficulty. In eight days they reached Tutahaco,[1] where they learned that there were other towns down the river. These people were peaceful. The villages are terraced, like those at Tiguex, and of the same style.

The general went up the river from here, visiting the whole province, until he reached Tiguex, where he found Hernando de Alvarado and the Turk. He felt no slight joy at such good news, because the Turk said in his country there was a river in the level country which was two leagues wide, in which there were fishes as big as horses, and large numbers of very big canoes, with more than twenty rowers on a side, and that they carried sails, and that their lords sat on the poop under awnings, and on the prow they had a great golden eagle. He said also that the lord of that country took his afternoon nap under a great tree on which were hung a great number of little gold bells, which put him to sleep as they swung in the air. He said also that everyone had his ordinary dishes made of wrought plate, and the jugs and bowls were of gold. He called gold *acochis*. For the present he was believed, on account of the ease with which he told it and because they showed him metal ornaments and he recognized them and said they were not gold, and he knew gold and silver very well and did not care anything about other metals.[2]

The general sent Hernando de Alvarado back to Cicuye to demand some gold bracelets which this Turk said they had taken from him at the time they captured him. Alvarado went, and was received as a friend at the village, & when he demanded the bracelets they said they knew nothing at all about them, saying the Turk was deceiving him & was lying. Captain Alvarado, seeing that there were no other means, got the Captain Whiskers and the governor to come to his tent, and when they had come he put them in chains. The villagers prepared to fight, and let fly their arrows, denouncing Hernando de Alvarado, and saying that he was a man who had no respect for peace & friendship. Hernando de Alvarado started back to Tiguex, where the general kept them prisoners more than six months. This began the want of confidence in the word of the Spaniards whenever there was talk of peace from this time on, as will be seen by what happened afterward.

CHAPTER XIV. C Of how the army went from Cibola to Ti/ guex & what happened to them on the way, on account of the snow.

WE HAVE already said that when the general started from Cibola, he left orders for Don Tristan de Arellano to start twenty days later. He did so as soon as he saw the men were well rested and provided with food and eager to start off to find their general. He set off with his force toward Tiguex and the first day they made their camp in the best, largest, and finest village of that (Cibola) province.[1] This is the only village that has houses with seven stories. In this village certain houses are used as fortresses; they are higher than the others and set up above them like towers, and there are embrasures and hoopholes in them for defending the roofs of the different stories, because, like the other villages, they do not have streets, and the flat roofs are all of a height and are used in common. The roofs have to be reached first, and these upper houses are the means of defending them. It began to snow on us there, and the force took refuge under the wings of the village, which extend out like balconies, with wooden pillars beneath, because they generally use ladders to go up to those balconies, since they do not have any doors below.

The army continued its march from here after it stopped snowing, and as the season had already advanced into December, during the ten days that the army was delayed, it did not fail to snow during the evenings and nearly every night, so that they had to clear away a large amount of snow when they came to where they wanted to make a route camp. The road could not be seen, but the guides managed to find it, as they knew the country. There are junipers and pines all over the country, which they used in making large brushwood fires, the smoke and heat of which melted the snow from two to four yards all around the fire. It was a dry snow, so that although it fell on the baggage and covered it for half a man's height it did not hurt it. It fell all night long, covering the baggage and the soldiers and their beds, piling up in the air, so that if anyone had suddenly come upon the army nothing would have been seen but mountains of snow. The horses stood half buried in it. It kept those who were underneath warm instead of cold.[2] The army passed by the great rock of Acuco, and the natives, who were peaceful, entertained our men well, giving them provisions and birds, although there are not many people here, as I have said. Many of the gentlemen went up to the top to see it, and they had great difficulty in going up the steps in the rock, because they were not used to them, for the natives go up and down so easily that they carry loads & the women carry water, and they do not seem even to touch their hands, although our men had to pass their weapons up from one to another.

From here they went on to Tiguex, where they were well received and taken care of, and the great good news of the Turk gave no little joy and helped lighten their hard labors, although when the army arrived we found the whole country or province in revolt, for reasons which were not slight in themselves, as will be shown, and our men had also burnt a village the day before the army arrived, and returned to the camp.

CHAPTER XV. ℂ Of how the people of Tiguex revolted, and how they were punished, without being to blame for it.

IT HAS been related how the general reached Tiguex, where he found Don Garcia Lopez de Cardenas & Hernando de Alvarado, & how he sent the latter back to Cicuye, where he took the Captain Whiskers and the governor of the village, who was an old man, prisoners.[1] The people of Tiguex did not feel well about this seizure.

In addition to this, the general wished to obtain some clothing to divide among his soldiers, and for this purpose he summoned one of the chief Indians of Tiguex, with whom he had already had much intercourse and with whom he was on good terms, who was called Juan Aleman by our men, after a Juan Aleman who lived in Mexico, whom he was said to resemble.[2] The general told him that he must furnish about three hundred or more pieces of cloth, which he needed to give his people. He said that he was not able to do this, but that it pertained to the governors; and that besides this, they would have to consult together and divide it among the villages, and that it was necessary to make the demand of each town separately. The general did this, and ordered certain of the gentlemen who were with him to go and make the demand; and as there were twelve villages, some of them went on one side of the river and some on the other. As they were in very great need, they did not give the natives a chance to consult about it, but when they came to a village they demanded what they had to give, so that they could proceed at once. Thus these people could do nothing except take off their own cloaks and give them to make up the number demanded of them. And some of the soldiers who were in these parties, when the collectors gave them some blankets or cloaks which were not such as they wanted, if they saw any Indian with a better one on, they exchanged with him without more ado, not stopping to find out the rank of the man they were stripping, which caused not a little hard feeling.

Besides what I have just said, one whom I will not name, out of regard for him, left the village where the camp was and went to another village about a league distant, and seeing a pretty woman there he called her husband down to hold his horse by the bridle while he went up; and as the village was entered by the upper story, the Indian supposed he was going to some other part of it. While he was there the Indian heard some slight noise, and then the Spaniard came down, took his horse, and went away. The Indian went up and learned that he had violated, or tried to violate, his wife, and so he came with the important men of the town to complain that a man had violated his wife, and he told how it had happened. When the general made all the soldiers and the persons who were with him come together, the Indian did not recognize the man, either because he had changed his clothes or for whatever other reason there may have been, but he said he could tell the horse, because he had held his bridle, and so he was taken to the stables, and found the horse, and said that the master of the horse must be the man. He denied doing it, seeing that he had not been recognized, and it may be that the Indian was mistaken in the horse; anyway, he went off without getting any satisfaction.[3] The next day one of the Indians, who was guarding the horses of the army, came running in, saying that a companion of his had been killed, and that the Indians of the country were driving off the horses toward their villages. The Spaniards tried to collect the horses again, but many were lost, besides seven of the general's mules.

The next day Don Garcia Lopez de Cardenas went to see the villages and talk with the natives. He found the villages closed by palisades and a great noise inside, the horses being chased as in a bull fight and shot with arrows. They were all ready for fighting. Nothing could be done, because they would not come down on to the plain and the villages are so strong that the Spaniards could not dislodge them. The general then ordered Don Garcia Lopez de Cardenas to go and surround one village with all the rest of the force. This village was the one where the greatest injury had been done and where the affair with the Indian woman occurred. Several captains who had gone on in advance with the general, Juan de Saldivar and Barrionuevo and Diego Lopez and Melgosa, took the Indians so much by surprise that they gained the upper story, with great danger, for they wounded many of our men from within the houses. Our men were on top of the houses in great danger for a day and a night and part of the next day, and they made some good shots with their crossbows and muskets. The horsemen on the plain with many of the Indian allies from New Spain smoked them out from the cellars[4] into which they had broken, so that they begged for peace.

Pablo de Melgosa and Diego Lopez, the alderman from Seville, were left on the roof and answered the Indians with the same signs they were making for peace, which was to make a cross. They then put down their arms and received pardon. They were taken to the tent of Don Garcia, who, according to what he said, did not know about the peace and thought that they had given themselves up of their own accord because they had been conquered. As he had been ordered by the general not to take them alive, but to make an example of them so that the other natives would fear the Spaniards, he ordered 200 stakes to be prepared at once to burn them alive. Nobody told him about the peace that had been granted them, for the soldiers knew as little as he, and those who should have told him about it remained silent, not thinking that it was any of their business. Then when the enemies saw that the Spaniards were binding them and beginning to roast them, about a hundred men who were in the tent began to struggle and defend themselves with what there was there and with the stakes they could seize. Our men who were on foot attacked the tent on all sides, so that there was great confusion around it, and then the horsemen chased those who escaped. As the country was level, not a man of them remained alive, unless it was some who remained hidden in the village and escaped that night to spread throughout the country the news that the strangers did not respect the peace they had made, which afterward proved a great misfortune. After this was over, it began to snow, and they abandoned the village and returned to the camp just as the army came from Cibola.[5]

CHAPTER XVI. ℂOf how they besieged Tiguex & took it, and of what happened during the siege.

AS I have already related, it began to snow in that country just after they captured the village, and it snowed so much that for the next two months it was impossible to do anything except to go along the roads to advise them to make peace and tell them that they would be pardoned and might consider themselves safe, to which they replied that they did not trust those who did not know how to keep good faith after they had once given it, and that the Spaniards should remember that they were keeping Whiskers prisoner and that they did not keep their word when they burned those who surrendered in the village. Don Garcia Lopez de Cardenas was one of those who went to give this notice. He started out with about 30 companions and went to the village of Tiguex to talk with Juan Aleman. Although they were hostile, they talked with him and said that if he wished to talk with them he must dismount and they would come out and talk with him about a peace, and that if he would send away the horsemen and make his men keep away, Juan Aleman and another captain would come out of the village and meet him. Everything was done as they required, and then when they approached they said that they had no arms and that he must take his off. Don Garcia Lopez did this in order to give them confidence, on account of his great desire to get them to make peace. When he met them, Juan Aleman approached and embraced him vigorously, while the other two who had come with him drew two mallets[1] which they had hidden behind their backs and gave him two such blows over his helmet that they almost knocked him senseless. Two of the soldiers on horseback had been unwilling to go very far off, even when he ordered them, and so they were near by and rode up so quickly that they rescued him from their hands, although they were unable to catch the enemies because the meeting was so near the village that of the great shower of arrows which were shot at them one arrow hit a horse and went through his nose. The horsemen all rode up together and hurriedly carried off their captain, without being able to harm the enemy, while many of our men were dangerously wounded.

They then withdrew, leaving a number of men to continue the attack. Don Garcia Lopez de Cardenas went on with a part of the force to another village about half a league distant, because almost all the people in this region had collected into these two villages. As they paid no attention to the demands made on them except by shooting arrows from the upper stories with loud yells, and would not hear of peace, he returned to his companions whom he had left to keep up the attack at Tiguex. A large number of those in the village came out and our men rode off slowly, pretending to flee, so that they drew the enemy on to the plain, and then turned on them and caught several of their leaders. The rest collected on the roofs of the village and the captain returned to his camp.

After this affair the general ordered the army to go and surround the village. He set out with his men in good order, one day, with several scaling ladders. When he reached the village, he encamped his force near by, and then began the siege; but as the enemy had had several days to provide themselves with stores, they threw down such quantities of rocks upon our men that many of them were laid out, and they wounded nearly a hundred with arrows, several of whom afterward died on account of the bad treatment by an unskillful surgeon who was with the army. The siege lasted fifty days, during which time several assaults were made. The lack of water was what troubled the Indians most. They dug a very deep well inside the village, but were not able to get water, and while they were making it, it fell in and killed 30 persons. Two hundred of the besieged died in the fights. One day when there was a hard fight, they killed Francisco de Obando, a captain who had been army-master all the time that Don Garcia Lopez de Cardenas was away making the discoveries already described, and also Francisco Pobares, a fine gentleman. Our men were unable to prevent them from carrying Francisco de Obando inside the village, which was regretted not a little, because he was a distinguished person, besides being honored on his own account, affable and much beloved, which was noticeable.

One day, before the capture was completed, they asked to speak to us, and said that, since they knew we would not harm the women and children, they wished to surrender their women and sons, because they were using up their water. It was impossible to persuade them to make peace, as they said that the Spaniards would not keep an agreement made with them. So they gave up about a hundred persons, women and boys, who did not want to leave them. Don Lope de Urrea rode up in front of the town without his helmet and received the boys and girls in his arms, and when all of these had been surrendered, Don Lope begged them to make peace, giving them the strongest promises for their safety. They told him to go away, as they did not wish to trust themselves to people who had no regard for friendship or their own word which they had pledged. As he seemed unwilling to go away, one of them put an arrow in his bow ready to shoot, and threatened to shoot him with it unless he went off, and they warned him to put on his helmet, but he was unwilling to do so, saying that they would not hurt him as long as he stayed there. When the Indian saw that he did not want to go away, he shot and planted his arrow between the fore feet of the horse, and then put another arrow in his bow and repeated that if he did not go away he would really shoot him. Don Lope put on his helmet and slowly rode back to where the horsemen were, without receiving any harm from them. When they saw that he was really in safety, they began to shoot arrows in showers, with loud yells and cries. The general did not want to make an assault that day, in order to see if they could be brought in some way to make peace, which they would not consider.

Fifteen days later they decided to leave the village one night, and did so, taking the women in their midst. They started about the fourth watch, in the very early morning, on the side where the cavalry was. The alarm was given by those in the camp of Don Rodrigo Maldonado. The enemy attacked them and killed one Spaniard and a horse and wounded others, but they were driven back with great slaughter until they came to the river, where the water flowed swiftly and very cold. They threw themselves into this, and as the men had come quickly from the whole camp to assist the cavalry, there were few who escaped being killed or wounded. Some men from the camp went across the river next day and found many of them who had been overcome by the great cold. They brought these back, cured them, and made servants of them. This ended that siege, and the town was captured, although there were a few who remained in one part of the town and were captured a few days later.

Two captains, Don Diego de Guevara and Juan de Saldivar, had captured the other large village after a siege. Having started out very early one morning to make an ambuscade in which to catch some warriors who used to come out every morning to try to frighten our camp, the spies, who had been placed where they could see when they were coming, saw the people come out and proceed toward the country. The soldiers left the ambuscade and went to the village and saw the people fleeing. They pursued and killed large numbers of them. At the same time those in the camp were ordered to go over the town, and they plundered it, making prisoners of all the people who were found in it, amounting to about a hundred women and children. This siege ended the last of March, in the year '42.[2] Other things had happened in the meantime, which would have been noticed, but that it would have cut the thread. I have omitted them, but will relate them now, so that it will be possible to understand what follows.

CHAPTER XVII. ⌈ Of how messengers reached the army from the valley of Señora and how Captain Melchior Diaz died on the expedition to the Firebrand River.

E HAVE already related how Captain Melchior Diaz crossed the Firebrand river on rafts, in order to continue his discoveries farther in that direction. About the time the siege ended, messengers reached the army from the city of SanHieronimo with letters from Diego de Alarcon,[1] who had remained there in the place of Melchior Diaz. These contained the news that Melchior Diaz had died while he was conducting his search, and that the force had returned without finding any of the things they were after. It all happened in this fashion:

After they had crossed the river they continued their search for the coast, which here turned back toward the south, or between south & east, because that arm of the sea enters the land due north and this river, which brings its waters down from the north, flowing toward the south, enters the head of the gulf. Continuing in the direction they had been going, they came to some sand banks of hot ashes which it was impossible to cross without being drowned as in the sea. The ground they were standing on trembled like a sheet of paper, so that it seemed as if there were lakes underneath them. It seemed wonderful and like something infernal, for the ashes to bubble up here in several places. After they had gone away from this place, on account of the danger they seemed to be in and of the lack of water, one day a greyhound belonging to one of the soldiers chased some sheep which they were taking along for food. When the captain noticed this, he threw his lance at the dog while his horse was running, so that it stuck up in the ground, and not being able to stop his horse he went over the lance so that it nailed him through the thighs and the iron came out behind, rupturing his bladder. After this the soldiers turned back with their captain, having to fight every day with the Indians, who had remained hostile. He lived about twenty days, during which they proceeded with great difficulty on account of the necessity of carrying him. They returned in good order without losing a man, until he died, & after that they were relieved of the greatest difficulty. When they reached Señora, Alcaraz dispatched the messengers already referred to, so that the general might know of this and also that some of the soldiers were ill disposed and had caused several mutinies, and that he had sentenced two of them to the gallows, but they had afterward escaped from the prison.

When the general learned this, he sent Don Pedro de Tovar to that city to sift out some of the men. He was accompanied by messengers whom the general sent to Don Antonio de Mendoza the viceroy, with an account of what had occurred and with the good news given by the Turk. When Don Pedro de Tovar arrived there, he found that the natives of that province had killed a soldier with a poisoned arrow, which had made only a very little wound in one hand. Several soldiers went to the place where this happened to see about it, and they were not very well received. Don Pedro de Tovar sent Diego de Alcaraz with a force to seize the chiefs & lords of a village in what they call the valley of Knaves (de los Vellacos), which is in the hills. After getting there and taking these men prisoners, Diego de Alcaraz decided to let them go in exchange for some thread & cloth & other things which the soldiers needed. Finding themselves free, they renewed the war and attacked them, and as they were strong and had poison, they killed several Spaniards and wounded others so that they died on the way back. They retired toward the town, & if they had not had Indian allies from the country of the Hearts, it would have gone worse with them. They got back to the town, leaving 17 soldiers dead from the poison. They would die in agony from only a small wound, the bodies breaking out with an insupportable pestilential stink. When Don Pedro de Tovar saw the harm done, and as it semed to them that they could not safely stay in that city, he moved 40 leagues toward Cibola into the valley of Suya, where we will leave them, in order to relate what happened to the general and his army after the siege of Tiguex.

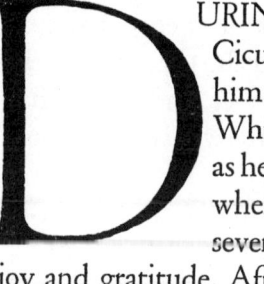

URING the siege of Tiguex the general decided to go to Cicuye and take the governor with him, in order to give him his liberty and to promise them that he would give Whiskers his liberty and leave him in the village, as soon as he should start for Quivira. He was received peacefully when he reached Cicuye, and entered the village with several soldiers. They received their governor with much joy and gratitude. After looking over the village and speaking with the natives he returned to his army, leaving Cicuye at peace, in the hope of getting back their Captain Whiskers.

After the siege was ended, as we have already related, he sent a captain to Chia,[1] a fine village with many people, which had sent to offer its submission. It was four leagues distant to the west of the river. They found it peaceful and gave it four bronze cannon, which were in poor condition, to take care of. Six gentlemen also went to Quirix, a province with seven villages.[2] At the first village, which had about a hundred inhabitants, the natives fled, not daring to wait for our men; but they headed them off by a short cut, riding at full speed, and then they returned to their houses in the village in perfect safety, and then told the other villagers about it and reassured them. In this way the entire region was reassured, little by little, by the time the ice in the river was broken up and it became possible to ford the river and so continue the journey. The twelve villages of Tiguex, however, were not repopulated at all during the time the army was there, in spite of every promise of security that could possibly be given to them.

And when the river, which for almost four months had been frozen over so that they crossed the ice on horseback, had thawed out, orders were given for the start to Quivira, where the Turk said there was some gold and silver, although not so much as in Arche and the Guaes.[3] There were already some in the army who suspected the Turk, because a Spaniard named Servantes,[4] who had charge of him during the siege, solemnly swore that he had seen the Turk talking with the devil in a pitcher of water, and also that while he had him under lock so that no one could speak to him, the Turk had asked him what Christians had been killed by the people at Tiguex. He told him "nobody," and then the Turk answered:

"You lie; five Christians are dead, including a captain." And as Cervantes knew that he told the truth, he confessed it so as to find out who had told him about it, and the Turk said he knew it all by himself and that he did not need to have anyone tell him in order to know it. And it was on account of this that he watched him and saw him speaking to the devil in the pitcher, as I have said.

While all this was going on, preparations were being made to start from Tiguex. At this time people came from Cibola to see the general, and he charged them to take good care of the Spaniards who were coming from Señora with Don Pedro de Tovar. He gave them letters to give to Don Pedro, informing him what he ought to do and how he should go to find the army, and that he would find letters under the crosses which the army would put up along the way. The army left Tiguex on the 5th of May[5] and returned to Cicuye, which, as I have said, is twenty-five marches, which means leagues, from there, taking Whiskers with them. Arrived there, he gave them their captain, who already went about freely with a guard. The village was very glad to see him, and the people were peaceful and offered food. The governor and Whiskers gave the general a young fellow named Xabe, a native of Quivira, who could give them information about the country. This fellow said that there was gold and silver, but not so much of it as the Turk had said. The Turk, however, continued to declare that it was as he had said. He went as a guide, and thus the army started off from here.

CHAPTER XIX. ℂ Of how they started in search of Quivira and of what happened on the way.

THE army started from Cicuye, leaving the village at peace and, as it seemed, contented, & under obligations to maintain the friendship because their governor and captain had been restored to them. Proceeding toward the plains, which are all on the other side of the mountains, after four days' journey they came to a river with a large, deep current, which flowed down from toward Cicuye, and they named this the Cicuye river.[1] They had to stop here to make a bridge so as to cross it. It was finished in four days, by much diligence and rapid work, and as soon as it was done the whole army and the animals crossed. After ten days more they came to some settlements of people who lived like Arabs and who are called Querechos in that region.[2] They had seen the cows for two days. These folks live in tents made of the tanned skins of the cows. They travel around near the cows, killing them for food. They did nothing unusual when they saw our army, except to come out of their tents to look at us, after which they came to talk with the advance guard, and asked who we were. The general talked with them, but as they had already talked with the Turk, who was with the advance guard, they agreed with what he had said. That they were very intelligent is evident from the fact that although they conversed by means of signs they made themselves understood so well that there was no need of an interpreter. They said there was a very large river over toward where the sun came from, and that one could go along this river through an inhabited region for ninety days without a break from settlement to settlement. They said that the first of these settlements was called Haxa, and that the river was more than a league wide and that there were many canoes on it. These folk started off from here next day with a lot of dogs which dragged their possessions.

For two days, during which the army marched in the same direction as that in which they had come from the settlements—that is, between north and east, but more toward the north—they saw other roaming Querechos and such great numbers of cows that it already seemed something incredible. These people gave a great deal of information about settlements, all toward the east from where we were. Here Don Garcia broke his arm and a Spaniard got lost who went off hunting so far that he was unable to return to the camp, because the country is very level. The Turk said it was one or two days to Haya (Haxa). The general sent Captain Diego Lopez with ten companions lightly equipped & a guide to go at full speed toward the sunrise for two days and discover Haxa, and then return to meet the army, which set out in the same direction next day. They came across so many animals that those who were on the advance guard killed a large number of bulls. As these fled they trampled one another in their haste until they came to a ravine. So many of the animals fell into this that they filled it up, and the rest went on across the top of them. The men who were chasing them on horseback fell in among the animals without noticing where they were going. Three of the horses that fell in among the cows, all saddled and bridled, were lost sight of completely.

As it seemed to the general that Diego Lopez ought to be on his way back, he sent six of his companions to follow up the banks of the little river, and as many more down the banks, to look for traces of the horses at the trails to and from the river. It was impossible to find tracks in this country, because the grass straightened up again as soon as it was trodden down. They were found by some Indians from the army who had gone to look for fruit. These got track of them a good league off, and soon came up with them. They followed the river down to the camp, and told the general that in the twenty leagues they had been over they had seen nothing but cows and the sky. There was another native of Quivira with the army, a tattooed Indian named Ysopete. This Indian had always declared that the Turk was lying, and on account of this the army paid no attention to him, and even now, although he said that the Querechos had consulted with him, Ysopete was not believed.[3]

The general sent Don Rodrigo Maldonado, with his company, forward from here. He traveled four days and reached a large ravine like those of Colima,[4] in the bottom of which he found a large settlement of people. Cabeza de Vaca and Dorantes had passed through this place, so that they presented Don Rodrigo with a pile of tanned skins and other things, and a tent as big as a house, which he directed them to keep until the army came up. He sent some of his companions to guide the army to that place, so that they should not get lost, although he had been making piles of stones and cow dung for the army to follow. This was the way in which the army was guided by the advance guard.

When the general came up with the army and saw the great quantity of skins, he thought he would divide them among the men, & placed guards so that they could look at them. But when the men arrived and saw that the general was sending some of his companions with orders for the guards to give them some of the skins, & that these were to select the best, they were angry because they were not going to be divided evenly, & made a rush, & in less than a quarter of an hour nothing was left but the empty ground.

The natives who happened to see this also took a hand in it. The women and some others were left crying, because they thought that the strangers were not going to take anything, but would bless them as Cabeza de Vaca and Dorantes had done when they passed through here. They found an Indian girl here who was as white as a Castilian lady, except that she had her chin tattooed like a Moorish woman. In general they all tattoo themselves in this way here, and they decorate their eyes.

CHAPTER XX. ⟨ Of how great stones fell in the camp; & how they discovered a ravine, where the army divided into two parts.

HILE the army was resting in this ravine, as we have related, a tempest came up one afternoon with a very high wind & hail, & in a very short space of time a great quantity of hailstones, as big as bowls, or bigger, fell as thick as raindrops, so that in places they covered the ground two or three spans or more deep. And one hit the horse— or I should say, there was not a horse that did not break away, except two or three which the negroes protected by holding large sea nets over them, with the helmets and shields which all the rest wore; and some of them dashed up on to the sides of the ravine so that they got them down with great difficulty. If this had struck them while they were upon the plain, the army would have been in great danger of being left without its horses, as there were many which they were not able to cover. The hail broke many tents, and battered many helmets, and wounded many of the horses, and broke all the crockery of the army, and the gourds, which was no small loss, because they do not have any crockery in this region. They do not make gourds, nor sow corn, nor eat bread, but instead raw meat—or only half cooked—and fruit.

From here the general sent out to explore the country, and they found another settlement four days from there.[1] . . . The country was well inhabited, and they had plenty of kidney beans and prunes like those of Castile, and tall vineyards. These village settlements extended for three days. This was called Cona. Some Teyas,[2] as these people are called, went with the army from here and traveled as far as the end of the other settlements with their packs of dogs & women & children, and then they gave them guides to proceed to a large ravine where the army was. They did not let these guides speak with the Turk and did not receive the same statements from these as they had from the others. These said that Quivira was toward the north, and that we would not find any good road thither. After this they began to believe Ysopete. The ravine which the army had now reached was a league wide from one side to the other, with a little bit of a river at the bottom, and there were many groves of mulberry trees near it, and rosebushes with the same sort of fruit that they have in France. They made verjuice from the unripe grapes at this ravine, although there were ripe ones. There were walnuts and the same kind of fowls as in New Spain, and large quantities of prunes like those of Castile. During this journey a Teya was seen to shoot a bull right through both shoulders with an arrow, which would be a good shot for a musket. These people are very intelligent; the women are well made and modest. They cover their whole body. They wear shoes and buskins made of tanned skin. The women wear cloaks over their small under petticoats, with sleeves gathered up at the shoulders, all of skin, and some wore something like little sanbenitos[3] with a fringe, which reached half-way down the thigh over the petticoat.

The army rested several days in this ravine and explored the country. Up to this point they had made thirty-seven days' marches, traveling six or seven leagues a day. It had been the duty of one man to measure and count his steps. They found that it was 250 leagues to the settlements.[4] When the general Francisco Vazquez realized this, and saw that they had been deceived by the Turk heretofore, & as the provisions were giving out and there was no country around here where they could procure more, he called the captains and ensigns together to decide on what they thought ought to be done. They all agreed that the general should go in search of Quivira with thirty horsemen and half a dozen foot-soldiers, and that Don Tristan de Arellano should go back to Tiguex with all the army. When the men in the army learned of this decision, they begged their general not to leave them to conduct the further search, but declared that they all wanted to die with him and did not want to go back. This did not do any good, although the general agreed to send messengers to them within eight days saying whether it was best for them to follow him or not, and with this he set off with the guides he had and with Ysopete. The Turk was taken along in chains.

CHAPTER XXI. 〔Of how the army returned to Tiguex and the general reached Quivira.

THE general started from the ravine with the guides that the Teyas had given him. He appointed the alderman Diego Lopez his army-master, and took with him the men who seemed to him to be most efficient, and the best horses. The army still had some hope that the general would send for them, and sent two horsemen, lightly equipped and riding post, to repeat their petition.

The general arrived—I mean, the guides ran away during the first few days and Diego Lopez had to return to the army for guides, bringing orders for the army to return to Tiguex to find food and wait there for the general. The Teyas, as before, willingly furnished him with new guides. The army waited for its messengers and spent a fortnight here, preparing jerked beef to take with them. It was estimated that during this fortnight they killed 500 bulls. The number of these that were there without any cows was something incredible. Many fellows were lost at this time who went out hunting and did not get back to the army for two or three days, wandering about the country as if they were crazy, in one direction or another, not knowing how to get back where they started from, although this ravine extended in either direction so that they could find it. Every night they took account of who was missing, fired guns and blew trumpets and beat drums and built great fires, but yet some of them went off so far and wandered about so much that all this did not give them any help, although it helped others. The only way was to go back where they had killed an animal and start from there in one direction and another until they struck the ravine or fell in with somebody who could put them on the right road. It is worth noting that the country there is so level that at midday, after one has wandered about in one direction and another in pursuit of game, the only thing to do is to stay near the game quietly until sunset, so as to see where it goes down, and even then they have to be men who are practiced to do it. Those who are not, had to trust themselves to others.

The general followed his guides until he reached Quivira, which took 48 days' marching, on account of the great detour they had made toward Florida. He was received peacefully on account of the guides whom he had. They asked the Turk why he had lied and had guided them so far out of their way. He said that his country was in that direction and that, besides this, the people at Cicuye had asked him to lead them off on to the plains and lose them, so that the horses would die when their provisions gave out, and they would be so weak if they ever returned that they would be killed without any trouble, and thus they could take revenge for what had been done to them. This was the reason why he had led them astray, supposing that they did not know how to hunt or to live without corn, while as for the gold, he did not know where there was any of it. He said this like one who had given up hope and who found that he was being persecuted, since they had begun to believe Ysopete, who had guided them better than he had, &

fearing lest those who were there might give some advice by which some harm would come to him. They garroted him, which pleased Ysopete very much, because he had always said that Ysopete was a rascal and that he did not know what he was talking about & had always hindered his talking with anybody. Neither gold nor silver nor any trace of either was found among these people. Their lord wore a copper plate on his neck and prized it highly.

The messengers whom the army had sent to the general returned, as I said, and then, as they brought no news except what the alderman had delivered, the army left the ravine and returned to the Teyas, where they took guides who led them back by a more direct road. They readily furnished these, because these people are always roaming over this country in pursuit of the animals and so know it thoroughly. They keep their road in this way: In the morning they notice where the sun rises and observe the direction they are going to take, and then shoot an arrow in this direction. Before reaching this they shoot another over it, and in this way they go all day toward the water where they are to end the day. In this way they covered in 25 days what had taken them 37 days going, besides stopping to hunt cows on the way. They found many salt lakes on this road, and there was a great quantity of salt. There were thick pieces of it on top of the water bigger than tables, as thick as four or five fingers. Two or three spans down under water there was salt which tasted better than that in the floating pieces, because this was rather bitter. It was crystalline. All over these plains there were large numbers of animals like squirrels and a great number of their holes.[1]

On its return the army reached the Cicuye river more than 30 leagues below there—I mean below the bridge they had made when they crossed it, and they followed it up to that place. In general, its banks are covered with a sort of rose bushes, the fruit of which tastes like muscatel grapes. They grow on little twigs about as high up as a man. It has the parsley leaf. There were unripe grapes and currants [?] and wild marjoram. The guides said this river joined that of Tiguex more than 20 days from here, and that its course turned toward the east. It is believed that it flows into the mighty river of the Holy Spirit (Espiritu Santo), which the men with Don Hernando de Soto discovered in Florida.[2] A tattooed Indian woman ran away from Juan de Saldivar and hid in the ravines about this time, because she recognized the country of Tiguex where she had been a slave. She fell into the hands of some Spaniards who had entered the country from Florida to explore it in this direction. After I got back to New Spain I heard them say that the Indian told them that she had run away from other men like them nine days, and that she gave the names of some captains; from which we ought to believe that we were not far from the region they discovered, although they said they were more than 200 leagues inland. I believe the land at that point is more than 600 leagues across from sea to sea.

As I said, the army followed the river up as far as Cicuye, which it found ready for war and unwilling to make any advances toward peace or to give any food to the army. From there we went on to Tiguex where several villages had been reinhabited, but the people were afraid and left them again.

CHAPTER XXII. ☾ Of how the general returned from Quivira and of other expeditions toward the north.

AFTER Don Tristan de Arellano reached Tiguex, about the middle of July, in the year '42,[1] he had provisions collected for the coming winter. Captain Francisco de Barrionuevo was sent up the river toward the north with several men. He saw two provinces, one of which was called Hemes[2] and had seven villages, and the other Yuqueyunque.[3] The inhabitants of Hemes came out peaceably and furnished provisions. At Yuqueyunque the whole nation left two very fine villages which they had on either side of the river entirely vacant, and went into the mountains, where they had four very strong villages in a rough country, where it was impossible for horses to go. In the two villages there was a great deal of food & some very beautiful glazed earthenware with many figures & different shapes. Here they also found many bowls full of a carefully selected shining metal with which they glazed the earthenware. This shows that mines of silver would be found in that country if they should hunt for them.

There was a large and powerful river, I mean village, which was called Braba, 20 leagues farther up the river, which our men called Valladolid.[4] The river flowed through the middle of it. The natives crossed it by wooden bridges, made of very long, large, squared pines. At this village they saw the largest & finest hot rooms or *estufas* that there were in the entire country, for they had a dozen pillars, each one of which was twice as large around

as one could reach and twice as tall as a man. Hernando de Alvarado visited
this village when he discovered Cicuye. The country is very high and very
cold. The river is deep and very swift, without any ford. Captain Barrionuevo returned from here, leaving the province at peace.

Another captain went down the river in search of the settlements which
the people at Tutahaco had said were several days distant from there. This
captain went down 80 leagues and found four large villages which he left at
peace. He proceeded until he found that the river sank into the earth, like
the Guadiana in Estremadura.[5] He did not go on to where the Indians said
that it came out much larger, because his commission did not extend for
more than 80 leagues march. After this captain got back, as the time had
arrived which the captain had set for his return from Quivira, and as he had
not come back, Don Tristan selected 40 companions and, leaving the army
to Francisco de Barrionuevo, he started with them in search of the general.

When he reached Cicuye the people came out of the village to fight,
which detained him there four days, while he punished them, which he did
by firing some volleys into the village. These killed several men, so that
they did not come out against the army, since two of their principal men
had been killed on the first day. Just then word was brought that the general was coming, and so Don Tristan had to stay there on this account also,
to keep the road open. Everybody welcomed the general on his arrival, with
great joy. The Indian Xabe, who was the young fellow who had been given
to the general at Cicuye when he started off in search of Quivira, was with
Don Tristan de Arellano & when he learned that the general was coming
he acted as if he was greatly pleased, and said, "Now, when the general
comes, you will see that there is gold and silver in Quivira, although not
so much as the Turk said." When the general arrived, and Xabe saw that
they had not found anything, he was sad and silent, and kept declaring
that there was some. He made many believe that it was so, because the general had not dared to enter into the country on account of its being thickly
settled and his force not very strong, and that he had returned to lead his
army there after the rains, because it had begun to rain there already, as it
was early in August when he left. It took him forty days to return, traveling lightly equipped. The Turk had said when they left Tiguex that they
ought not load the horses with too much provisions, which would tire them
so that they could not afterward carry the gold and silver, from which it is
very evident that he was deceiving them.

The general reached Cicuye with his force and at once set off for Tiguex, leaving the village more quiet, for they had met him peaceably and had talked with him. When he reached Tiguex, he made his plans to pass the winter there, so as to return with the whole army, because it was said that he brought information regarding large settlements and very large rivers, and that the country was very much like that of Spain in the fruits and vegetation and seasons. They were not ready to believe that there was no gold there, but instead had suspicions that there was some farther back in the country, because, although this was denied, they knew what the thing was and had a name for it among themselves—*acochis*. With this we end this first part, and now we will give an account of the provinces.

SECOND PART

C Which treats of the High Villages and Provinces and of their habits and customs, as collected by Pedro de Castañeda, native of the City of Najara.[1]   LAUS DEO ✠

IT does not seem to me that the reader will be satisfied with having seen and understood what I have already related about the expedition, although that has made it easy to see the difference between the report which told about vast treasures, and the places where nothing like this was either found or known. It is to be noted that in place of settlements great deserts were found, and instead of populous cities villages of 200 inhabitants and only 800 or 1,000 people in the largest. I do not know whether this will furnish grounds for pondering and considering the uncertainty of this life. To please these, I wish to give a detailed account of all the inhabited region seen & discovered by this expedition, and some of their ceremonies and habits, in accordance with what we came to know about them, and the limits within which each province falls, so that hereafter it may be possible to understand in what direction Florida lies and in what direction Greater India; and this land of New Spain is part of the mainland with Peru, and with Greater India or China as well, there not being any strait between to separate them. On the other hand, the country is so wide that there is room for these vast deserts which lie between the two seas, for the coast of the North Sea beyond Florida stretches toward the Bacallaos[2] and then turns toward Norway, while that of the South Sea turns toward the west, making another bend down toward the south almost like a bow and stretches away toward India, leaving room for the lands that border on the mountains on both sides to stretch out in such a way as to have between them these great plains which are full of cattle and many other animals of different sorts, since they are not inhabited, as I will relate farther on. There is every sort of game and fowl there, but no snakes, for they are free from these. I will leave the account of the return of the army to New Spain until I have shown what slight occasion there was for this. We will begin our account with the city of Culiacan, & point out the differences between the one country and the other, on account of which one ought to be settled by Spaniards and the other not. It should be the reverse, however, with Christians, since there are intelligent men in one, and in the other wild animals and worse than beasts.

CHAPTER I. Of the province of Culiacan and of its habits and customs.

CULIACAN is the last place in the New Kingdom of Galicia, and was the first settlement made by Nuño de Guzman when he conquered this kingdom.[1] It is 210 leagues west of Mexico. In this province there are three chief languages, besides other related dialects. The first is that of the Tahues,[2] who are the best & most intelligent race. They are now the most settled and have received the most light from the faith. They worship idols & make presents to the devil of their goods and riches, consisting of cloth & turquoises. They do not eat human flesh nor sacrifice it. They are accustomed to keep very large snakes, which they venerate.[3] Among them there are men dressed like women who marry other men and serve as their wives.[4] At a great festival they consecrate the women who wish to live unmarried, with much singing and dancing, at which all the chiefs of the locality gather and dance naked, and after all have danced with her they put her in a hut that has been decorated for this event and the chiefs adorn her with clothes and bracelets of fine turquoises, and then the chiefs go in one by one to lie with her, and all the others who wish, follow them. From this time on these women cannot refuse anyone

who pays them a certain amount agreed on for this. Even if they take husbands, this does not exempt them from obliging anyone who pays them.
The greatest festivals are on market days. The custom is for the husbands
to buy the women whom they marry, of their fathers and relatives, at a high
price, and then to take them to a chief, who is considered to be a priest, to
deflower them and see if she is a virgin; and if she is not, they have to return
the whole price, and he can keep her for his wife or not, or let her be conse-
crated, as he chooses. At these times they all get drunk.

The second language is that of the Pacaxes, the people who live in the
country between the plains and the mountains. These people are more barbarous. Some of them who live near the mountains eat human flesh. They
are great sodomites, & have many wives, even when these are sisters. They
worship painted and sculptured stones, and are much given to witchcraft
and sorcery.

The third language is that of the Acaxes, who are in possession of a large
part of the hilly country and all of the mountains. They go hunting for
men just as they hunt animals. They all eat human flesh, and he who has
the most human bones and skulls hung up around his house is most feared
and respected. They live in settlements and in very rough country, avoid-
ing the plains. In passing from one settlement to another, there is always a
ravine in the way which they can not cross, although they can talk together
across it. At the slightest call 500 men collect, and on any pretext kill and
eat one another. Thus it has been very hard to subdue these people, on
account of the roughness of the country, which is very great.

Many rich silver mines have been found in this country. They do not
run deep, but soon give out. The gulf of the sea begins on the coast of this
province, entering the land 250 leagues toward the north and ending at
the mouth of the Firebrand (Tizon) River.[5] This country forms its eastern
limit, and California the western. From what I have been told by men who
had navigated it, it is 30 leagues across from point to point, because they
lose sight of this country when they see the other. They say the gulf is over
150 leagues broad (or deep), from shore to shore. The coast makes a turn
toward the south at the Firebrand River, bending down to California, which
turns toward the west, forming that peninsula which was formerly held to
be an island, because it was a low sandy country. It is inhabited by brutish,
bestial, naked people who eat their own offal.[6] The men and women couple
like animals, the female openly getting down on all fours.

CHAPTER II. Of the province of Petlatlan and all the in-
habited country as far as Chichilticalli.

ETLATLAN is a settlement of houses covered with a sort of mats made of *petates*. These are collected into villages, extending along a river from the mountains to the sea. The people are of the same race and habits as the Culuacanian Tahues. There is much sodomy among them. In the mountain district there is a large population & more settlements. These people have a somewhat different language from the Tahues, although they understand each other. It is called Petlatlan because the houses are made of *petates* or palm-leaf mats.[1] Houses of this sort are found for more than 240 leagues in this region, to the beginning of the Cibola wilderness. The nature of the country changes here very greatly, because from this point on there are no trees except the pine, nor are there any fruits except a few tunas,[2] mesquites,[3] and pitahayas.[4]

Petlatlan is 20 leagues from Culiacan, and it is 130 leagues from here to the valley of Señora.[5] There are many rivers between the two, with settlements of the same sort of people—for example, Sinaloa, Boyomo, Teocomo, Yaquimi, and other smaller ones. There is also the Corazones or Hearts, which is in our possession, down the valley of Señora.

Señora is a river and valley thickly settled by able-bodied people. The women wear petticoats of tanned deerskin, and little sanbenitos reaching halfway down the body. The chiefs of the villages go up on some little heights they have made for this purpose, like public criers, and there make proclamations for the space of an hour, regulating those things they have to attend to. They have some little huts for shrines, all over the outside of which they stick many arrows, like a hedgehog. They do this when they are eager for war. All about this province toward the mountains there is a large population in separate little provinces containing ten or twelve villages. Seven or eight of them, of which I know the names, are Comupatrico, Mochilagua, Arispa, and the Little Valley. There are others which we did not see.[6]

It is 40 leagues from Señora to the valley of Suya. The town of Saint Jerome (San Hieronimo) was established in this valley, where there was a rebellion later, and part of the people who had settled there were killed, as will be seen in the third part.[7] There are many villages in the neighborhood of this valley. The people are the same as those in Señora and have the same dress and language, habits, and customs, like all the rest as far as the desert of Chichilticalli. The women paint their chins and eyes like the Moorish women of Barbary. They are great sodomites. They drink wine made of the pitahaya, which is the fruit of a great thistle which opens like the pomegranate. The wine makes them stupid. They make a great quantity of preserves from the tuna; they preserve it in a large amount of its sap without other honey. They make bread of the mesquite, like cheese, which keeps good for a whole year.[8] There are native melons in this country so large that a person can carry only one of them. They cut these into slices and dry them in the sun. They are good to eat, and taste like figs, & are better than dried meat; they are very good and sweet, keeping for a whole year when prepared in this way.[9]

In this country there were also tame eagles, which the chiefs esteemed to be something fine.[10] No fowls of any sort were seen in any of these villages except in this valley of Suya, where fowls like those of Castile were found. Nobody could find out how they came to be so far inland, the people being all at war with one another. Between Suya and Chichilticalli there are many sheep & mountain goats with very large bodies and horns. Some Spaniards declare that they have seen flocks of more than a hundred together, which ran so fast that they disappeared very quickly.

At Chichilticalli the country changes its character again and the spiky vegetation ceases. The reason is that the gulf reaches as far up as this place, and the mountain chain changes its direction at the same time that the coast does. Here they had to cross and pass through the mountains in order to get into the level country.

CHAPTER III. (Of Chichilticalli & the desert, of Cibola, its customs and habits, and of other things.

CHICHILTICALLI is so called because the friars found a house at this place which was formerly inhabited by people who separated from Cibola. It was made of colored or reddish earth.[1] The house was large and appeared to have been a fortress. It must have been destroyed by the people of the district, who are the most barbarous people that have yet been seen. They live in separate cabins and not in settlements. They live by hunting. The rest of the country is all wilderness, covered with pine forests. There are great quantities of the pine nuts. The pines are two or three times as high as a man before they send out branches. There is a sort of oak with sweet acorns, of which they make cakes like sugar plums with dried coriander seeds. It is very sweet, like sugar. Watercress grows in many springs, and there are rosebushes, and penny-royal, and wild marjoram.

There are barbels and *picones,* like those of Spain, in the rivers of this wilderness. Gray lions and leopards were seen.[2] The country rises continually from the beginning of the wilderness until Cibola is reached, which is 85 leagues, going north. From Culiacan to the edge of the wilderness the route had kept the north on the left hand.

Cibola is seven villages.[3] The largest is called Maçaque.[4] The houses are ordinarily three or four stories high, but in Maçaque there are houses with four and seven stories. These people are very intelligent. They cover their privy parts and all the immodest parts with cloths made like a sort of table napkin, with fringed edges & a tassel at each corner, which they tie over the hips. They wear long robes of feathers and of the skins of hares and cotton blankets.[5] The women wear blankets, which they tie or knot over the left shoulder leaving the right arm out. These serve to cover the body. They wear a neat well-shaped outer garment of skin. They gather their hair over the two ears, making a frame which looks like an old-fashioned headdress.[6]

This country is in a valley between mountains in the form of isolated cliffs. They cultivate the corn, which does not grow very high, in patches. There are three or four large fat ears having each eight hundred grains on every stalk growing upward from the ground, something not seen before in these parts.[7] There are large numbers of bears in this province, and lions, wild-cats, deer, and otter. There are very fine turquoises, although not so many as was reported.[8] They collect the pine nuts each year, and store them up in advance. A man does not have more than one wife. There are *estufas* or hot rooms in the villages, which are the courtyards or places where they gather for consultation. They do not have chiefs as in New Spain, but are ruled by a council of the oldest men. They have priests who preach to them, whom they call "papas."[9] These are the elders. They go up on the highest roof of the village and preach to the village from there, like public criers, in the morning while the sun is rising, the whole village being silent & sitting in the galleries to listen.[10] They tell them how they are to live, and I believe that they give certain commandments for them to keep, for there is no drunkenness among them nor sodomy nor sacrifices, neither do they eat human flesh nor steal, but they are usually at work. The *estufas* belong to the whole village. It is a sacrilege for the women to go into the *estufas* to sleep.[11] They make the cross as a sign of peace. They burn their dead, and throw the implements used in their work into the fire with the bodies.[12]

It is 20 leagues to Tusayan, going northwest.[13] This is a province with seven villages, of the same sort, dress, habits, and ceremonies as at Cibola. There may be as many as 3,000 or 4,000 men in the fourteen villages of these two provinces.[14] It is 40 leagues or more to Tiguex, the road trending toward the north. The rock of Acuco, which we described in the first part, is between these.

CHAPTER IV. ℂ Of how they live at Tiguex, & of the pro⁄ vince of Tiguex and its neighborhood.

TIGUEX is a province with twelve villages on the banks of a large, swift river; some villages on one side and some on the other. It is a spacious valley two leagues wide, & a very high, rough, snow-covered mountain chain lies east of it. There are seven villages in the ridges at the foot of this—four on the plain and three situated on the skirts of the mountain.[1]

There are seven villages seven leagues to the north [*i. e.* of Tiguex] at Quirix, and the seven villages of the province of Hemes are 40 leagues northeast.[2] It is four leagues north or east to Acha.[3] Tutahaco, a province with eight villages, is toward the southeast.[4] In general, these villages all have the same habits & customs, although some have some things in particular which the others have not. They are governed by the opinions of the elders.[5] They all work together to build the villages, the women being engaged in making the mixture and the walls, while the men bring the wood and put it in place. They have no lime, but they make a mixture of ashes, coals, and dirt which is almost as good as mortar, for when the house is to have four stories, they do not make the walls more than half a yard thick. They gather a great pile of twigs of thyme and sedge grass and set it afire, and when it is half coals and ashes they throw a quantity of dirt and water on it and mix it all together.[6] They make round balls of this, which they use instead of stones after they are dry, fixing them with the same mixture, which comes to be like a stiff clay. Before they are married the young men serve the whole village in general, and fetch the wood that is needed for use, putting it in a pile in the courtyard of the villages, from which the women take it to carry to their houses.

The young men live in the *estufas*, which are in the yards of the village. They are underground, square or round, with pine pillars. Some were seen with twelve pillars and with four in the center as large as two men could stretch around.[7] They usually had three or four pillars. The floor was made of large, smooth stones, like the baths which they have in Europe. They have a hearth made like the binnacle or compass box of a ship, in which they burn a handful of thyme at a time to keep up the heat, and they can stay in there just as in a bath. The top was on a level with the ground. Some that were seen were large enough for a game of ball. When any man wishes to marry, it has to be arranged by those who govern. The man has to spin and weave a blanket & place it before the woman, who covers herself with it and becomes his wife. The houses belong to the women, the *estufas* to the men. If a man repudiates his woman, he has to go to the *estufa*. It is forbidden for women to sleep in the *estufas*, or to enter these for any purpose except to give their husbands or sons something to eat. The men spin & weave. The women bring up the children and prepare the food. The country is so fertile that they do not have to break up the ground the year round, but only have to sow the seed, which is presently covered by the fall of snow, and the ears come up under the snow. In one year they gather enough for seven. A very large number of cranes & wild geese and crows & starlings live on what is sown, and for all this, when they come to sow for another year, the fields are covered with corn which they have not been able to finish gathering.[8]

There are a great many native fowl in these provinces, and cocks with great hanging chins.[9] When dead, these keep for sixty days, and longer in winter, without losing their feathers or opening, and without any bad smell, and the same is true of dead men.

The villages are free from nuisances, because they go outside to excrete, and they pass their water into clay vessels, which they empty at a distance from the village.[10]

They keep the separate houses where they prepare the food for eating and where they grind the meal, very clean. This is a separate room or closet, where they have a trough with three stones fixed in stiff clay. Three women go in here, each one having a stone, with which one of them breaks the corn, the next grinds it, and the third grinds it again. They take off their shoes, do up their hair, shake their clothes, & cover their heads before they enter the door. A man sits at the door playing on a fife while they grind, moving the stones to the music and singing together. They grind a large quantity at one time, because they make all their bread of meal soaked in warm water, like wafers. They gather a great quantity of brushwood and dry it to use for cooking all through the year.[11] There are no fruits good to eat in the country, except the pine nuts. They have their preachers. Sodomy is not found among them. They do not eat human flesh nor make sacrifices of it. The people are not cruel, for they had Francisco de Ovando in Tiguex about forty days, after he was dead, and when the village was captured, he was found among their dead, whole and without any other wound except the one which killed him, white as snow, without any bad smell. I found out several things about them from one of our Indians, who had been a captive among them for a whole year. I asked him especially for the reason why the young women in that province went entirely naked, however cold it might be, and he told me that the virgins had to go around this way until they took a husband, and that they covered themselves after they had known man. The men here wear little shirts of tanned deerskin & their long robes over this. In all these provinces they have earthenware glazed with antimony and jars of extraordinary labor and workmanship, which were worth seeing.[12]

CHAPTER V. ❲Of Cicuye and the villages in its neighbor-hood, and of how some people came to conquer this country.

E have already said that the people of Tiguex and of all the provinces on the banks of that river were all alike, having the same ways of living and the same customs. It will not be necessary to say anything particular about them. I wish merely to give an account of Cicuye & some depopulated villages which the army saw on the direct road which it followed thither, and of others that were across the snowy mountains near Tiguex, which also lay in that region above the river.

Cicuye[1] is a village of nearly 500 warriors, who are feared throughout that country. It is square, situated on a rock, with a large court or yard in the middle, containing the *estufas*. The houses are all alike, four stories high

One can go over the top of the whole village without there being a street to hinder. There are corridors going all around it at the first two stories, by which one can go around the whole village. These are like outside balconies, and they are able to protect themselves under these. The houses do not have doors below, but they use ladders, which can be lifted up like a drawbridge, and so go up to the corridors which are on the inside of the village. As the doors of the houses open on the corridor of that story, the corridor serves as a street. The houses that open on the plain are right back of those that open on the court, and in time of war they go through those behind them. The village is inclosed by a low wall of stone. There is a spring of water inside, which they are able to divert.[2] The people of this village boast that no one has been able to conquer them & that they conquer whatever villages they wish. The people & their customs are like those of the other villages. Their virgins also go nude until they take husbands, because they say that if they do anything wrong then it will be seen, & so they do not do it. They do not need to be ashamed because they go around as they were born.

There is a village, small and strong, between Cicuye and the province of Quirix, which the Spaniards named Ximena,[3] and another village almost deserted, only one part of which is inhabited.[4] This was a large village, and judging from its condition and newness it appeared to have been destroyed. They called this the village of the granaries or silos, because large underground cellars were found here stored with corn. There was another large village farther on, entirely destroyed and pulled down, in the yards of which there were many stone balls, as big as twelve-quart bowls, which seemed to have been thrown by engines or catapults, which had destroyed the village. All that I was able to find out about them was that, sixteen years before, some people called Teyas,[5] had come to this country in great numbers and had destroyed these villages. They had besieged Cicuye but had not been able to capture it, because it was strong, and when they left the region, they had made peace with the whole country. It seems as if they must have been a powerful people, and that they must have had engines to knock down the villages. The only thing they could tell about the direction these people came from was by pointing toward the north. They usually call these people Teyas or brave men, just as the Mexicans say *chichimecas* or braves, for the Teyas whom the army saw were brave.[6] These knew the people in the settlements, and were friendly with them, and they (the Teyas of the plains) went there to spend the winter under the wings of the settlements. The inhabitants do not dare to let them come inside, because they can not trust them. Although they are received as friends, and trade with them, they do not stay in the villages over night, but outside under the wings. The villages are guarded by sentinels with trumpets, who call to one another just as in the fortresses of Spain.

There are seven other villages along this route, toward the snowy mountains, one of which has been half destroyed by the people already referred to. These were under the rule of Cicuye. Cicuye is in a little valley between mountain chains and mountains covered with large pine forests. There is a little stream which contains very good trout and otters, and there are very large bears and good falcons hereabouts.

CHAPTER VI. **C** Which gives the number of villages which were seen in the country of the terraced houses, & their population.

BEFORE I proceed to speak of the plains, with the cows and settlements and tribes there, it seems to me that it will be well for the reader to know how large the settlements were, where the houses with stories, gathered into villages, were seen, and how great an extent of country they occupied.[1] As I say, Cibola is the first:

Cibola, seven villages.[2]

Tusayan, seven villages.

The rock of Acuco, one.

Tiguex, twelve villages.

Tutahaco, eight villages.

These villages were below the river.

Quirix, seven villages.

In the snowy mountains, seven villages.

Ximena, three villages.

Cicuye, one village.

Hemes, seven villages.

Aguas Calientes, or Boiling Springs, three villages.

Yuqueyunque, in the mountains, six villages.

Valladolid, called Braba, one village.

Chia,[3] one village.

In all, there are sixty-six villages.[4] Tiguex appears to be in the center of the villages. Valladolid is the farthest up the river toward the northeast. The four villages down the river are toward the southeast, because the river turns toward the east.[5] It is 130 leagues—10 more or less—from the farthest point that was seen down the river to the farthest point up the river, and all the settlements are within this region. Including those at a distance, there are sixty-six villages in all, as I have said, and in all of them there may be some 20,000 men, which may be taken to be a fair estimate of the population of the villages. There are no houses or other buildings between one village and another, but where we went it is entirely uninhabited. These people, since they are few, and their manners, government, and habits are so different from all the nations that have been seen and discovered in these western regions, must come from that part of Greater India, the coast of which lies to the west of this country, for they could have come down from that country, crossing the mountain chains and following down the river, settling in what seemed to them the best place. As they multiplied, they kept on making settlements until they lost the river when it buried itself underground, its course being in the direction of Florida. It comes down from the northeast, where they[6] could certainly have found signs of villages. He preferred, however, to follow the reports of the Turk, but it would have been better to cross the mountains where this river rises. I believe they would have found traces of riches and would have reached the lands from which these people started, which from its location is on the edge of Greater India, although the region is neither known nor understood, because from the trend of the coast it appears that the land between Norway and China is very far up. The country from sea to sea is very wide, judging from the location of both coasts, as well as from what Captain Villalobos discovered when he went in search of China by the sea to the west,[7] and from what has been discovered on the North Sea concerning the trend of the coast of Florida toward the Bacallaos, up toward Norway.

To return then to the proposition with which I began, I say that the settlements and people already named were all that were seen in a region 70 leagues wide and 130 long, in the settled country along the river Tiguex. In New Spain there are not one but many establishments, containing a larger number of people. Silver metals were found in many of their villages, which they use for glazing and painting their earthenware.[8]

CHAPTER VII. ℂ Which treats of the plains that were crossed, of the cows, and of the people who inhabit them.

WE HAVE spoken of the settlements of high houses which are situated in what seems to be the most level and open part of the mountains, since it is 150 leagues across before entering the level country between the two mountain chains which I said were near the North Sea and the South Sea, which might better be called the Western Sea along this coast. This mountain series is the one which is near the South Sea.[1] In order to show that the settlements are in the middle of the mountains, I will state that it is 80 leagues from Chichilticalli, where we began to cross this country, to Cibola; from Cibola, which is the first village, to Cicuye, which is the last on the way across, is 70 leagues; it is 30 leagues from Cicuye to where the plains begin. It may be we went across in an indirect or roundabout way, which would make it seem as if there was more country than if it had been crossed in a direct line, and it may be more difficult and rougher. This can not be known certainly, because the mountains change their direction above the bay at the mouth of the Firebrand (Tizon) River.

Now we will speak of the plains. The country is spacious and level, and is more than 400 leagues wide in the part between the two mountain ranges—one, that which Francisco Vazquez de Coronado crossed, and the other that which the force under Don Fernando de Soto crossed, near the North Sea, entering the country from Florida. No settlements were seen anywhere on these plains.

In traversing 250 leagues, the other mountain range was not seen, nor a hill nor a hillock which was three times as high as a man. Several lakes were found at intervals; they were round as plates, a stone's throw or more across, some fresh and some salt. The grass grows tall near these lakes; away from them it is very short, a span or less. The country is like a bowl, so that when a man sits down, the horizon surrounds him all around at the distance of a musket shot. There are no groves of trees except at the rivers, which flow at the bottom of some ravines where the trees grow so thick that they were not noticed until one was right on the edge of them. They are of dead earth. There are paths down into these, made by the cows when they go to the water, which is essential throughout these plains.

As I have related in the first part, people follow the cows, hunting them and tanning the skins to take to the settlements in the winter to sell, since they go there to pass the winter, each company going to those which are nearest, some to the settlements at Cicuye, others toward Quivira, and others to the settlements which are situated in the direction of Florida. These people are called Querechos and Teyas. They described some large settlements, and judging from what was seen of these people and from the accounts they gave of other places, there are a good many more of these people than there are of those at the settlements. They have better figures, are better warriors, and are more feared. They travel like the Arabs, with their tents and troops of dogs loaded with poles[2] and having Moorish pack saddles with girths. When the load gets disarranged, the dogs howl, calling some one to fix them right. These people eat raw flesh and drink blood. They do not eat human flesh. They are a kind people and not cruel. They are faithful friends. They are able to make themselves very well understood by means of signs. They dry the flesh in the sun, cutting it thin like a leaf, and when dry they grind it like meal to keep it and make a sort of sea soup of it to eat. A handful thrown into a pot swells up so as to increase very much. They season it with fat, which they always try to secure when they kill a cow.[3] They empty a large gut and fill it with blood, and carry this around the neck to drink when they are thirsty. When they open the belly of a cow, they squeeze out the chewed grass and drink the juice that remains behind, because they say that this contains the essence of the stomach. They cut the hide open at the back and pull it off at the joints, using a flint as large as a finger, tied in a little stick, with as much ease as if working with a good iron tool. They give it an edge with their own teeth. The quickness with which they do this is something worth seeing and noting.

There are very great numbers of wolves on these plains, which go around with the cows. They have white skins. The deer are pied with white. Their skin is loose, so that when they are killed it can be pulled off with the hand while warm, coming off like pigskin. The rabbits, which are very numerous, are so foolish that those on horseback killed them with their lances. This is when they are mounted among the cows. They fly from a person on foot.

CHAPTER VIII. C Of Quivira, of where it is and some information about it.

QUIVIRA is to the west of those ravines, in the midst of the country, somewhat nearer the mountains toward the sea, for the country is level as far as Quivira, and there they began to see some mountain chains.[1] The country is well settled. Judging from what was seen on the borders of it, this country is very similar to that of Spain in the varities of vegetation and fruits. There are plums like those of Castile, grapes, nuts, mulberries, oats, pennyroyal, wild marjoram, and large quantities of flax, but this does not do them any good, because they do not know how to use it.[1] The people are of almost the same sort and appearance as the Teyas. They have villages like those in New Spain. The houses are round, without a wall, and they have one story like a loft, under the roof, where they sleep and keep their belongings. The roofs are of straw.[2] There are other thickly settled provinces around it containing large numbers of men. A friar named Juan de Padilla remained in this province, together with a Spanish-Portuguese and a negro and a half-blood and some Indians from the province of Capothan, in New Spain. They killed the friar because he wanted to go to the province of the Guas, who were their enemies. The Spaniard escaped by taking flight on a mare, and afterward reached New Spain, coming out by way of Panuco. The Indians from New Spain who accompanied the friar were allowed by the murderers to bury him, and then they followed the Spaniard and overtook him. This Spaniard was a Portuguese, named Campo.

The great river of the Holy Spirit (Espiritu Santo),[3] which Don Fernando de Soto discovered in the country of Florida, flows through this country. It passes through a province called Arache, according to the reliable accounts which were obtained here.[4] The sources were not visited, because, according to what they said, it comes from a very distant country in the mountains of the South Sea, from the part that sheds its waters onto the plains. It flows across all the level country and breaks through the mountains of the North Sea, and comes out where the people with Don Fernando de Soto navigated it. This is more than 300 leagues from where it enters the sea. On account of this, and also because it has large tributaries, it is so mighty when it enters the sea that they lost sight of the land before the water ceased to be fresh.[5]

This country of Quivira was the last that was seen, of which I am able to give any description or information. Now it is proper for me to return and speak of the army, which I left in Tiguex, resting for the winter, so that it would be able to proceed or return in search of these settlements of Quivira, which was not accomplished after all, because it was God's pleasure that these discoveries should remain for other peoples and that we who had been there should content ourselves with saying that we were the first who discovered it and obtained any information concerning it, just as Hercules knew the site where Julius Cæsar was to found Seville or Hispales. May the all-powerful Lord grant that His will be done in everything. It is certain that if this had not been His will Francisco Vazquez would not have returned to New Spain without cause or reason, as he did, and that it would not have been left for those with Don Fernando de Soto to settle such a good country, as they have done, and besides settling it to increase its extent, after obtaining, as they did, information from our army.[6]

THIRD PART

℃ Which describes what happened to Francisco Vasquez
de Coronado during the winter, & how he gave up the
expedition and returned to New Spain. LAUS DEO ✠

CHAPTER I. ℃ Of how Don Pedro de Tovar came from Señora with some men, & Don García Lopez de Cardenas started back to New Spain.

AT THE end of the first part of this book, we told how Francisco Vazquez de Coronado, when he got back from Quivira, gave orders to winter at Tiguex, in order to return, when the winter was over, with his whole army to discover all the settlements in those regions. Don Pedro de Tovar, who had gone, as we related, to conduct a force from the city of Saint Jerome (San Hieronimo), arrived in the meantime with the men whom he had brought. He had not selected the rebels and seditious men there, but the most experienced ones and the best soldiers—men whom he could trust—wisely considering that he ought to have good men in order to go in search of his general in the country of the Indian called Turk.

Although they found the army at Tiguex when they arrived there, this did not please them much, because they had come with great expectations, believing that they would find their general in the rich country of the

Indian called Turk. They consoled themselves with the hope of going back there, and lived in anticipation of the pleasure of undertaking this return expedition, which the army would soon make to Quivira. Don Pedro de Tovar brought letters from New Spain, both from the viceroy, Don Antonio de Mendoza, and from individuals. Among these was one from Don Garcia Lopez de Cardenas, which informed him of the death of his brother, the heir, and summoned him to Spain to receive the inheritance. On this account he was given permission, and left Tiguex with several other persons who received permission to go and settle their affairs. There were many others who would have liked to go, but did not, in order not to appear fainthearted. During this time the general endeavored to pacify several villages in the neighborhood which were not well disposed, and to make peace with the people at Tiguex. He tried also to procure some of the cloth of the country, because the soldiers were almost naked and poorly clothed, full of lice, which they were unable to get rid of or avoid.

The general, Francisco Vazquez de Coronado, had been beloved and obeyed by his captains and soldiers as heartily as any of those who have ever started out in the Indies. Necessity knows no law, and the captains who collected the cloth divided it badly, taking the best for themselves and their friends and soldiers, and leaving the rest for the soldiers, and so there began to be some angry murmuring on account of this. Others also complained because they noticed that some favored ones were spared in the work and in the watches and received better portions of what was divided, both of cloth and food. On this account it is thought that they began to say that there was nothing in the country of Quivira which was worth returning for, which was no slight cause of what afterward happened, as will be seen.

CHAPTER II. C Of the general's fall, and how the return to New Spain was ordered.

A FTER the winter was over, the return to Quivira was announced, and the men began to prepare the things needed. Since nothing in this life is at the disposition of men, but all is under the ordination of Almighty God, it was His will that we should not accomplish this, and so it happened that one feast day the general went out on horseback to amuse himself, as usual, riding with the

Captain Don Rodrigo Maldonado. He was on a powerful horse, and his servants had put on a new girth, which must have been rotten at the time, for it broke during the race and he fell over on the side where Don Rodrigo was, and as his horse passed over him it hit his head with its hoof, which laid him at the point of death, and his recovery was slow and doubtful.

During this time, while he was in his bed, Don Garcia Lopez de Cardenas, who had started to go to New Spain, came back in flight from Suya, because he had found that town deserted and the people and horses and cattle all dead. When he reached Tiguex and learned the sad news that the general was near his end, as already related, they did not dare to tell him until he had recovered, and when he finally got up and learned of it, it affected him so much that he had to go back to bed again. He may have done this in order to bring about what he afterward accomplished, as was believed later.

It was while he was in this condition that he recollected what a scientific friend of his in Salamanca had told him, that he would become a powerful lord in distant lands, and that he would have a fall from which he would never be able to recover. This expectation of death made him desire to return and die where he had a wife and children. As the physician and surgeon who was doctoring him, and also acted as a talebearer, suppressed the murmurings that were going about among the soldiers, he treated secretly and underhandedly with several gentlemen who agreed with him. They set the soldiers to talking about going back to New Spain, in little knots and gatherings, and induced them to hold consultations about it, and had them send papers to the general, signed by all the soldiers, through their ensigns, asking for this. They all entered into it readily, and not much time needed to be spent, since many desired it already. When they asked him, the general acted as if he did not want to do it, but all the gentlemen and captains supported them, giving him their signed opinions, and as some were in this, they could give it at once, and they even persuaded others to do the same.

Thus they made it seem as if they ought to return to New Spain, because they had not found any riches, nor had they discovered any settled country out of which estates could be formed for all the army. When he had obtained their signatures, the return to New Spain was at once announced, and since nothing can ever be concealed, the double dealing began to be understood, and many of the gentlemen found that they had been deceived and had made a mistake. They tried in every way to get their signatures back again from the general, who guarded them so carefully that he did not go out of one room, making his sickness seem very much worse, and putting guards about his person and room, and at night about the floor on which he slept. In spite of all this, they stole his chest, and it is said that they did not find their signatures in it, because he kept them in his mattress; on the other hand, it is said that they did recover them. They asked the general to give them 60 picked men, with whom they would remain and hold the country until the viceroy could send them support, or recall them, or else that the general would leave them the army and pick out 60 men to go back with him. But the soldiers did not want to remain either way, some because they had turned their prow toward New Spain, and others because they saw clearly the trouble that would arise over who should have the command. The gentlemen, I do not know whether because they had sworn fidelity or because they feared that the soldiers would not support them, did what had been decided on, although with an ill-will, and from this time on they did not obey the general as readily as formerly, and they did not show any affection for him. He made much of the soldiers and humored them, with the result that he did what he desired and secured the return of the whole army.

CHAPTER III. Of the rebellion at Suya and the reasons the settlers gave for it.

E HAVE already stated in the last chapter that Don Garcia Lopez de Cardenas came back from Suya in flight, having found that country risen in rebellion. He told how and why that town was deserted, which occurred as I will relate. The entirely worthless fellows were all who had been left in that town, the mutinous and seditious men, besides a few who were honored with the charge of public affairs and who were left to govern the others. Thus the bad dispositions of the worthless secured the power, and they held daily meetings and councils and declared that they had been betrayed and were not going to be rescued, since the others had been directed to go through another part of the country, where there was a more convenient route to New Spain, which was not so because they were still almost on the direct road. This talk led some of them to revolt, and they chose one Pedro de Avila as their captain.

They went back to Culiacan, leaving the captain, Diego de Alcaraz, sick in the town of San Hieronimo, with only a small force. He did not have anyone whom he could send after them to compel them to return. They killed a number of people at several villages along the way. Finally they reached Culiacan, where Hernandarias de Saabedra, who was waiting for Juan Gallego to come back from New Spain with a force, detained them by means of promises, so that Gallego could take them back. Some who feared what might happen to them ran away one night to New Spain. Diego de Alcaraz, who had remained at Suya with a small force, sick, was not able to hold his position, although he would have liked to, on account of the poisonous herb which the natives use. When these noticed how weak the Spaniards were, they did not continue to trade with them as they formerly had done. Veins of gold had already been discovered before this, but they were unable to work these, because the country was at war. The disturbance was so great that they did not cease to keep watch and to be more than usually careful.[1]

The town was situated on a little river. One night all of a sudden they saw fires which they were not accustomed to, and on this account they doubled the watches, but not having noticed anything during the whole night, they grew careless along toward morning, and the enemy entered the village so silently that they were not seen until they began to kill and plunder. A number of men reached the plain as well as they could, but while they were getting out the captain was mortally wounded. Several Spaniards came back on some horses after they had recovered themselves and attacked the enemy, rescuing some, though only a few. The enemy went off with the booty, leaving three Spaniards killed, besides many of the servants and more than twenty horses.

The Spaniards who survived started off the same day on foot, not having any horses. They went toward Culiacan, keeping away from the roads, and did not find any food until they reached Corazones, where the Indians, like the good friends they have always been, provided them with food. From here they continued to Culiacan, undergoing great hardships. Hernandarias de Saabedra, the mayor, received them and entertained them as well as he could until Juan Gallego arrived with the reinforcements which he was conducting, on his way to find the army. He was not a little troubled at finding that post deserted, when he expected that the army would be in the rich country which had been described by the Indian called Turk, because he looked like one.

CHAPTER IV. C Of how Friar Juan de Padilla & Friar Luis remained in the country & the army prepared to return to Mexico.

WHEN the general, Francisco Vazquez, saw that everything was now quiet, and that his schemes had gone as he wished, he ordered that everything should be ready to start on the return to New Spain by the beginning of the month of April, in the year 1543.[1]

Seeing this, Friar Juan de Padilla, a regular brother of the lesser order,[2] and another, Friar Luis, a lay brother, told the general that they wanted to remain in that country—Friar Juan de Padilla in Quivira, because his teachings seemed to promise fruit there, and Friar Luis at Cicuye. On this account, as it was Lent at the time, the father made this the subject of his sermon to the companies one Sunday, establishing his proposition on the authority of the Holy Scriptures. He declared his zeal for the conversion of these peoples and his desire to draw them to the faith, and stated that he had received permission to do it, although this was not necessary. The general sent a company to escort them as far as Cicuye, where Friar Luis stopped, while Friar Juan went on back to Quivira with the guides who had conducted the general, taking with him the Portuguese, as we related, and the half-blood, and the Indians from New Spain. He was martyred a short time after he arrived there, as we related in the second part, chapter 8. Thus we may be sure that he died a martyr, because his zeal was holy and earnest.

Friar Luis remained at Cicuye. Nothing more has been heard about him since, but before the army left Tiguex some men who went to take him a number of sheep that were left for him to keep, met him as he was on his way to visit some other villages, which were 15 or 20 leagues from Cicuye, accompanied by some followers. He felt very hopeful that he was liked at the village and that his teachings would bear fruit, although he complained that the old men were falling away from him. I, for my part, believe that as he was a man of good and holy life, Our Lord will protect him and give him grace to convert many of those peoples, and end his days in guiding them in the faith. We do not need to believe otherwise, for the people in those parts are pious and not at all cruel. They are friends, or rather, enemies of cruelty, and they remain faithful and loyal friends.[3]

After the friars had gone, the general, fearing that they might be injured if people were carried away from that country to New Spain, ordered the soldiers to let any of the natives who were held as servants go free to their villages whenever they might wish. In my opinion, though I am not sure, it would have been better if they had been kept and taught among Christians.

The general was very happy and contented when the time arrived and everything needed for the journey was ready, and the army started from Tiguex on its way back to Cibola. One thing of no small note happened during this part of the trip. The horses were in good condition for their work when they started, fat and sleek, but more than thirty died during the ten days which it took to reach Cibola, and there was not a day in which two or three or more did not die. A large number of them also died afterward before reaching Culiacan, a thing that did not happen during all the rest of the journey.

After the army reached Cibola, it rested before starting across the wilderness, because this was the last of the settlements in that country. The whole country was left well disposed and at peace, and several of our Indian allies remained there.

CHAPTER V. ❲Of how the army left the settlements and marched to Culiacan, and of what happened on the way.

EAVING astern, as we might say, the settlements that had been discovered in the new land, of which, as I have said, the seven villages of Cibola were the first to be seen and the last that were left, the army started off, marching across the wilderness. The natives kept following the rear of the army for two or three days, to pick up any baggage or servants, for although they were still at peace and had always been loyal friends, when they saw that we were going to leave the country entirely, they were glad to get some of our people in their power, although I do not think that they wanted to injure them, from what I was told by some who were not willing to go back with them when they teased and asked them to. Altogether, they carried off several people besides those who had remained of their own accord, among whom good interpreters could be found today.

The wilderness was crossed without opposition, and on the second day before reaching Chichilticalli Juan Gallego met the army, as he was coming from New Spain with re-enforcements of men and necessary supplies for the army, expecting that he would find the army in the country of the Indian called Turk. When Juan Gallego saw that the army was returning, the first thing he said was not, "I am glad you are coming back," and he did not like it any better after he had talked with the general. After he had reached the army, or rather the quarters, there was quite a little movement among the gentlemen toward going back with the new force which had made no slight exertions in coming thus far, having encounters every day with the Indians of these regions who had risen in revolt, as will be related. There was talk of making a settlement somewhere in that region until the viceroy could receive an account of what had occurred. Those soldiers who had come from the new lands would not agree to anything except the return to New Spain, so that nothing came of the proposals made at the consultations, and although there was some opposition, they were finally quieted. Several of the mutineers who had deserted the town of Corazones came with Juan Gallego, who had given them his word as surety for their safety, and even if the general had wanted to punish them, his power was slight, for he had been disobeyed already and was not much respected. He began to be afraid again after this, and made himself sick, and kept a guard.

In several places yells were heard and Indians seen, and some of the horses were wounded and killed, before Batuco[1] was reached, where the friendly Indians from Corazones came to meet the army and see the general. They were always friendly and had treated all the Spaniards who passed through their country well, furnishing them with what food they needed, and men, if they needed these. Our men had always treated them well and repaid them for these things. During this journey the juice of the quince was proved to be a good protection against the poison of the natives, because at one place, several days before reaching Señora, the hostile Indians wounded a Spaniard called Mesa, and he did not die, although the wound of the fresh poison is fatal, and there was a delay of over two hours before curing him with the juice. The poison, however, had left its mark upon him. The skin rotted and fell off until it left the bones and sinews bare, with a horrible smell. The wound was in the wrist, and the poison had reached as far as the shoulder when he was cured. The skin on all this fell off.

The army proceeded without taking any rest, because the provisions had begun to fail by this time. These districts were in rebellion, and so there were not any victuals where the soldiers could get them until they reached Petlatlan, although they made several forays into the cross country in search of provisions. Petlatlan is in the province of Culiacan, and on this account was at peace, although they had several surprises after this. The army rested here several days to get provisions. After leaving here they were able to travel more quickly than before, through the 30 leagues of the valley of Culiacan, where they were welcomed back again as people who came with their governor, who had suffered ill treatment.

CHAPTER VI. Of how the general started from Culiacan to give the viceroy an account of the army with which he had been entrusted.

IT SEEMED, indeed, as if the arrival in the valley of Culiacan had ended the labors of this journey, partly because the general was governor there and partly because it was inhabited by Christians. On this account some began to disregard their superiors and the authority which their captains had over them, and some captains even forgot the obedience due to their general. Each one played his own game, so that while the general was marching toward the town, which was still 10 leagues away, many of the men, or most of them, left him in order to rest in the valley, and some even proposed not to follow him. The general understood that he was not strong enough to compel them, although his position as governor gave him fresh authority. He determined to accomplish it by a better method, which was to order all the captains to provide food and meat from the stores of several villages that were under his control as governor. He pretended to be sick, keeping his bed, so that those who had any business with him could speak to him or he with them more freely, without hindrance or observation, and he kept sending for his particular friends in order to ask them to be sure to speak to the soldiers and encourage them to accompany him back to New Spain, and to tell them that he would request the viceroy, Don Antonio de Mendoza, to show them especial favor, and that he would do so himself for those who might wish to remain in his government. After this had been done, he started with his army at a very bad time, when the rains were beginning, for it was about Saint John's day, at which season it rains continuously.

In the uninhabited country which they passed through as far as Compostela there are numerous, very dangerous rivers, full of large and fierce alligators. While the army was halting at one of these rivers, a soldier who was crossing from one side to the other was seized, in sight of everybody, and carried off by an alligator without it being possible to help him. The general proceeded, leaving the men who did not want to follow him all along the way, and reached Mexico with fewer than 100 men. He made his report to the viceroy, Don Antonio de Mendoza, who did not receive him very graciously, although he gave him his discharge. His reputation was gone from this time on. He kept the government of New Galicia, which had been entrusted to him, for only a short time, when the viceroy took it himself, until the arrival of the court, or audiencia, which still governs it. And this was the end of those discoveries and of the expedition which was made to these new lands.

It now remains for us to describe the way in which to enter the country by a more direct route, although there is never a short cut without hard work. It is always best to find out what those know who have prepared the way, who know what will be needed. This can be found elsewhere, and I will now tell where Quivira lies, what direction the army took, and the direction in which Greater India lies, which was what they pretended to be in search of, when the army started thither. Today, since Villalobos has discovered that this part of the coast of the South Sea trends toward the west, it is clearly seen and acknowledged that, since we were in the north, we ought to have turned to the west instead of toward the east, as we did. With this, we will leave this subject and will proceed to finish this treatise, since there are several noteworthy things of which I must give an account, which I have left to be treated more extensively in the two following chapters.

CHAPTER VII.❧Of the adventures of Captain Juan Gallego while he was bringing re-enforcements through the revolted country.

NE might well have complained when in the last chapter I passed in silence over the exploits of Captain Juan Gallego with his 20 companions. I will relate them in the present chapter, so that in times to come those who read about it or tell of it may have a reliable authority on whom to rely. I am not writing fables, like some of the things which we read about nowadays in the books of chivalry. If it were not that those stories contained enchantments, there are some things which our Spaniards have done in our own day in these parts, in their conquests and encounters with the Indians, which, for deeds worthy of admiration, surpass not only the books already mentioned, but also those which have been written about the twelve peers of France, because, if the deadly strength which the authors of those times attributed to their heroes and the brilliant and resplendent arms with which they adorned them, are fully considered, and compared with the small stature of the men of our time and the few and poor weapons which they have in these parts,[1] the remarkable things which our people have undertaken and accomplished with such weapons are more to be wondered at today than those of which the ancients write, and just because, too, they fought with barbarous naked people, as ours have with Indians, among whom there are always men who are brave and valiant and very sure bowmen, for we have seen them pierce the wings while flying, and hit hares while running after them. I have said all this in order to show that some things which we consider fables may be true, because we see greater things every day in our own times, just as in future times people will greatly wonder at the deeds of Don Fernando Cortez, who dared to go into the midst of New Spain with 300 men against the vast number of people in Mexico, and who with 500 Spaniards succeeded in subduing it, and made himself lord over it in two years.

The deeds of Don Pedro de Alvarado in the conquest of Guatemala, and those of Montejo in Tabasco, the conquests of the mainland and of Peru, were all such as to make me remain silent concerning what I now wish to relate; but since I have promised to give an account of what happened on this journey, I want the things I am now going to relate to be known as well as those others of which I have spoken.

The Captain Juan Gallego, then, reached the town of Culiacan with a very small force. There he collected as many as he could of those who had escaped from the town of Hearts, or, more correctly, from Suya, which made in all 22 men, and with these he marched through all of the settled country, across which he traveled 200 leagues with the country in a state of war and the people in rebellion, although they had formerly been friendly toward the Spaniards, having encounters with the enemy almost every day. He always marched with the advance guard, leaving two-thirds of his force behind with the baggage. With six or seven Spaniards, and without any of the Indian allies whom he had with him, he forced his way into their villages, killing and destroying and setting them on fire, coming upon the enemy so suddenly and with such quickness and boldness that they did not have a chance to collect or even to do anything at all, until they became so afraid of him that there was not a town which dared wait for him, but they fled before him as from a powerful army; so much so, that for ten days, while he was passing through the settlements, they did not have an hour's rest.

He did all this with his seven companions, so that when the rest of the force came up with the baggage there was nothing for them to do except to pillage, since the others had already killed and captured all the people they could lay their hands on and the rest had fled. They did not pause anywhere, so that although the villages ahead of him received some warning, they were upon them so quickly that they did not have a chance to collect. Especially in the region where the town of Hearts had been, he killed and hung a large number of people to punish them for their rebellion. He did not lose a companion during all this, nor was anyone wounded, except one soldier, who was wounded in the eyelid by an Indian who was almost dead, whom he was stripping. The weapon broke the skin and, as it was poisoned, he would have had to die if he had not been saved by the quince juice; he lost his eye as it was.

These deeds of theirs were such that I know those people will remember them as long as they live, and especially four or five friendly Indians who went with them from Corazones, who thought that they were so wonderful that they held them to be something divine rather than human. If he had not fallen in with our army as he did, they would have reached the country of the Indian called Turk, which they expected to march to, & they would have arrived there without danger on account of their good order and the skill with which he was leading them, & their knowledge and ample practice in war. Several of these men are still in this town of Culiacan, where I am now writing this account and narrative, where they, as well as I and the others who have remained in this province, have never lacked for labor in keeping this country quiet, in capturing rebels, and increasing in poverty and need, and more than ever at the present hour, because the country is poorer and more in debt than ever before.

CHAPTER VIII. ℂ Which describes some remarkable things that were seen on the plains, with a description of the bulls.

M Y silence was not without mystery and dissimulation when, in chapter 7 of the second part of this book, I spoke of the plains and of the things of which I will give a detailed account in this chapter, where all these things may be found together; for these things were remarkable and something not seen in other parts. I dare to write of them because I am writing at a time when many men are still living who saw them and who will vouch for my account. Who could believe that 1,000 horses and 500 of our cows and more than 5,000 rams and ewes and more than 1,500 friendly Indians and servants, in traveling over those plains, would leave no more trace where they had passed than if nothing had been there—nothing—so that it was necessary to make piles of bones and cow dung now and then, so that the rear guard could follow the army. The grass never failed to become erect after it had been trodden down, and, although it was short, it was as fresh and straight as before.

Another thing was a heap of cow bones, a crossbow shot long, or a very little less, almost twice a man's height in places, and some 18 feet or more wide, which was found on the edge of a salt lake in the southern part, and this in a region where there are no people who could have made it. The only explanation of this which could be suggested was that the waves which the north winds must make in the lake had piled up the bones of the cattle which had died in the lake, when the old and weak ones who went into the water were unable to get out. The noticeable thing is the number of cattle that would be necessary to make such a pile of bones.[1]

Now that I wish to describe the appearance of the bulls, it is to be noticed first that there was not one of the horses that did not take flight when he saw them first, for they have a narrow, short face, the brow two palms across from eye to eye, the eyes sticking out at the side, so that, when they are running, they can see who is following them. They have very long beards, like goats, and when they are running they throw their heads back with the beard dragging on the ground. There is a sort of girdle round the middle of the body. The hair is very woolly, like a sheep's, very fine, and in front of the girdle the hair is very long and rough like a lion's. They have a great hump, larger than a camel's. The horns are short & thick, so that they are not seen much above the hair. In May they change the hair in the middle of the body for a down, which makes perfect lions of them. They rub against the small trees in the little ravines to shed their hair, and they continue this until only the down is left, as a snake changes his skin. They have a short tail, with a bunch of hair at the end. When they run, they carry it erect like a scorpion. It is worth noticing that the little calves are red and just like ours, but they change their color and appearance with time and age.

Another strange thing was that all the bulls that were killed had their left ears slit, although these were whole when young. The reason for this was a puzzle that could not be guessed. The wool ought to make good cloth on account of its fineness, although the color is not good, because it is the color of burel.[2]

Another thing worth noticing is that the bulls traveled without cows in such large numbers that nobody could have counted them, and so far away from the cows that it was more than 40 leagues from where we began to see the bulls to the place where we began to see the cows. The country they traveled over was so level and smooth that if one looked at them the sky could be seen between their legs, so that if some of them were at a distance they looked like smooth-trunked pines whose tops joined, and if there was only one bull it looked as if there were four pines. When one was near them, it was impossible to see the ground on the other side of them. The reason for all this was that the country seemed as round as if a man should imagine himself in a three-pint measure, and could see the sky at the edge of it, about a crossbow shot from him, and even if a man only lay down on his back he lost sight of the ground.[3]

I have not written about other things which were seen nor made any mention of them, because they were not of so much importance, although it does not seem right for me to remain silent concerning the fact that they venerate the sign of the cross in the region where the settlements have high houses. For at a spring which was in the plain near Acuco they had a cross two palms high and as thick as a finger, made of wood with a square twig for its crosspiece, and many little sticks decorated with feathers around it, and numerous withered flowers, which were the offerings.[4] In a graveyard outside the village of Tutahaco there appeared to have been a recent burial. Near the head there was another cross made of two little sticks tied with cotton thread, & dry withered flowers. It certainly seems to me that in some way they must have received some light from the cross of Our Redeemer, Christ, & it may have come by way of India, from whence they proceeded.

CHAPTER IX. ℂ Which treats of the direction which the army took, and of how another more direct way might be found, if anyone was to return to that country.

I VERY much wish that I possessed some knowledge of cosmography or geography, so as to render intelligible what I wish to say, and so that I could reckon up or measure the advantage those people who might go in search of that country would have if they went directly through the center of the country, instead of following the road the army took. However, with the help of the favor of the Lord, I will state it as well as I can, making it as plain as possible.

It is, I think, already understood that the Portuguese, Campo, was the soldier who escaped when Friar Juan de Padilla was killed at Quivira, and that he finally reached New Spain from Panuco,[1] having traveled across the plains country until he came to cross the North Sea mountain chain, keeping the country that Don Hernando de Soto discovered all the time on his left hand, since he did not see the river of the Holy Spirit (Espiritu Santo) at all.[2] After he had crossed the North Sea mountains, he found that he was in Panuco, so that if he had not tried to go to the North Sea, he would have come out in the neighborhood of the border land, or the country of the Sacatecas,[3] of which we now have some knowledge.[4]

This way would be somewhat better and more direct for anyone going back there in search of Quivira, since some of those who came with the Portuguese are still in New Spain to serve as guides. Nevertheless, I think it would be best to go through the country of the Guachichules,[5] keeping near the South Sea mountains all the time, for there are more settlements and a food supply, for it would be suicide to launch out on to the plains country, because it is so vast and is barren of anything to eat, although, it is true, there would not be much need of this after coming to the cows.

This is only when one goes in search of Quivira, and of the villages which were described by the Indian called Turk, for the army of Francisco Vazquez de Coronado went the very farthest way round to get there, since they started from Mexico and went 110 leagues to the west, and then 100 leagues to the northeast, and 250 to the north, and all this brought them as far as the ravines where the cows were, and after traveling 850 leagues they were not more than 400 leagues distant from Mexico by a direct route. If one desires to go to the country of Tiguex, so as to turn from there toward the west in search of the country of India, he ought to follow the road taken by the army, for there is no other, even if one wished to go by a different way, because the arm of the sea which reaches into this coast toward the north does not leave room for any. But what might be done is to have a fleet and cross this gulf and disembark in the neighborhood of the Island of Negroes[6] and enter the country from there, crossing the mountain chains in search of the country from which the people at Tiguex came, or other peoples of the same sort.

As for entering from the country of Florida and from the North Sea, it has already been observed that the many expeditions which have been undertaken from that side have been unfortunate and not very successful, because that part of the country is full of bogs and poisonous fruits, barren, and the very worst country that is warmed by the sun. But they might disembark after passing the river of the Holy Spirit, as Don Hernando de Soto did. Nevertheless, despite the fact that I underwent much labor, I still think that the way I went to that country is the best. There ought to be river courses, because the necessary supplies can be carried on these more easily in large quantities. Horses are the most necessary things in the new countries, and they frighten the enemy most. . . . Artillery is also much feared by those who do not know how to use it. A piece of heavy artillery would be very good for settlements like those which Francisco Vazquez de Coronado discovered, in order to knock them down, because he had nothing but some small machines for slinging and nobody skillful enough to make a catapult or some other machine which would frighten them, which is very necessary.

I say, then, that with what we now know about the trend of the coast of the South Sea, which has been followed by the ships which explored the western part, and what is known of the North Sea toward Norway, the coast of which extends up from Florida, those who now go to discover the country which Francisco Vazquez entered, and reach the country of Cibola or of Tiguex, will know the direction in which they ought to go in order to discover the true direction of the country which the Marquis of the Valley, Don Hernando Cortes, tried to find, following the direction of the gulf of the Firebrand (Tizon) River. This will suffice for the conclusion of our narrative. Everything else rests on the powerful Lord of all things, God Omnipotent, who knows how and when these lands will be discovered and for whom He has guarded this good fortune.   LAUS DEO ✠

℃ Finished copying, Saturday the 26th of October, 1596, in Seville.

℄ Letter from Mendoza to the King, April 17, 1540

℄ Letter from Coronado to Mendoza, August 3, 1540

℄ Traslado de las Nuevas

℄ Relacion del Suceso

℄ Letter from Coronado to the King, October 20, 1541

℄ Narrative of Jaramillo

℄ Report of Hernando de Alvarado

℄ Testimony concerning those who went on the expedition with Francisco Vazquez de Coronado

LETTER FROM MENDOZA TO THE KING

April 17, 1540[1]

S.C.C.M.:

I WROTE to Your Majesty from Compostela the last of February, giving you an account of my arrival there and of the departure of Francisco Vazquez with the force which I sent to pacify and settle in the newly discovered country, and of how the warden, Lope de Samaniego, was going as army-master, both because he was a responsible person and a very good Christian, and because he has had experience in matters of this sort; as Your Majesty had desired to know. And the news which I have received since then is to the effect that after they had passed the uninhabited region of Culuacan and were approaching Chiametla, the warden went off with some horsemen to find provisions, and one of the soldiers who was with him, who had strayed from the force, called out that they were killing him. The warden hastened to his assistance, and they wounded him in the eye with an arrow, from which he died. In regard to the fortress,[2] besides the fact that it is badly built and going to pieces, it seems to me that the cost of it is excessive, and that Your Majesty could do without the most of it, because there is one man who takes charge of the munitions and artillery, and an armorer to repair it, and a gunner, and as this is the way it was under the Audiencia, before the fortresses were made conformable to what I have written to Your Majesty, we can get along without the rest, because that fortress was built on account of the brigantines, and not for any other purpose.[3] And as the lagoon is so dry that it can do no good in this way for the present, I think that, for this reason, the cost is superfluous. I believe that it will have fallen in before a reply can come from Your Majesty.

Some days ago I wrote to Your Majesty that I had ordered Melchior Diaz, who was in the town of San Miguel de Culuacan, to take some horsemen and see if the account given by the father, Friar Marcos, agreed with what he could discover. He set out from Culuacan with fifteen horsemen, the 17th of November last. The 20th of this present March I received a letter from him, which he sent me by Juan de Zaldyvar and three other horsemen. In this he says that after he left Culuacan and crossed the river of Petlatlan he was everywhere very well received by the Indians. The way he did was to send a cross to the place where he was going to stop, because this was a sign which the Indians received with deep veneration, making a house out of mats in which to place it, & somewhat away from this they made a lodging for the Spaniards, & drove stakes where they could tie the horses, and supplied fodder for them, and abundance of corn wherever they had it. They say that they suffered from hunger in many places, because it had been a bad year. After going 100 leagues from Culuacan, he began to find the country cold, with severe frosts, & the farther he went on the colder it became, until he reached a point where some Indians whom he had with him were frozen, and two Spaniards were in great danger. Seeing this, he decided not to go any farther until the winter was over, and to send back, by those whom I mentioned, an account of what he had learned concerning Cibola and the country beyond, which is as follows, taken literally from his letter:

"I have given Your Lordship an account of what happened to me along the way; and seeing that it is impossible to cross the uninhabited region which stretches from here to Cibola, on account of the heavy snows and the cold, I will give Your Lordship an account of what I have learned about Cibola, which I have ascertained by asking many persons who have been there fifteen and twenty years; and I have secured this in many different ways, taking some Indians together and others separately, and on comparison they all seem to agree in what they say. After crossing this large wilderness, there are seven places, being a short day's march from one to another, all of which are together called Cibola. The houses are of stone and mud, coarsely worked. They are made in this way: One large wall, and at each end of this wall some rooms are built, partitioned off 20 feet square, according to the description they give, which are planked with square beams. Most of the houses are reached from the flat roofs, using their ladders to go to the streets. The houses have three and four stories. They declare that there are few having two stories. The stories are mostly half as high again as a man, except the first one, which is low, and only a little more than a man's height. One ladder is used to communicate with ten or twelve houses together. They make use of the low ones and live in the highest ones. In the lowest ones of all they have some loopholes made sideways, as in the fortresses of Spain. The Indians say that when these people are attacked, they station themselves in their houses and fight from there;[4] and that when they go to make war, they carry shields and wear leather jackets, which are made of cows' hide, colored, and that they fight with arrows and with a sort of stone maul and with some other weapons made of sticks, which I have not been able to make out. They eat human flesh, and they keep those whom they capture in war as slaves. There are many fowls in the country, tame.[5] They have much corn and beans and melons [squashes]. In their houses they keep some hairy animals, like the large Spanish hounds, which they shear, and they make long colored wigs from the hair, like this one which I send to Your Lordship, which they wear, and they also put this same stuff in the cloth which they make.[6] The men are of small stature; the women are light colored and of good appearance, and they wear shirts or chemises which reach down to their feet. They wear their hair on each side done up in a sort of twist, which leaves the ears outside, in which they hang many turquoises, as well as on their necks and on the wrists of their arms. The clothing of the men is a cloak, and over this the skin of a cow, like the one which Cabeza de Vaca and Dorantes brought, which Your Lordship saw; they wear caps[7] on their heads; in summer they wear shoes made of painted or colored skin, and high buskins in winter.

"They were also unable to tell me of any metal, nor did they say that they had it. They have turquoises in quantity, although not so many as the father provincial said. They have some little stone crystals, like this which I send to Your Lordship, of which Your Lordship has seen many here in New Spain.[8] They cultivate the ground in the same way as in New Spain. They carry things on their heads, as in Mexico. The men weave cloth and spin cotton. They have salt from a marshy lake, which is two days from the province of Cibola.[9] The Indians have their dances and songs, with some flutes which have holes on which to put the fingers. They make much noise. They sing in unison with those who play, and those who sing clap their hands in our fashion. One of the Indians that accompanied the negro Stephen, who had been a captive there, saw the playing as they practiced it, and others singing as I have said, although not very vigorously. They say that five or six play together, and that some of the flutes are better than others.[10] They say the country is good for corn and beans, and that they do not have any fruit trees, nor do they know what such a thing is.[11] They have very good mountains. The country lacks water. They do not raise cotton, but bring it from Totonteac.[12] They eat out of flat bowls, like the Mexicans. They raise considerable corn and beans and other similar things. They do not know what sea fish is, nor have they ever heard of it. I have not obtained any information about the cows, except that these are found beyond the province of Cibola. There is a great abundance of wild goats, of the color of bay horses; there are many of these here where I am, and although I have asked the Indians if those are like these, they tell me no. Of the seven settlements, they describe three of them as very large; four not so big. They describe them, as I understand, to be about three crossbow shots square for each place, and from what the Indians say, and their descriptions of the houses and their size, and as these are close together, and considering that there are people in each house, it ought to make a large multitude. Totonteac is declared to be seven short days from the province of Cibola, and of the same sort of houses and people, and they say that cotton grows there. I doubt this, because they tell me that it is a cold country. They say that there are twelve villages, every one of which is larger than the largest at Cibola. They also tell me that there is a village which is one day from Cibola, and that the two are at war.[13] They have the same sort of houses and people and customs. They declare this to be greater than any of those described; I take it that there is a great multitude of people there. They are very well known, on account of having these houses and abundance of food and turquoises. I have not been able to learn more than what I have related, although, as I have said, I have had with me Indians who have lived there fifteen and twenty years.

"The death of Stephen the negro took place in the way the father, Friar Marcos, described it to Your Lordship, and so I do not make a report of it here, except that the people at Cibola sent word to those of this village and in its neighborhood that if any Christian should come, they ought not to consider them as anything peculiar, and ought to kill them, because they were mortal—saying that they had learned this because they kept the bones of the one who had come there; and that, if they did not dare to do this, they should send word so that those (at Cibola) could come and do it. I can very easily believe that all this has taken place, and that there has been some communication between these places, because of the coolness with which they received us and the sour faces they have shown us."

Melchior Diaz says that the people whom he found along the way do not have any settlements at all, except in one valley which is 150 leagues from Culuacan, which is well settled and has houses with lofts, and that there are many people along the way, but that they are not good for anything except to make them Christians, as if this was of small account. May Your Majesty remember to provide for the service of God, and keep in mind the deaths and the loss of life and of provinces which has taken place in these Indies. And, moreover, up to this present day none of the things Your Majesty has commanded, which have been very holy and good, have been attended to, nor priests provided, either for that country or for this. For I assure Your Majesty that there is no trace of Christianity where they have not yet arrived, neither little nor much, and that the poor people are ready to receive the priests and come to them even when they flee from us like deer in the mountains. And I state this because I am an eyewitness, & I have seen it clearly during this trip. I have importuned Your Majesty for friars, and yet again I can not cease doing it much more, because unless this be done I can not accomplish that which I am bound to do.

After I reach Mexico, I will give Your Majesty an account of everything concerning these provinces, for while I should like to do it today, I can not, because I am very weak from a slow fever which I caught in Colima, which attacked me very severely, although it did not last more than six days. It has pleased Our Lord to make me well already, and I have traveled here to Jacona, where I am.

May Our Lord protect the Holy Catholic Cæsarian person of Your Majesty and aggrandize it with increase of better kingdoms and lordships, as we your servants desire.

From Jacona, April 17, 1540.

S. C. C. M.

Your Holy Majesty's humble servant, who salutes your royal feet and hands,   D. Antonio de Mendoza.

LETTER
FROM CORONADO TO MENDOZA
August 3, 1540[1]

℃ The account given by Francisco Vazquez de Coronado, Captain/ General of the force which was sent in the Name of His Majesty to the newly discovered country, of what happened to the expedition after April 22 of the year 1540, when he started forward from Culiacan, and of what he found in the country through which he passed.

I

℃ Francisco Vazquez starts from Culiacan with his army, and after suffering various inconveniences on account of the badness of the way, reaches the Valley of Hearts, where he failed to find any corn, to procure which he sends to the valley called Señora. He receives an account of the important Valley of Hearts and of the people there, and of some lands lying along that coast.

ON THE 22d of the month of April last, I set out from the province of Culiacan with a part of the army, having made the arrangements of which I wrote to Your Lordship. Judging by the outcome, I feel sure that it was fortunate that I did not start the whole of the army on this undertaking, because the labors have been so very great and the lack of food such that I do not believe this undertaking could have been completed before the end of this year, and that there would be a great loss of life if it should be accomplished. For, as I wrote to Your Lordship, I spent eighty days in traveling to Culiacan,[2] during which time I and the gentlemen of my company, who were horsemen, carried on our backs and on our horses a little food, in such wise that after leaving this place none of us carried any necessary effects weighing more than a pound. For all this, and although we took all possible care and forethought of the small supply of provisions which we carried, it gave out. And this is not to be wondered at, because the road is rough and long, and what with our harquebuses, which had to be carried up the mountains and hills and in the passage of the rivers, the greater part of the corn was lost.

And since I send Your Lordship a drawing of this route, I will say no more about it here.

Thirty leagues before reaching the place which the father provincial spoke so well of in his report,[3] I sent Melchior Diaz forward with fifteen horsemen, ordering him to make but one day's journey out of two, so that he could examine everything there before I arrived. He traveled through some very rough mountains for four days, and did not find anything to live on, nor people, nor information about anything, except that he found two or three poor villages, with twenty or thirty huts apiece. From the people here he learned that there was nothing to be found in the country beyond except the mountains, which continued very rough, entirely uninhabited by people. And, because this was labor lost, I did not want to send Your Lordship an account of it. The whole company felt disturbed at this, that a thing so much praised, and about which the father had said so many things, should be found so very different; and they began to think that all the rest would be of the same sort.

When I noticed this, I tried to encourage them as well as I could, telling them that Your Lordship had always thought that this part of the trip would be a waste of effort, and that we ought to devote our attention to those Seven Cities and the other provinces about which we had information —that these should be the end of our enterprise. With this resolution and purpose, we all marched cheerfully along a very bad way, where it was impossible to pass without making a new road or repairing the one that was there, which troubled the soldiers not a little, considering that everything which the friar had said was found to be quite the reverse; because, among other things which the father had said and declared, he said that the way would be plain and good, and that there would be only one small hill of about half a league. And the truth is, that there are mountains where, however well the path might be fixed, they could not be crossed without there being great danger of the horses falling over them. And it was so bad that a large number of the animals which Your Lordship sent as provisions for the army were lost along this part of the way, on account of the roughness of the rocks. The lambs and wethers lost their hoofs along the way, and I left the greater part of those which I brought from Culiacan at the river of Lachimi,[4] because they were unable to travel, and so that they might proceed more slowly.

Four horsemen remained with them, who have just arrived. They have not brought more than 24 lambs and 4 wethers; the rest died from the toil, although they did not travel more than two leagues daily. I reached the Valley of Hearts[5] at last, on the 26th day of the month of May, and rested there a number of days. Between Culiacan and this place I could sustain myself only by means of a large supply of corn bread, because I had to leave all the corn, as it was not yet ripe. In this Valley of Hearts we found more people than in any part of the country which we had left behind, and a large extent of tilled ground. There was no corn for food among them, but as I heard that there was some in another valley called Señora, which I did not wish to disturb by force, I sent Melchior Diaz with goods to exchange for it, so as to give this to the friendly Indians whom we brought with us, & to some who had lost their animals along the way & had not been able to carry the food which they had taken from Culiacan. By the favor of Our Lord, some little corn was obtained by this trading, which relieved the friendly Indians and some Spaniards. Ten or twelve of the horses had died of overwork by the time that we reached this Valley of Hearts, because they were unable to stand the strain of carrying heavy burdens and eating little. Some of our negroes and some of the Indians also died here, which was not a slight loss for the rest of the expedition. They told me that the Valley of Hearts is a long five days' journey from the Western Sea. I sent to summon Indians from the coast in order to learn about their condition, and while I was waiting for these the horses rested. I stayed there four days, during which the Indians came from the sea, who told me that there were seven or eight islands two days' journey from that seacoast, directly opposite, well populated with people, but poorly supplied with food, and the people were savages.[6] They told me they had seen a ship pass not very far from the land. I do not know whether to think that it was the one which was sent to discover the country, or perhaps some Portuguese.[7]

II

℃ They come to Chichilticale; after having taken two days' rest, they enter a country containing very little food and hard to travel for 30 leagues, beyond which the country becomes pleasant, and there is a river called the River of the Flax (del Lino); they fight against the Indians, being attacked by these; and having by their victory secured the city, they relieve themselves of the pangs of their hunger.

I SET out from the Hearts and kept near the seacoast as well as I could judge, but in fact I found myself continually farther off, so that when I reached Chichilticale I found that I was fifteen days' journey distant from the sea, although the father provincial had said that it was only 5 leagues distant and that he had seen it. We all became very distrustful, and felt great anxiety and dismay to see that everything was the reverse of what he had told Your Lordship. The Indians of Chichilticale say that when they go to the sea for fish, or for anything else that they need, they go across the country, and that it takes them ten days; and this information which I have received from the Indians appears to me to be true. The sea turns toward the west directly opposite the Hearts for 10 or 12 leagues, where I learned that the ships of Your Lordship had been seen, which had gone in search of the port of Chichilticale, which the father said was on the thirty-fifth degree.[8]

God knows what I have suffered, because I fear that they may have met with some mishap. If they follow the coast, as they said they would, as long as the food lasts which they took with them, of which I left them a supply in Culiacan, and if they have not been overtaken by some misfortune, I maintain my trust in God that they have already discovered something good, for which the delay which they have made may be pardoned. I rested for two days at Chichilticale, and there was good reason for staying longer, because we found that the horses were becoming so tired; but there was no chance to rest longer, because the food was giving out. I entered the borders of the wilderness region on Saint John's eve, and, for a change from our past labors, we found no grass during the first days, but a worse way through mountains and more dangerous passages than we had experienced previously. The horses were so tired that they were not equal to it, so that in this last desert we lost more horses than before; and some Indian allies and a Spaniard called Spinosa, besides two negroes, died from eating some herbs because the food had given out.

I sent the army-master, Don Garcia Lopez de Cardenas, with 15 horsemen, a day's march ahead of me, in order to explore the country and prepare the way, which he accomplished like the man that he is, and agreeably to the confidence which Your Lordship has had in him. I am the more certain that he did so, because, as I have said, the way is very bad for at least 30 leagues and more, through impassable mountains. But when we had passed these 30 leagues, we found fresh rivers and grass like that of Castile, and especially one sort like what we call *Scaramoio;* many nut and mulberry trees, but the leaves of the nut trees are different from those of Spain. There was a considerable amount of flax near the banks of one river, which was called on this account El Rio del Lino.[9] No Indians were seen during the first day's march, after which four Indians came out with signs of peace, saying that they had been sent to that desert place to say that we were welcome, and that on the next day the tribe would provide the whole force with food. The army-master gave them a cross, telling them to say to the people in their city that they need not fear, and that they should have their people stay in their own houses, because I was coming in the name of His Majesty to defend and help them.

After this was done, Ferrando Alvarado came back to tell me that some Indians had met him peaceably, & that two of them were with the army-master waiting for me. I went to them forthwith and gave them some paternosters and some little cloaks, telling them to return to their city and say to the people there that they could stay quietly in their houses and that they need not fear. After this I ordered the army-master to go and see if there were any bad passages which the Indians might be able to defend, and to seize and hold any such until the next day, when I would come up. He went, and found a very bad place in our way where we might have received much harm. He immediately established himself there with the force which he was conducting. The Indians came that very night to occupy that place so as to defend it, and finding it taken, they assaulted our men. According to what I have been told, they attacked like valiant men, although in the end they had to retreat in flight, because the army-master was on the watch and kept his men in good order. The Indians sounded a little trumpet as a sign of retreat, and did not do any injury to the Spaniards. The army-master sent me notice of this the same night, so that on the next day I started with as good order as I could, for we were in such great need of food that I thought we should all die of hunger if we continued to be without provisions for another day, especially the Indians, since altogether we did not have two bushels of corn, and so I was obliged to hasten forward without delay. The Indians lighted their fires from point to point, and these were answered from a distance with as good understanding as we could have shown. Thus notice was given concerning how we went and where we had arrived.

As soon as I came within sight of this city, I sent the army-master, Don

Garcia Lopez, Friar Daniel and Friar Luis, and Ferrando Vermizzo, with some horsemen, a little way ahead, so that they might find the Indians and tell them that we were not coming to do them any harm, but to defend them in the name of our lord the Emperor. The summons, in the form which His Majesty commanded in his instructions, was made intelligible to the people of the country by an interpreter. But they, being a proud people, were little affected, because it seemed to them that we were few in number, and that they would not have any difficulty in conquering us. They pierced the gown of Friar Luis with an arrow, which, blessed be God, did him no harm. Meanwhile I arrived with all the rest of the horse and the footmen, and found a large body of the Indians on the plain, who began to shoot with their arrows. In obedience to the orders of Your Lordship and of the marquis,[10] I did not wish my company, who were begging me for permission, to attack them, telling them that they ought not to offend them, and that what the enemy was doing was nothing, and that so few people ought not to be insulted. On the other hand, when the Indians saw that we did not move, they took greater courage, and grew so bold that they came up almost to the heels of our horses to shoot their arrows. On this account I saw that it was no longer time to hesitate, and as the priests approved the action, I charged them. There was little to do, because they suddenly took to flight, part running toward the city, which was near and well fortified, and others toward the plain, wherever chance led them. Some Indians were killed, and others might have been slain if I could have allowed them to be pursued. But I saw that there would be little advantage in this, because the Indians who were outside were few, and those who had retired to the city were numerous, besides many who had remained there in the first place.

As that was where the food was, of which we stood in such great need, I assembled my whole force and divided them as seemed to me best for the attack on the city, and surrounded it. The hunger which we suffered would not permit of any delay, and so I dismounted with some of these gentlemen and soldiers. I ordered the musketeers and crossbowmen to begin the attack and drive back the enemy from the defenses, so that they could not do us any injury. I assaulted the wall on one side, where I was told that there was a scaling ladder and that there was also a gate. But the crossbowmen broke all the strings of their crossbows and the musketeers could do nothing, because they had arrived so weak & feeble that they could scarcely stand on their feet. On this account the people who were on top were not prevented at all from defending themselves and doing us whatever injury they were able. Thus, for myself, they knocked me down to the ground twice with countless great stones which they threw down from above, and if I had not been protected by the very good headpiece which I wore, I think that the outcome would have been bad for me. They picked me up from the ground, however, with two small wounds in my face and an arrow in my foot, and with many bruises on my arms and legs, and in this condition I retired from the battle, very weak. I think that if Don Garcia Lopez de Cardenas had not come to my help, like a good cavalier, the second time that they knocked me to the ground, by placing his own body above mine, I should have been in much greater danger than I was. But, by the pleasure of God, these Indians surrendered, and their city was taken with the help of Our Lord, and a sufficient supply of corn was found there to relieve our necessities.[11]

The army-master & Don Pedro de Tovar & Ferrando de Alvarado & Paulo de Melgosa, the infantry captain, sustained some bruises, although none of them were wounded. Agoniez Quarez was hit in the arm by an arrow, and one Torres, who lived in Panuco, in the face by another, and two other footmen received slight arrow wounds. They all directed their attack against me because my armor was gilded and glittered, and on this account I was hurt more than the rest, and not because I had done more or was farther in advance than the others; for all these gentlemen and soldiers bore themselves well, as was expected of them. I praise God that I am now well, although somewhat sore from the stones. Two or three other soldiers were hurt in the battle which we had on the plain, and three horses were killed—one that of Don Lopez[12] & another that of Vigliega & the third that of Don Alfonso Manrich—and seven or eight other horses were wounded; but the men, as well as the horses, have now recovered and are well.

III

℄ Of the situation and condition of the Seven Cities called the kingdom of Cevola, and the sort of people and their customs, and of the animals which are found there.

IT now remains for me to tell about this city and kingdom and province, of which the father provincial gave Your Lordship an account. In brief, I can assure you that in reality he has not told the truth in a single thing that he said, but everything is the reverse of what he said, except the name of the city and the large stone houses. For, although they are not decorated with turquoises, or made of lime nor of good bricks, nevertheless they are very good houses, with three and four and five stories, where there are very good apartments and good rooms with corridors, and some very good rooms under ground and paved, which are made for winter, and are something like a sort of hot baths.[13] The ladders which they have for their houses are all movable and portable, which are taken up and placed wherever they please. They are made of two pieces of wood, with rounds like ours.

The Seven Cities are seven little villages, all having the kind of houses I have described. They are all within a radius of five leagues. They are all called the kingdom of Cevola, and each has its own name and no single one is called Cevola, but all together are called Cevola.[14] This one which I have called a city I have named Granada, partly because it has some similarity to it, as well as out of regard for Your Lordship. In this place where I am now lodged there are perhaps 200 houses, all surrounded by a wall, and it seems to me that with the other houses, which are not so surrounded, there might be altogether 500 families. There is another town near by, which is one of the seven, but somewhat larger than this, and another of the same size as this, & the other four are somewhat smaller. I send them all to Your Lordship, painted with the route. The skin on which the painting is made was found here with other skins.

The people of the towns seem to me to be of ordinary size and intelligent, although I do not think that they have the judgment & intelligence which they ought to have to build these houses in the way in which they have, for most of them are entirely naked except the covering of their privy parts, and they have painted mantles like the one which I send to Your Lordship. They do not raise cotton, because the country is very cold, but they wear mantles, as may be seen by the exhibit which I send. It is also true that some cotton thread was found in their houses. They wear the hair on their heads like the Mexicans. They all have good figures, and are well bred. I think that they have a quantity of turquoises, which they had removed with the rest of their goods, except the corn, when I arrived, because I did not find any women here nor any men under 15 years or over 60, except two or three old men who remained in command of all the other men and the warriors. Two points of emerald and some little broken stones which approach the color of rather poor garnets[15] were found in a paper, besides other stone crystals, which I gave to one of my servants to keep until they could be sent to Your Lordship. He has lost them, as they tell me. We found fowls, but only a few, and yet there are some. The Indians tell me that they do not eat these in any of the seven villages, but that they keep them merely for the sake of procuring the feathers.[16] I do not believe this, because they are very good, and better than those of Mexico.

The climate of this country and the temperature of the air is almost like that of Mexico, because it is sometimes hot and sometimes it rains. I have not yet seen it rain, however, except once when there fell a little shower with wind, such as often falls in Spain. The snow and the cold are usually very great, according to what the natives of the country all say. This may very probably be so, both because of the nature of the country and the sort of houses they build and the skins and other things which these people have to protect them from the cold. There are no kinds of fruit or fruit trees. The country is all level, & is nowhere shut in by high mountains, although there are some hills and rough passages.[17] There are not many birds, probably because of the cold, and because there are no mountains near. There are no trees fit for firewood here, because they can bring enough for their needs from a clump of very small cedars four leagues distant. Very good grass is found a quarter of a league away, where there is pasturage for our horses as well as mowing for hay, of which we had great need, because our horses were so weak and feeble when they arrived.[18]

The food which they eat in this country is corn, of which they have a great abundance, & beans & venison, which they probably eat (although they say that they do not), because we found many skins of deer and hares and rabbits. They make the best corn cakes I have ever seen anywhere, and this is what everybody ordinarily eats. They have the very best arrangement and machinery for grinding that was ever seen. One of these Indian women here will grind as much as four of the Mexicans. They have very good salt in crystals, which they bring from a lake a day's journey distant from here. No information can be obtained among them about the North Sea or that on the west, nor do I know how to tell Your Lordship which we are nearest to. I should judge that it is nearer to the western, and 150 leagues is the nearest that it seems to me it can be thither. The North Sea ought to be much farther away. Your Lordship may thus see how very wide the country is. They have many animals—bears, tigers, lions, porcupines, and some sheep as big as a horse, with very large horns and little tails. I have seen some of their horns the size of which was something to marvel at. There are also wild goats, whose heads I have seen, and the paws of the bears and the skins of the wild boars. For game they have deer, leopards, & very large deer,[19] & everyone thinks that some of them are larger than that animal which Your Lordship favored me with, which belonged to Juan Melaz. They inhabit some plains eight days' journey toward the north. They have some of their skins here very well dressed, & they prepare and paint them where they kill the cows, according to what they tell me.

IV

⊂Of the nature and situation of the kingdoms of Totonteac, Marata, and Acus, wholly different from the account of Friar Marcos. The conference which they had with the Indians of the city of Granada, which they had captured, who had been forewarned of the coming of Christians into their country fifty years before. The account which was obtained from them concerning seven other cities, of which Tucano is the chief, and how he sent to discover them. A present sent to Mendoza of various things found in this country by Vazquez de Coronado.

THESE Indians say that the kingdom of Totonteac, which the father provincial praised so much, saying that it was something marvelous, and of such a very great size, & that cloth was made there, is a hot lake, on the edge of which there are five or six houses. There used to be some others, but these have been destroyed by war. The kingdom of Marata can not be found, nor do these Indians know anything about it. The kingdom of Acus is a single small city, where they raise cotton, and this is called Acucu.[20] I say that this is the country, because Acus, with or without the aspiration, is not a word in this region; & because it seems to me that Acucu may be derived from Acus, I say that it is this town which has been converted into the kingdom of Acus. They tell me that there are some other small ones not far from this settlement, which are situated on a river which I have seen and of which the Indians have told me. God knows that I wish I had better news to write to Your Lordship, but I must give you the truth, and, as I wrote you from Culuacan, I must advise you of the good as well as of the bad. But you may be assured that if there had been all the riches and treasures of the world, I could not have done more in His Majesty's service and in that of Your Lordship than I have done, in coming here where you commanded me to go, carrying, both my companions & myself, our food on our backs for 300 leagues, and traveling on foot many days, making our way over hills and rough mountains, besides other labors which I refrain from mentioning. Nor do I think of stopping until my death, if it serves His Majesty or Your Lordship to have it so.

Three days after I captured this city, some of the Indians who lived here came to offer to make peace. They brought me some turquoises and poor mantles, and I received them in His Majesty's name with as good a speech as I could, making them understand the purpose of my coming to this country, which is, in the name of His Majesty and by the commands of Your Lordship, that they and all others in this province should become Christians and should know the true God for their Lord, and His Majesty for their king and earthly lord. After this they returned to their houses and suddenly, the next day, they packed up their goods and property, their women and children, & fled to the hills, leaving their towns deserted, with only some few remaining in them. Seeing this, I went to the town which I said was larger than this, eight or ten days later, when I had recovered from my wounds. I found a few of them there, whom I told that they ought not to feel any fear, and I asked them to summon their lord to me. By what I can find out or observe, however, none of these towns have any, since I have not seen any principal house by which any superiority over others could be shown.[21] Afterward, an old man, who said he was their lord, came with a mantle made of many pieces, with whom I argued as long as he stayed with me. He said that he would come to see me with the rest of the chiefs of the country, three days later, in order to arrange the relations which should exist between us. He did so, and they brought me some little ragged mantles and some turquoises. I said that they ought to come down from their strongholds and return to their houses with their wives and children, and that they should become Christians, and recognize His Majesty as their king and lord. But they still remain in their strongholds, with their wives and all their property.

I commanded them to have a cloth painted for me, with all the animals that they know in that country, and although they are poor painters, they quickly painted two for me, one of the animals and the other of the birds and fishes. They say that they will bring their children so that our priests may instruct them, & that they desire to know our law. They declare that it was foretold among them more than fifty years ago that a people such as we are should come, and the direction they should come from, and that the whole country would be conquered. So far as I can find out, the water is what these Indians worship, because they say that it makes the corn grow and sustains their life, and that the only other reason they know is because their ancestors did so.[22] I have tried in every way to find out from the natives of these settlements whether they know of any other peoples or provinces or cities. They tell me about seven cities which are at a considerable distance, which are like these, except that the houses there are not like these, but are made of earth [adobe], and small, and that they raise much cotton there. The first of these four places about which they know is called, they say, Tucano. They could not tell me much about the others. I do not believe that they tell me the truth, because they think that I shall soon have to depart from them and return home. But they will quickly find that they are deceived in this. I sent Don Pedro de Tobar there, with his company & some other horsemen, to see it. I would not have dispatched this packet to Your Lordship until I had learned what he found there, if I thought that I should have any news from him within twelve or fifteen days. However, as he will remain away at least thirty, and, considering that this information is of little importance and that the cold and the rains are approaching, it seemed to me that I ought to do as Your Lordship commanded me in your instructions, which is, that as soon as I arrived here, I should advise you thereof, and this I do, by sending you the plain narrative of what I have seen, which is bad enough, as you may perceive. I have determined to send throughout all the surrounding regions, in order to find out whether there is anything, and to suffer every extremity before I give up this enterprise, and to serve His Majesty, if I can find any way in which to do it, and not to lack in diligence until Your Lordship directs me as to what I ought to do.

We have great need of pasture, and you should know, also, that among all those who are here there is not one pound of raisins, nor sugar, nor oil, nor wine, except barely half a quart, which is saved to say mass, since everything is consumed, and part was lost on the way. Now, you can provide us with what appears best; but if you are thinking of sending us cattle, you should know that it will be necessary for them to spend at least a year on the road, because they can not come in any other way, nor any quicker. I would have liked to send to Your Lordship, with this dispatch, many samples of the things which they have in this country, but the trip is so long & rough that it is difficult for me to do so. However, I send you twelve small mantles, such as the people of this country ordinarily wear, and a garment which seems to me to be very well made. I kept it because it seemed to me to be of very good workmanship, and because I do not think that anyone else has ever seen in these Indies any work done with a needle, unless it were done since the Spaniards settled here. And I also send two cloths painted with the animals which they have in this country, although, as I said, the painting is very poorly done, because the artist did not spend more than one day in painting it. I have seen other paintings on the walls of these houses which have much better proportion and are done much better.

I send you a cow skin, some turquoises, and two earrings of the same, and fifteen of the Indian combs,[23] and some plates decorated with these turquoises, and two baskets made of wicker, of which the Indians have a large supply. I also send two rolls, such as the women usually wear on their heads when they bring water from the spring, the same way that they do in Spain. One of these Indian women, with one of these rolls on her head, will carry a jar of water up a ladder without touching it with her hands.[24] And, lastly, I send you samples of the weapons with which the natives of this country fight, a shield, a hammer, and a bow with some arrows, among which there are two with bone points, the like of which have never been seen, according to what these conquerors say.[25] As far as I can judge, it does not appear to me that there is any hope of getting gold or silver, but I trust in God that, if there is any, we shall get our share of it, and it shall not escape us through any lack of diligence in the search.[26] I am unable to give Your Lordship any certain information about the dress of the women, because the Indians keep them guarded so carefully that I have not seen any, except two old women. These had on two long skirts reaching down to their feet and open in front, & a girdle, & they are tied together with some cotton strings. I asked the Indians to give me one of those which they wore, to send to you, since they were not willing to show me the women. They brought me two mantles, which are these that I send, almost painted over.[27] They have two tassels, like the women of Spain, which hang somewhat over their shoulders.

The death of the negro is perfectly certain, because many of the things which he wore have been found, and the Indians say that they killed him here because the Indians of Chichilticale said that he was a bad man, and not like the Christians, because the Christians never kill women, and he killed them, and because he assaulted their women, whom the Indians love better than themselves. Therefore they determined to kill him, but they did not do it in the way that was reported, because they did not kill any of the others who came with him, nor did they kill the lad from the province of Petatlan, who was with him, but they took him and kept him in safe custody until now. When I tried to secure him, they made excuses for not giving him to me, for two or three days, saying that he was dead, and at other times that the Indians of Acucu had taken him away. But when I finally told them that I should be very angry if they did not give him to me, they gave him to me. He is an interpreter; for although he cannot talk much, he understands very well.

Some gold & silver has been found in this place, which those who know about minerals say is not bad. I have not yet been able to learn from these people where they got it. I perceive that they refuse to tell me the truth in everything, because they think that I shall have to depart from here in a short time, as I have said. But I trust in God that they will not be able to avoid answering much longer. I beg Your Lordship to make a report of the success of this expedition to His Majesty, because there is nothing more than what I have already said. I shall not do so until it shall please God to grant that we find what we desire. Our Lord God protect and keep your most illustrious Lordship. From the province of Cevola, and this city of Granada, the 3d of August, 1540. Francisco Vazquez de Coronado kisses the hand of your most illustrious Lordship.

THE TRASLADO DE LAS NUEVAS

C Copy of the Reports and Descriptions that have been received regarding the Discovery of a City which is called Cibola, situated in the New Country.[1]

IS GRACE left the larger part of his army in the valley of Culiacan, & with only 75 companions on horseback & 30 footmen, he set out for here Thursday, April 22. The army which remained there was to start about the end of the month of May, because they could not find any sort of sustenance for the whole of the way that they had to go, as far as this province of Cibola, which is 350 long leagues, and on this account he did not dare to put the whole army on the road. As for the men he took with him, he ordered them to make provision for eighty days, which was carried on horses, each having one for himself and his followers. With very great danger of suffering hunger, and not less labor, since they had to open the way, and every day discovered waterways & rivers with bad crossings, they stood it after a fashion, and on the whole journey as far as this province there was not a peck of corn.

He reached this province on Wednesday, the 7th of July last, with all the men whom he led from the valley very well, praise be to Our Lord, except one Spaniard who died of hunger four days from here and some negroes and Indians who also died of hunger and thirst. The Spaniard was one of those on foot, and was named Espinosa. In this way his grace spent seventy-seven days on the road before reaching here, during which God knows in what sort of a way we lived, and whether we could have eaten much more than we ate the day that his grace reached this city of Granada, for so it has been named out of regard for the viceroy, and because they say it resembles the Albaicin.[2] The force he led was not received the way it should have been, because they all arrived very tired from the great labor of the journey. This, and the loading and unloading like so many muleteers, and not eating as much as they should have, left them more in need of resting several days than of fighting, although there was not a man in the army who would not have done his best in everything if the horses, which suffered the same as their masters, could have helped them.

The city was deserted by men over sixty years and under twenty, and by women and children. All who were there were the fighting men who remained to defend the city, and many of them came out, about a crossbow shot, uttering loud threats. The general himself went forward with two priests and the army-master, to urge them to surrender, as is the custom in new countries. The reply that he received was from many arrows which they let fly, and they wounded Hernando Bermejo's horse and pierced the loose flap of the frock of father Friar Luis, the former companion of the Lord Bishop of Mexico. When this was seen, taking as their advocate the Holy Saint James,[3] he rushed upon them with all his force, which he had kept in very good order, and although the Indians turned their backs and tried to reach the city, they were overtaken and many of them killed before they could reach it. They killed three horses and wounded seven or eight.

When my lord the general reached the city, he saw that it was surrounded by stone walls, and the houses very high, four and five and even six stories apiece, with their flat roofs and balconies. As the Indians had made themselves secure within it, and would not let anyone come near without shooting arrows at him, and as we could not obtain anything to eat unless we captured it, his grace decided to enter the city on foot and to surround it by men on horseback, so that the Indians who were inside could not get away. As he was distinguished among them all by his gilt arms & a plume on his headpiece, all the Indians aimed at him, because he was noticeable among all, and they knocked him down to the ground twice by chance stones thrown from the flat roofs, and stunned him in spite of his headpiece, and if this had not been so good, I doubt if he would have come out alive from that enterprise, and besides all this—praised be Our Lord that he came out on his own feet—they hit him many times with stones on his head and shoulders and legs, and he received two small wounds on his face and an arrow wound in the right foot; but despite all this his grace is as sound and well as the day he left that city. And you[4] may assure my lord of all this, and also that on the 19th of July last he went four leagues from this city to see a rock where they told him that the Indians of this province had fortified themselves,[5] and he returned the same day, so that he went eight leagues in going and returning.

I think I have given you an account of everything, for it is right that I should be the authority for you and his lordship, to assure you that everything is going well with the general my lord, and without any hesitation I can assure you that he is as well and sound as the day he left the city. He is located within the city, for when the Indians saw that his grace was determined to enter the city, then they abandoned it, since they let them go with their lives. We found in it what we needed more than gold and silver, and that was much corn and beans and fowls, better than those of New Spain, and salt, the best and whitest that I have seen in all my life.

☾ This is the latest account of Cibola, and of more than four hundred leagues beyond.[6]

IT is more than 300 leagues from Culiacan to Cibola, uninhabited most of the way. There are very few people there; the country is sterile; the roads are very bad. The people go around entirely naked, except the women, who wear white tanned deer skins from the waist down, something like little skirts, reaching to the feet. Their houses are of mats made of reeds; the houses are round and small, so that there is hardly room inside for a man on his feet. The country is sandy where they live near together and where they plant. They raise corn, but not very much, and beans and melons, and they also live on game —rabbits, hares and deer. They do not have sacrifices. This is between Culiacan and Cibola.

Cibola is a village of about 200 houses. They have two and three and four and five stories. The walls are about a handbreadth thick; the sticks of timber are as large as the wrist, and round; for boards, they have very small bushes, with their leaves on, covered with a sort of greenish-colored mud; the walls are of dirt and mud,[7] the doors of the houses are like hatchways of ships. The houses are close together, each joined to the others. Outside of the houses they have some hot-houses (or *estufas*) of dirt mud, where they take refuge from the cold in the winter—because this is very great, since it snows six months in the year.

Some of these people wear cloaks of cotton and of the maguey (or Mexican aloe)[8] and of tanned deer skin, and they wear shoes made of these skins, reaching up to the knees. They also make cloaks of the skins of hares and rabbits, with which they cover themselves. The women wear cloaks of the maguey, reaching down to the feet, with girdles; they wear their hair gathered about the ears like little wheels. They raise corn and beans and melons, which is all they need to live on, because it is a small tribe. The land where they plant is entirely sandy; the water is brackish; the country is very dry. They have some fowls, although not many. They do not know what sort of a thing fish is. There are seven villages in this province of Cibola within a space of five leagues; the largest may have about 200 houses & two others about 200, and the others somewhere between 60 or 50 and 30 houses.

It is 60 leagues from Cibola to the river and province of Tibex [Tiguex]. The first village is 40 leagues from Cibola, and is called Acuco. This village is on top of a very strong rock; it has about 200 houses, built in the same way as at Cibola, where they speak another language. It is 20 leagues from here to the river of Tiguex. The river is almost as wide as that of Seville, although not so deep; it flows through a level country; the water is good; it contains some fish; it rises in the north. He who relates this, saw twelve villages within a certain distance of the river; others saw more, they say, up the river. Below, all the villages are small, except two that have about 200 houses. The walls of these houses are something like mud walls of dirt and sand, very rough; they are as thick as the breadth of a hand. The houses have two and three stories; the construction is like those at Cibola. The country is very cold. They have hot-houses, as in Cibola, and the river freezes so thick that loaded animals cross it, and it would be possible for carts to do so. They raise as much corn as they need, and beans and melons. They have some fowls, which they keep so as to make cloaks of their feathers. They raise cotton, although not much; they wear cloaks made of this, and shoes of hide, as at Cibola. These people defend themselves very well, and from within their houses, since they do not care to come out. The country is all sandy.

Four days' journey from the province and river of Tiguex four villages are found. The first has 30 houses; the second is a large village destroyed in their wars, and has about 35 houses occupied; the third about [?]. These three are like those at the river in every way. The fourth is a large village which is among some mountains. It is called Cicuic,[9] and has about 50 houses, with as many stories as those at Cibola. The walls are of dirt and mud like those at Cibola. It has plenty of corn, beans and melons, and some fowls. Four days from this village they came to a country as level as the sea, and in these plains there was such a multitude of cows that they are numberless. These cows are like those of Castile, and somewhat larger, as they have a little hump on the withers, and they are more reddish, approaching black; their hair, more than a span long, hangs down around their horns and ears and chin, and along the neck and shoulders like manes, and down from the knees; all the rest is a very fine wool, like merino; they have very good, tender meat, and much fat.

Having proceeded many days through these plains, they came to a settlement of about 200 inhabited houses. The houses were made of the skins of the cows, tanned white, like pavilions or army tents. The maintenance or sustenance of these Indians comes entirely from the cows, because they neither sow nor reap corn. With the skins they make their houses, with the skins, they clothe and shoe themselves, of the skins they make rope, and also of the wool; from the sinews they make thread, with which they sew their clothes and also their houses; from the bones they make awls; the dung serves them for wood, because there is nothing else in that country; the stomachs serve them for pitchers and vessels from which they drink; they live on the flesh; they sometimes eat it half roasted and warmed over the dung, at other times raw; seizing it with their fingers, they pull it out with one hand and with a flint knife in the other they cut off mouthfuls, and thus swallow it half chewed; they eat the fat raw, without warming it; they drink the blood just as it leaves the cows, and at other times after it has run out, cold and raw; they have no other means of livelihood.[10]

These people have dogs like those in this country, except that they are somewhat larger, and they load these dogs like beasts of burden, and make saddles for them like our pack saddles, and they fasten them with their leather thongs, and these make their backs sore on the withers like pack animals. When they go hunting, they load these with their necessities, & when they move—for these Indians are not settled in one place, since they travel wherever the cows move, to support themselves—these dogs carry their houses, and they have the sticks of their houses dragging along tied on to the pack-saddles, besides the load which they carry on top, and the load may be, according to the dog, from 35 to 50 pounds.[11] It is 30 leagues, or even more, from Cibola to these plains where they went. The plains stretch away beyond, nobody knows how far. The captain, Francisco Vazquez, went farther across the plains, with 30 horsemen, and Friar Juan de Padilla with him; all the rest of the force returned to the settlement at the river to wait for Francisco Vazquez, because this was his command. It is not known whether he has returned.

The country is so level that men became lost when they went off half a league. One horseman was lost, who never reappeared, and two horses, all saddled and bridled, which they never saw again. No track was left of where they went, and on this account it was necessary to mark the road by which they went with cow dung, so as to return, since there were no stones or anything else.

Marco Polo, the Venetian, in his treatise, in chapter 1 5, relates and says that (he saw) the same cows, with the same sort of hump; and in the same chapter he says that there are sheep as big as horses.

Nicholas, the Venetian, gave an account to Micer Pogio, the Florentine, in his second book, toward the end, which says that in Ethiopia there are oxen with a hump, like camels, and they have horns three cubits long, and they carry their horns up over their backs, and one of these horns makes a wine pitcher.

Marco Polo, in chapter 1 34, says that in the country of the Tartars, toward the north, they have dogs as large or little smaller than asses. They harness these into a sort of cart and with these enter a very miry country, all a quagmire, where other animals can not enter and come out without getting submerged, and on this account they take dogs.

ℭ Account of what happened on the journey which Francisco Vazquez made to discover Cibola.

WHEN the army reached the valley of Culiacan, Francisco Vazquez divided the army on account of the bad news which was received regarding Cibola, and because the food supply along the way was small, according to the report of Melchior Diaz, who had just come back from seeing it. He himself took 80 horsemen and 25 foot soldiers, and a small part of the artillery, and set out from Culiacan, leaving Don Tristan de Arellano with the rest of the force, with orders to set out 20 days later, and when he reached the Valley of Hearts (Corazones) to wait there for a letter from him, which would be sent after he had reached Cibola, and had seen what was there; and this was done. The Valley of Hearts is 150 leagues from the valley of Culiacan, and the same distance from Cibola.

This whole distance, up to about fifty leagues before reaching Cibola, is inhabited, although it is away from the road in some places. The population is all of the same sort of people, since the houses are all of palm mats, & some of them have low lofts. They all have corn, although not much, and in some places very little. They have melons and beans. The best settlement of all is a valley called Señora, which is ten leagues beyond the Hearts, where a town was afterward settled. There is some cotton among these, but deer skins are what most of them use for clothes.

Francisco Vazquez passed by all these on account of the small crops. There was no corn the whole way, except at this valley of Señora, where they collected a little, and besides this he had what he took from Culiacan, where he provided himself for 80 days. In 73 days we reached Cibola, although after hard labor and the loss of many horses and the death of several Indians, and after we saw it these were all doubled, although we did find corn enough. We found the natives peaceful for the whole way.

The day we reached the first village part of them came out to fight us, and the rest stayed in the village and fortified themselves. It was not possible to make peace with these, although we tried hard enough, so it was necessary to attack them and kill some of them. The rest then drew back to the village, which was then surrounded and attacked. We had to withdraw, on account of the great damage they did us from the flat roofs, and we began to assault them from a distance with the artillery and muskets, and that afternoon they surrendered. Francisco Vazquez came out of it badly hurt by some stones, and I am certain, indeed, that he would have been there yet if it had not been for the army-master, D. Garcia Lopez de Cardenas, who rescued him. When the Indians surrendered, they abandoned the village and went to the other villages, and as they left the houses we made ourselves at home in them.

Father Friar Marcos understood, or gave to understand, that the region and neighborhood in which there are seven villages was a single village which he called Cibola, but the whole of this settled region is called Cibola. The villages have from 150 to 200 and 300 houses; some have the houses of the village all together, although in some villages they are divided into two or three sections, but for the most part they are all together, and their courtyards are within, and in these are their hot rooms for winter, and they have their summer ones outside the villages. The houses have two or three stories, the walls of stone and mud, and some have mud walls. The villages have for the most part the walls of the houses; the houses are too good for Indians, especially for these, since they are brutish and have no decency in anything except in their houses.

For food they have much corn and beans and melons, and some fowls, like those of Mexico, and they keep these more for their feathers than to eat, because they make long robes of them, since they do not have any cotton; and they wear cloaks of heniquen (a fibrous plant),[2] and of the skins of deer, and sometimes of cows.

Their rites and sacrifices are somewhat idolatrous, but water is what they worship most, to which they offer small painted sticks & feathers & yellow powder made of flowers, and usually this offering is made to springs. Sometimes, also, they offer such turquoises as they have, although poor ones.[3]

From the valley of Culiacan to Cibola it is 240 leagues in two directions. It is north to about the thirty-fourth-and-a-half degree, and from there to Cibola, which is nearly the thirty-seventh degree, toward the northeast.[4]

Having talked with the natives of Cibola about what was beyond, they said that there were settlements toward the west. Francisco Vazquez then sent Don Pedro de Tobar to investigate, who found seven other villages, which were called the province of Tuzan[5]; this is 35 leagues to the west. The villages are somewhat larger than those of Cibola, & in other respects, in food and everything, they are of the same sort, except that these raise cotton. While Don Pedro de Tobar had gone to see these, Francisco Vaz-quez dispatched messengers to the viceroy, with an account of what had happened up to this point.[7] He also prepared instructions for these to take to Don Tristan, who as I have said, was at Hearts, for him to proceed to Cibola, and to leave a town established in the valley of Señora, which he did, and in it he left 80 horsemen of the men who had but one horse and the weakest men, and Melchior Diaz with them as captain and leader, because Francisco Vazquez had so arranged for it. He ordered him to go from there with half the force to explore toward the west; and he did so, and traveled 150 leagues, to the river which Hernando de Alarcon entered from the sea, which he called Buenaguia. The settlements & people that are in this direc-tion are mostly like those at the Hearts, except at the river and around it, where the people have much better figures and have more corn, although the houses in which they live are hovels, like pig pens, almost underground, with a covering of straw, and made without any skill whatever. This river is reported to be large. They reached it 30 leagues from the coast, where, and as far again above, Alarcon had come up with his boats two months before they reached it. This river runs north & south there. Melchior Diaz passed on toward the west five or six days, from which he returned for the reason that he did not find any water or vegetation, but only many stretches of sand; and he had some fighting on his return to the river and its vicinity, because they wanted to take advantage of him while crossing the river. While returning Melchior Diaz died from an accident, by which he killed himself, throwing a lance at a dog.

After Don Pedro de Tobar returned and had given an account of those villages, he then dispatched Don Garcia Lopez de Cardenas, the army-master, by the same road Don Pedro had followed, to go beyond that prov-ince of Tuzan to the west, and he allowed him eighty days in which to go and return, for the journey, and to make the discoveries. He was conducted beyond Tuzan by native guides, who said there were settlements beyond, although at a distance. Having gone 50 leagues west of Tuzan, and 80 from Cibola, he found the edge of a river down which it was impossible to find a path for a horse in any direction, or even for a man on foot, except in one very difficult place, where there was a descent for almost two leagues. The sides were such a steep rocky precipice that it was scarcely possible to see the river, which looks like a brook from above, although it is half as large again as that of Seville, according to what they say, so that although they sought for a passage with great diligence, none was found for a long distance, during which they were for several days in great need of water, which could not be found, and they could not approach that of the river, although they could see it, and on this account Don Garcia Lopez was forced to return. This river comes from the northeast and turns toward the south-southwest at the place where they found it, so that it is without any doubt the one that Melchior Diaz reached.

Four days after Francisco Vazquez had dispatched Don Garcia Lopez to make this discovery, he dispatched Hernando de Alvarado to explore the route toward the east. He started off, and 30 leagues from Cibola found a rock with a village on top, the strongest position that ever was seen in the world, which was called Acuco[8] in their language, and father Friar Marcos called it the kingdom of Hacus. They came out to meet us peacefully, although it would have been easy to decline to do this and to have stayed on their rock, where we would not have been able to trouble them. They gave us cloaks of cotton, skins of deer and of cows, and turquoises, and fowls and other food which they had, which is the same as in Cibola.

Twenty leagues to the east of this rock we found a river which runs north and south,[9] well settled; there are in all, small and large, 70 villages near it, a few more or less, the same sort as those at Cibola, except that they are almost all of well-made mud walls. The food is neither more nor less. They raise cotton—I mean those who live near the river—the others not. There is much corn here. These people do not have markets. They are settled for 50 leagues along this river, north and south, and some villages are 15 or 20 leagues distant, in one direction and the other. This river rises where these settlements end at the north, on the slope of the mountains there, where there is a larger village different from the others, called Yuraba.[10] It is settled in this fashion: It has 18 divisions; each one has a situation as if for two ground plots; the houses are very close together, and have five or six stories, three of them with mud walls and two or three with thin wooden walls, which become smaller as they go up, and each one has its little balcony outside of the mud walls, one above the other, all around, of wood. In this village, as it is in the mountains, they do not raise cotton nor breed fowls; they wear the skins of deer and cows entirely. It is the most populous village of all that country; we estimated there were 15,000 souls in it.[11] There is one of the other kind of villages larger than all the rest, and very strong, which is called Cicuique.[12] It has four & five stories, has eight large courtyards, each one with its balcony, and there are fine houses in it.

They do not raise cotton nor keep fowls, because it is 15 leagues away from the river to the east, toward the plains where the cows are.[13] After Alvarado had sent an account of this river to Francisco Vazquez, he proceeded forward to these plains, and at the borders of these he found a little river which flows to the southwest, & after four days' march he found the cows, which are the most monstrous thing in the way of animals which has ever been seen or read about. He followed this river for 100 leagues, finding more cows every day. We provided ourselves with some of these, although at first, until we had had experience, at the risk of the horses. There is such a quantity of them that I do not know what to compare them with, except with the fish in the sea, because on this journey, as also on that which the whole army afterward made when it was going to Quivira, there were so many that many times when we started to pass through the midst of them and wanted to go through to the other side of them, we were not able to, because the country was covered with them. The flesh of these is as good as that of Castile, and some said it was even better.

The bulls are large and brave, although they do not attack very much; but they have wicked horns, & in a fight use them well, attacking fiercely; they killed several of our horses & wounded many. We found the pike to be the best weapon to use against them, & the musket for use when this misses.

When Hernando de Alvarado returned from these plains to the river which was called Tiguex, he found the army-master Don Garcia Lopez de Cardenas getting ready for the whole army, which was coming there. When it arrived, although all these people had met Hernando de Alvarado peacefully, part of them rebelled when all the force came. There were 12 villages near together, and one night they killed 40 of our horses and mules which were loose in the camp. They fortified themselves in their villages, and war was then declared against them. Don Garcia Lopez went to the first and took it and executed justice on many of them. When the rest saw this, they abandoned all except two of the villages, one of these the strongest one of all, around which the army was kept for two months. And although after we invested it, we entered it one day and occupied a part of the flat roof, we were forced to abandon this on account of the many wounds that were received and because it was so dangerous to maintain ourselves there, and although we again entered it soon afterward, in the end it was not possible to get it all, and so it was surrounded all this time. We finally captured it because of their thirst, and they held out so long because it snowed twice when they were just about to give themselves up. In the end we captured it, and many of them were killed because they tried to get away at night.[14]

Francisco Vazquez obtained an account from some Indians who were found in this village of Cicuique, which, if it had been true, was of the richest thing that has been found in the Indies. The Indian who gave the news and the account came from a village called Harale, 300 leagues east of this river.[15] He gave such a clear account of what he told, as if it were true and he had seen it, that it seemed plain afterward that it was the devil who was speaking in him. Francisco Vazquez and all of us placed much confidence in him, although he was advised by several gentlemen not to move the whole army, but rather to send a captain to find out what was there. He did not wish to do this, but wanted to take every one, and even to send Don Pedro de Tobar to the Hearts for half the men who were in that village. So he started with the whole army, and proceeded 150 leagues, 100 to the east and 50 to the south,[16] and the Indian failing to make good what he had said about there being a settlement there, and corn, with which to proceed farther, the other two guides were asked how that was, and one confessed that what the Indian said was a lie, except that there was a province which was called Quivira, and that there was corn and houses of straw there, but that they were very far off, because we had been led astray a distance from the road. Considering this, and the small supply of food that was left, Francisco Vazquez, after consulting with the captains, determined to proceed with 30 of the best men who were well equipped, and that the army should return to the river; and this was done at once. Two days before this, Don Garcia Lopez' horse had happened to fall with him, and he threw his arm out of joint, from which he suffered much, and so Don Tristan de Arellano returned to the river with the army. On this journey they had a very hard time, because almost all of them had nothing to eat except meat, and many suffered on this account. They killed a world of bulls and cows, for there were days when they brought 60 and 70 head into camp, and it was necessary to go hunting every day, and on this account, and from not eating any corn during all this time, the horses suffered much.

Francisco Vazquez set out across these plains in search of Quivira, more on account of the story which had been told us at the river than from the confidence which was placed in the guide here, and after proceeding many days by the needle (*i. e.*, to the north) it pleased God that after thirty days' march we found the river Quivira, which is 30 leagues below the settlement. While going up the valley, we found people who were going hunting, who were natives of Quivira.[17]

All that there is at Quivira is a very brutish people, without any decency whatever in their houses nor in anything. These are of straw, like the Tarascan settlements; in some villages there are as many as 200 houses; they have corn and beans and melons; they do not have cotton nor fowls, nor do they make bread which is cooked, except under the ashes. Francisco Vazquez went 25 leagues through these settlements, to where he obtained an account of what was beyond, and they said that the plains come to an end, and that down the river there are people who do not plant, but live wholly by hunting.

They also gave an account of two other large villages, one of which was called Tareque and the other Arae,[18] with straw houses at Tareque, and at Arae some of straw and some of skins. Copper was found here, and they said it came from a distance. From what the Indian had said, it is possible that this village of Arae contains more,[19] from the clear description of it which he gave. We did not find any trace or news of it here. Francisco Vazquez returned from here to the river of Tiguex, where he found the army. We went back by a more direct route, because in going by the way we went we traveled 330 leagues, and it is not more than 200 by that by which we returned.[20] Quivira is in the fortieth degree and the river in the thirty-sixth.[21] It was so dangerous to travel or to go away from the camp in these plains, that it is as if one was traveling on the sea, since the only roads are those of the cows, & they are so level & have no mountain or prominent landmark, that if one went out of sight of it, he was lost, and in this way we lost one man, & others who went hunting wandered around two or three days, lost.

Two kinds of people travel around these plains with the cows; one is called Querechos and the others Teyas; they are very well built, and painted, and are enemies of each other. They have no other settlement or location than comes from traveling around with the cows. They kill all of these they wish, and tan the hides, with which they clothe themselves and make their tents, and they eat the flesh, sometimes even raw, and they also even drink the blood when thirsty. The tents they make are like field tents, and they set them up over some poles they have made for this purpose, which come together and are tied at the top, and when they go from one place to another they carry them on some dogs they have, of which they have many, and they load them with the tents and poles and other things, for the country is so level, as I said, that they can make use of these, because they carry the poles dragging along on the ground.[22] The sun is what they worship most. The skin for the tents is cured on both sides, without the hair, and they have the skins of deer and cows left over.[23] They exchange some cloaks with the natives of the river for corn.

After Francisco Vazquez reached the river, where he found the army, Don Pedro de Tobar came with half the people from the Hearts, and Don Garcia Lopez de Cardenas started off for Mexico, who, besides the fact that his arm was very bad, had permission from the viceroy on account of the death of his brother. Ten or twelve who were sick went with him, and not a man among them all who could fight. He reached the town of the Spaniards and found it burned and two Spaniards and many Indians and horses dead, and he returned to the river on this account, escaping from them by good fortune and great exertions. The cause of this misfortune was that after Don Pedro started and left 40 men there, half of these raised a mutiny and fled, and the Indians, who remembered the bad treatment they had received, attacked them one night and overpowered them because of their carelessness and weakness, and they fled to Culiacan. Francisco Vazquez fell while running a horse about this time and was sick a long time, and after the winter was over he determined to come back, and although they may say something different, he did so, because he wanted to do this more than anything, and so we all came together as far as Culiacan, and each one went where he pleased from there, and Francisco Vazquez came here to Mexico to make his report to the viceroy, who was not at all pleased with his coming, although he pretended so at first. He was pleased that Father Friar Juan de Padilla had stayed there, who went to Quivira, and a Spaniard and a negro with him, and Friar Luis, a very holy lay brother, stayed in Cicuique. We spent two very cold winters at this river, with much snow and thick ice. The river froze one night and remained so for more than a month, so that loaded horses crossed on the ice. The reason these villages are settled in this fashion is supposed to be the great cold, although it is also partly the wars which they have with one another. And this is all that was seen and found out about all that country, which is very barren of fruits and groves. Quivira is a better country, having many huts and not being so cold, although it is more to the north.

LETTER
FROM CORONADO TO THE KING
October 20, 1541[1]

℃ Letters from Francisco Vazquez de Coronado to His Majesty, in which he gives an Account of the Discovery of the Province of Tiguex.

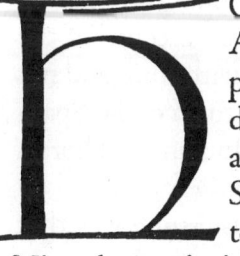

OLY CATHOLIC CÆSARIAN MAJESTY: On April 20 of this year I wrote to Your Majesty from this province of Tiguex, in reply to a letter from Your Majesty dated in Madrid, June 11 a year ago. I gave a detailed account of this expedition, which the viceroy of New Spain ordered me to undertake in Your Majesty's name to this country which was discovered by Friar Marcos de Niza, the provincial of the order of Holy Saint Francis. I described it all, and the sort of force I have, as Your Majesty had ordered me to relate in my letters; and stated that while I was engaged in the conquest and pacification of the natives of this province, some Indians who were natives of other provinces beyond these had told me that in their country there were much larger villages and better houses than those of the natives of this country, and that they had lords who ruled them, who were served with dishes of gold, and other very magnificent things; and although, as I wrote Your Majesty, I did not believe it before I had set eyes on it, because it was the report of Indians and given for the most part by means of signs, yet as the report appeared to me to be very fine and that it was important that it should be investigated for Your Majesty's service, I determined to go and see it with the men I have here. I started from this province on the 23d of last April, for the place where the Indians wanted to guide me.

After nine days' march I reached some plains, so vast that I did not find their limit anywhere that I went, although I traveled over them for more than 300 leagues. And I found such a quantity of cows in these, of the kind that I wrote Your Majesty about, which they have in this country, that it is impossible to number them, for while I was journeying through these plains, until I returned to where I first found them, there was not a day that I lost sight of them. And after seventeen days' march I came to a settlement of Indians who are called Querechos, who travel around with these cows, who do not plant, and who eat the raw flesh and drink the blood of the cows they kill, and they tan the skins of the cows, with which all the people of this country dress themselves here. They have little field tents made of the hides of the cows, tanned and greased, very well made, in which they live while they travel around near the cows, moving with these. They have dogs which they load, which carry their tents and poles and belongings. These people have the best figures of any that I have seen in the Indies. They could not give me any account of the country where the guides were taking me. I traveled five days more as the guides wished to lead me, until I reached some plains, with no more landmarks than as if we had been swallowed up in the sea, where they strayed about, because there was not a stone, nor a bit of rising ground, nor a tree, nor a shrub, nor anything to go by. There is much very fine pasture land, with good grass. And while we were lost in these plains, some horsemen who went off to hunt cows fell in with some Indians who also were out hunting, who are enemies of those that I had seen in the last settlement, and of another sort of people who are called Teyas; they have their bodies and faces all painted, are a large people like the others, of a very good build; they eat the raw flesh just like the Querechos, and live and travel round with the cows in the same way as these. I obtained from these an account of the country where the guides were taking me, which was not like what they had told me, because these made out that the houses there were not built of stones, with stories, as my guides had described it, but of straw and skins, and a small supply of corn there.

This news troubled me greatly, to find myself on these limitless plains, where I was in great need of water, and often had to drink it so poor that it was more mud than water. Here the guides confessed to me that they had not told the truth in regard to the size of the houses, because these were of straw, but that they had done so regarding the large number of inhabitants and the other things about their habits. The Teyas disagreed with this, and on account of this division between some of the Indians and the others, and also because many of the men I had with me had not eaten anything except meat for some days, because we had reached the end of the corn which we carried from this province, and because they made it out more than forty days' journey from where I fell in with the Teyas to the country where the guides were taking me, although I appreciated the trouble and danger there would be in the journey owing to the lack of water and corn, it seemed to me best, in order to see if there was anything there of service to Your Majesty, to go forward with only 30 horsemen until I should be able to see the country, so as to give Your Majesty a true account of what was to be found in it. I sent all the rest of the force I had with me to this province, with Don Tristan de Arellano in command, because it would have been impossible to prevent the loss of many men, if all had gone on, owing to the lack of water and because they also had to kill bulls and cows on which to sustain themselves. And with only the 30 horsemen whom I took for my escort, I traveled forty-two days after I left the force, living all this while solely on the flesh of the bulls and cows which we killed, at the cost of several of our horses which they killed, because, as I wrote Your Majesty, they are very brave and fierce animals; and going many days without water, and cooking the food with cow dung, because there is not any kind of wood in all these plains, away from the gullies and rivers, which are very few.

It was the Lord's pleasure that, after having journeyed across these deserts seventy-seven days, I arrived at the province they call Quivira, to which the guides were conducting me, and where they had described to me houses of stone, with many stories; and not only are they not of stone, but of straw, but the people in them are as barbarous as all those whom I have seen and passed before this; they do not have cloaks, nor cotton of which to make these, but use the skins of the cattle they kill, which they tan, because they are settled among these on a very large river. They eat the raw flesh like the Querechos and Teyas; they are enemies of one another, but are all of the same sort of people, and these at Quivira have the advantage in the houses they build and in planting corn. In this province of which the guides who brought me are natives, they received me peaceably, and although they told me when I set out for it that I could not succeed in seeing it all in two months, there are not more than 25 villages of straw houses there & in all the rest of the country that I saw & learned about, which gave their obedience to Your Majesty and placed themselves under your royal overlordship.

The people here are large. I had several Indians measured, and found that they were 10 palms in height; the women are well proportioned and their features are more like Moorish women than Indians. The natives here gave me a piece of copper which a chief Indian wore hung around his neck; I sent it to the viceroy of New Spain, because I have not seen any other metal in these parts except this and some little copper bells which I sent him, and a bit of metal which looks like gold. I do not know where this came from, although I believe that the Indians who gave it to me obtained it from those whom I brought here in my service, because I can not find any other origin for it nor where it came from. The diversity of languages which exists in this country and my not having anyone who understood them, because they speak their own language in each village, has hindered me, because I have been forced to send captains and men in many directions to find out whether there was anything in this country which could be of service to Your Majesty. And although I have searched with all diligence I have not found or heard of anything, unless it be these provinces, which are a very small affair.

The province of Quivira is 950 leagues from Mexico. Where I reached it, it is in the fortieth degree.² The country itself is the best I have ever seen for producing all the products of Spain, for besides the land itself being very fat and black and being very well watered by the rivulets and springs and rivers, I found prunes like those of Spain [or I found everything they have in Spain] & nuts and very good sweet grapes and mulberries. I have treated the natives of this province, and all the others whom I found wherever I went, as well as was possible, agreeably to what Your Majesty had commanded, and they have received no harm in any way from me or from those who went in my company.³ I remained twenty-five days in this province of Quivira, so as to see and explore the country and also to find out whether there was anything beyond which could be of service to Your Majesty, because the guides who had brought me had given me an account of other provinces beyond this. And what I am sure of is that there is not any gold nor any other metal in all that country, and the other things of which they had told me are nothing but little villages, and in many of these they do not plant anything and do not have any houses except of skins and sticks, and they wander around with the cows; so that the account they gave me was false, because they wanted to persuade me to go there with the whole force, believing that as the way was through such uninhabited deserts, and from the lack of water, they would get us where we and our horses would die of hunger. And the guides confessed this, and said they had done it by the advice and orders of the natives of these provinces. At this, after having heard the account of what was beyond, which I have given above, I returned to these provinces to provide for the force I had sent back here and to give Your Majesty an account of what this country amounts to, because I wrote Your Majesty that I would do so when I went there.

I have done all that I possibly could to serve Your Majesty and to discover a country where God Our Lord might be served and the royal patrimony of Your Majesty increased, as your loyal servant and vassal. For since I reached the province of Cibola, to which the viceroy of New Spain sent me in the name of Your Majesty, seeing that there were none of the things there of which Friar Marcos had told, I have managed to explore this country for 200 leagues and more around Cibola, and the best place I have found is this river of Tiguex where I am now, and the settlements here. It would not be possible to establish a settlement here, for besides being 400 leagues from the North Sea and more than 200 from the South Sea, with which it is impossible to have any sort of communication, the country is so cold, as I have written to Your Majesty, that apparently the winter could not possibly be spent here, because there is no wood, nor cloth with which to protect the men, except the skins which the natives wear and some small amount of cotton cloaks. I send the viceroy of New Spain an account of everything I have seen in the countries where I have been, and as Don Garcia Lopez de Cardenas is going to kiss Your Majesty's hands, who has done much and has served Your Majesty very well on this expedition, and he will give Your Majesty an account of everything here, as one who has seen it himself, I give way to him. And may Our Lord protect the Holy Imperial Catholic person of Your Majesty, with increase of greater kingdoms and powers, as your loyal servants and vassals desire. From this province of Tiguex, October 20, in the year 1541. Your Majesty's humble servant and vassal, who would kiss the royal feet and hands:

FRANCISCO VAZQUEZ DE CORONADO.

JARAMILLO'S NARRATIVE

❦ Account given by Captain Juan Jaramillo of the journey which he made to the New Country, on which Francisco Vazquez de Coronado was the General.[1]

E started from Mexico, going directly to Compostela, the whole way populated and at peace, the direction being west, and the distance 112 leagues. From there we went to Culiacan, perhaps about 80 leagues; the road is well known and much used, because there is a town inhabited by Spaniards in the said valley of Culiacan, under the government of Compostela. The 70 horsemen who went with the general went in a northwesterly direction from this town. He left his army here, because information had been obtained that the way was uninhabited and almost the whole of it without food. He went with the said horsemen to explore the route and prepare the way for those who were to follow. He pursued this direction, though with some twisting, until we crossed a mountain chain, where they knew about New Spain, more than 300 leagues distant. To this pass we gave the name of Chichiltic Calli, because we learned that this was what it was called, from some Indians whom we left behind.

Leaving the said valley of Culiacan, he crossed a river called Pateatlan (*or* Peteatlan), which was about four days distant.[2] We found these Indians peaceful, and they gave us some few things to eat. From here we went to another river called Cinaloa, which was about three days from the other.[3] From here the general ordered ten of us horsemen to make double marches, lightly equipped, until we reached the stream of the Cedars (arroyo de los Cedros),[4] and from there we were to enter a break in the mountains on the right of the road and see what there was in and about this. If more time should be needed for this than we gained on him, he would wait for us at the said Cedros stream. This was done, and all that we saw there was a few poor Indians in some settled valleys like farms or estates, with sterile soil. It was about five more days from the river to this stream. From there we went to the river called Yaquemi, which took about three days.[5] We proceeded along a dry stream, and after three days more of marching, although the dry stream lasted only for a league, we reached another stream where there were some settled Indians, who had straw huts and storehouses of corn and beans and melons. Leaving here, we went to the stream and village which is called Hearts (Corazones),[6] the name which was given it by Dorantes and Cabeza de Vaca and Castillo and the negro Estebanillo, because they gave them a present of the hearts of animals and birds to eat.

About two days were spent in this village of the Hearts. There is an irrigation stream, and the country is warm. Their dwellings are huts made of a frame of poles, almost like an oven, only very much better, which they cover with mats. They have corn and beans and melons for food, which I believe never fail them. They dress in deer skins. This appeared to be a good place, & so orders were given the Spaniards who were behind to establish a village here, where they lived until almost the failure of the expedition. There was a poison here, the effect of which is, according to what was seen of it, the worst that could possibly be found; and from what we learned about it, it is the sap of a small tree like the mastick tree, or lentisk, and it grows in gravelly and sterile land. We went on from here, passing through a sort of gateway, to another valley very near this stream, which opens off from this same stream, which is called Señora. It is also irrigated, and the Indians are like the others and have the same sort of settlements and food. This valley continues for six or seven leagues, a little more or less.

At first these Indians were peaceful; and afterward not, but instead they and those whom they were able to summon thither were our worst enemies. They have a poison with which they killed several Christians. There are mountains on both sides of them, which are not very fertile. From here we went along near this said stream, crossing it where it makes a bend, to another Indian settlement called Ispa.[7] It takes one day from the last of these others to this place. It is of the same sort as those we had passed. From here we went through deserted country for about four days to another river, which we heard called Nexpa,[8] where some poor Indians came out to see the general, with presents of little value, with some stalks of roasted maguey & pitahayas.[9] We went down this stream two days, and then left the stream, going toward the right to the foot of the mountain chain in two days' journey, where we heard news of what is called Chichiltic Calli. Crossing the mountains, we came to a deep and reedy river, where we found water and forage for the horses.[10] From this river back at Nexpa, as I have said, it seems to me that the direction was nearly northeast. From here, I believe that we went in the same dirction for three days to a river which we called Saint John (San Juan), because we reached it on his day.[11] Leaving here, we went to another river,[12] through a somewhat rough country, more toward the north, to a river which we called the Rafts (de las Balsas), because we had to cross on these, as it was rising. It seems to me that we spent two days between one river and the other, and I say this because it is so long since we went there that I may be wrong in some days, though not in the rest. From here we went to another river, which we called Slough (de la Barranca).[13] It is two short days from one to the other, and the direction almost northeast. From here we went to another river, which we called the Cold River (el rio Frio),[14] on account of its water being so, in one day's journey, & from here we went by a pine mountain, where we found, almost at the top of it, a cool spring and streamlet, which was another day's march. In the neighborhood of this stream a Spaniard, who was called Espinosa, died, besides two other persons, on account of poisonous plants which they ate, owing to the great need in which they were.

From here we went to another river, which we called the Red River (Bermejo),[15] two days' journey in the same direction, but less toward the northeast. Here we saw an Indian or two, who afterward appeared to belong to the first settlement of Cibola. From here we came in two days' journey to the said village, the first of Cibola. The houses have flat roofs and walls of stone and mud, and this was where they killed Steve (Estebanillo), the negro who had come with Dorantes from Florida and returned with Friar Marcos de Niza. In this province of Cibola there are five little villages besides this, all with flat roofs and of stone and mud, as I said.[16] The country is cold, as is shown by their houses and hothouses (estufa). They have food enough for themselves, of corn and beans and melons. These villages are about a league or more apart from each other, within a circuit of perhaps six leagues. The country is somewhat sandy and not very salty (or barren of vegetation[17]), and on the mountains the trees are for the most part evergreen.[18] The clothing of the Indians is of deerskins, very carefully tanned, and they also prepare some tanned cowhides, with which they cover themselves, which are like shawls, and a great protection. They have square cloaks of cotton, some larger than others, about a yard and a half long. The Indians wear them thrown over the shoulder like a gipsy, & fastened with one end over the other, with a girdle, also of cotton. From this first village of Cibola, looking toward the northeast and a little less, on the left hand, there is a province called Tucayan, about five days off, which has seven flat-roof villages, with a food supply as good or better than these, and an even larger population; and they also have the skins of cows and of deer, and cloaks of cotton, as I described.

All the waterways we found as far as this one at Cibola—and I do not know but what for a day or two beyond—the rivers and streams run into the South Sea, and those from here on into the North Sea.[19]

From this first village of Cibola, as I have said, we went to another in the same province,[20] which was about a short day's journey off, on the way to Tihuex. It is nine days, of such marches as we made, from this settlement of Cibola to the river of Tihuex. Half way between, I do not know but it may be a day more or less, there is a village of earth and dressed stone, in a very strong position, which is called Tutahaco.[21] All these Indians, except the first in the first village of Cibola, received us well. At the river of Tihuex there are 15 villages within a distance of about 20 leagues, all with flat-roof houses of earth, instead of stone, after the fashion of mud walls. There are other villages besides these on other streams which flow into this, and three of these are, for Indians, well worth seeing, especially one that is called Chia, and another Uraba, and another Cicuique.[22] Uraba and Cicuique have many houses two stories high. All the rest, and these also, have corn and beans and melons, skins, and some long robes of feathers which they braid, joining the feathers with a sort of thread; and they also make them of a sort of plain weaving with which they make the cloaks with which they protect themselves. They all have hot rooms underground, which, although not very clean, are very warm. They raise and have a very little cotton, of which they make the cloaks which I have spoken of above. This river comes from the northwest and flows about southeast, which shows that it certainly flows into the North Sea.

Leaving this settlement[23] and the said river, we passed two other villages whose names I do not know,[24] and in four days came to Cicuique, which I have already mentioned. The direction of this is toward the northeast. From there we came to another river, which the Spaniards named after Cicuique, in three days;[25] if I remember rightly, it seems to me that we went rather toward the northeast to reach this river where we crossed it, & after crossing this, we turned more to the left hand, which would be more to the northeast, and began to enter the plains where the cows are, although we did not find them for some four or five days, after which we began to come across bulls, of which there are great numbers, and after going on in the same direction and meeting the bulls for two or three days, we began to find ourselves in the midst of very great numbers of cows, yearlings and bulls all in together. We found Indians among these first cows, who were, on this account, called Querechos by those in the flat-roof houses. They do not live in houses, but have some sets of poles which they carry with them to make some huts at the places where they stop, which serve them for houses. They tie these poles together at the top and stick the bottoms into the ground, covering them with some cowskins which they carry around, and which, as I have said, serve them for houses. From what was learned of these Indians, all their human needs are supplied by these cows, for they are fed and clothed and shod from these. They are a people who wander around here and there, wherever seems to them best. We went on for eight or ten days in the same direction, along those streams which are among the cows.

The Indian who guided us from here was the one that had given us the news about Quevira and Arache (*or* Arahei) and about its being a very rich country with much gold and other things, and he and the other one were from that country I mentioned, to which we were going, and we found these two Indians in the flat-roof villages. It seems that, as the said Indian wanted to go to his own country, he proceeded to tell us what we found was not true, and I do not know whether it was on this account or because he was counseled to take us into other regions by confusing us on the road, although there are none in all this region except those of the cows. We understood, however, that he was leading us away from the route we ought to follow and that he wanted to lead us on to those plains where he had led us, so that we would eat up the food, and both ourselves and our horses would become weak from the lack of this, because if we should go either backward or forward in this condition we could not make any resistance to whatever they might wish to do to us. From the time when, as I said, we entered the plains and from this settlement of Querechos, he led us off more to the east, until we came to be in extreme need from the lack of food, and as the other Indian, who was his companion and also from his country, saw that he was not taking us where we ought to go, since we had always followed the guidance of the Turk, for so he was called, instead of his, he threw himself down in the way, making a sign that although we cut off his head he ought not to go that way, nor was that our direction.

I believe we had been traveling twenty days or more in this direction, at the end of which we found another settlement of Indians of the same sort and way of living as those behind, among whom there was an old blind man with a beard, who gave us to understand, by signs which he made, that he had seen four others like us many days before, whom he had seen near there and rather more toward New Spain, and we so understood him, and presumed that it was Dorantes and Cabeza de Vaca and those whom I have mentioned.[26]

At this settlement the general, seeing our difficulties, ordered the captains, and the persons whose advice he was accustomed to take, to assemble, so that we might discuss with him what was best for all. It seemed to us that all the force should go back to the region we had come from, in search of food, so that they could regain their strength, and that 30 picked horsemen should go in search of what the Indian had told about; and we decided to do this. We all went forward one day to a stream which was down in a ravine in the midst of good meadows, to agree on who should go ahead and how the rest should return. Here the Indian Isopete, as we had called the companion of the said Turk, was asked to tell us the truth, and to lead us to that country which we had come in search of. He said he would do it, and that it was not as the Turk had said, because those were certainly fine things which he had said and had given us to understand at Tihuex, about gold and how it was obtained, and the buildings, and the style of them, & their trade, and many other things told for the sake of prolixity, which had led us to go in search of them, with the advice of all who gave it and of the priests. He asked us to leave him afterward in that country, because it was his native country, as a reward for guiding us, and also, that the Turk might not go along with him, because he would quarrel and try to restrain him in everything that he wanted to do for our advantage; and the general promised him this, and said he would be with one of the thirty, and he went in this way. And when everything was ready for us to set out and for the others to remain, we pursued our way, the direction all the time after this being toward the north, for more than thirty days' march, although not long marches, not having to go without water on any one of them, and among cows all the time, some days in larger numbers than others, according to the water which we came across, so that on Saint Peter and Paul's day we reached a river which we found to be there below Quibira.[27]

When he reached the said river, the Indian recognized it and said that was it, and that it was below the settlements. We crossed it there and went up the other side on the north, the direction turning toward the northeast, and after marching three days we found some Indians who were going hunting, killing the cows to take the meat to their village, which was about three or four days still farther away from us. Here where we found the Indians and they saw us, they began to utter yells and appeared to fly, and some even had their wives there with them. The Indian Isopete began to call them in his language, and so they came to us without any signs of fear. When we and these Indians had halted here, the general made an example of the Indian Turk, whom we had brought along, keeping him all the time out of sight among the rear guard, and having arrived where the place was prepared, it was done in such a way that the other Indian, who was called Isopete, should not see it, so as to give him the satisfaction he had asked.[28] Some satisfaction was experienced here on seeing the good appearance of the earth, and it is certainly such among the cows, and from there on. The general wrote a letter here to the governor of Harahey and Quibira, having understood that he was a Christian from the lost army of Florida, because what the Indian had said of their manner of government and their general character had made us believe this. So the Indians went to their houses, which were at the distance mentioned, and we also proceeded at our rate of marching until we reached the settlements, which we found along good river bottoms, although without much water, and good streams which flow into another, larger than the one I have mentioned. There were, if I recall correctly, six or seven settlements, at quite a distance from one another, among which we traveled for four or five days, since it was understood to be uninhabited between one stream and the other.

We reached what they said was the end of Quibira, to which they took us, saying that the things there were of great importance.[29] Here there was a river, with more water and more inhabitants than the others. Being asked if there was anything beyond, they said that there was nothing more of Quibira, but that there was Harahey, and that it was the same sort of a place, with settlements like these, and of about the same size. The general sent to summon the lord of those parts and the other Indians who they said resided in Harahey, and he came with about 200 men—all naked—with bows, and some sort of things on their heads, and their privy parts slightly covered. He was a big Indian, with a large body and limbs, and well proportioned. After he had heard the opinion of one and another about it, the general asked them what we ought to do, reminding us of how the army had been left and that the rest of us were there, so that it seemed to all of us that as it was already almost the opening of winter, for, if I remember rightly, it was after the middle of August, and because there was little to winter there for, and we were but very little prepared for it, and the uncertainty as to the success of the army that had been left, and because the winter might close the roads with snow and rivers which we could not cross, and also in order to see what had happened to the rest of the force left behind, it seemed to us all that his grace ought to go back in search of them, and when he had found out for certain how they were, to winter there and return to that country at the opening of spring, to conquer and cultivate it.

Since, as I have said, this was the last point which we reached, here the Turk saw that he had lied to us, and one night he called on all these people to attack us and kill us. We learned of it, and put him under guard and strangled him that night so that he never waked up. With the plan mentioned, we turned back it may have been two or three days, where we provided ourselves with picked fruit and dried corn for our return. The general raised a cross at this place, at the foot of which he made some letters with a chisel, which said that Francisco Vazquez de Coronado, general of that army, had arrived here.

This country presents a very fine appearance, than which I have not seen a better in all our Spain nor Italy nor a part of France, nor, indeed, in the other countries where I have traveled in His Majesty's service, for it is not a very rough country, but is made up of hillocks and plains, and very fine appearing rivers and streams, which certainly satisfied me and made me sure that it will be very fruitful in all sorts of products. Indeed, there is profit in the cattle ready to the hand, from the quantity of them, which is as great as one could imagine. We found a variety of Castilian prunes which are not all red, but some of them black and green; the tree and fruit is certainly like that of Castile, with a very excellent flavor. Among the cows we found flax, which springs up from the earth in clumps apart from one another, which are noticeable, as the cattle do not eat it, with their tops & blue flowers, and very perfect although small, resembling that of our own Spain (*or* and sumach like ours in Spain). There are grapes along some streams, of a fair flavor, not to be improved upon.

The houses which these Indians have were of straw, and most of them round, and the straw reached down to the ground like a wall, so that they did not have the symmetry or the style of these here; they have something like a chapel or sentry box outside and around these, with an entry, where the Indians appear seated or reclining. The Indian Isopete was left here where the cross was erected, and we took five or six of the Indians from these villages to lead and guide us to the flat-roof houses.[30] Thus they brought us back by the same road as far as where I said before that we came to a river called Saint Peter and Paul's, and here we left that by which we had come, and, taking the right hand, they led us along by watering places and among cows and by a good road,[31] although there are none either one way or the other except those of the cows, as I have said. At last we came to where we recognized the country, where I said we found the first settlement, where the Turk led us astray from the route we should have followed. Thus, leaving the rest aside, we reached Tiguex, where we found the rest of the army, and here the general fell while running his horse, by which he received a wound on his head which gave symptoms of turning out badly, and he conceived the idea of returning, which ten or twelve of us were unable to prevent by dissuading him from it.

When this return had been ordered, the Franciscan friars who were with us—one of them a regular and the other a lay brother—who were called, the regular one Friar Juan de Padilla and the lay one Friar Luis de Escalona, were told to get ready, although they had permission from their provincial so that they could remain. Friar Luis wished to remain in these flat-roof houses, saying that he would raise crosses for those villagers with a chisel & adze they left him, and would baptize several poor creatures who could be led, on the point of death, so as to send them to heaven, for which he did not desire any other company than a little slave of mine who was called Christopher, to be his consolation, and who he said would learn the language there quickly so as to help him; and he brought up so many things in favor of this that he could not be denied, and so nothing more has been heard from him. The knowledge that this friar would remain there was the reason that many Indians from hereabouts stayed there, & also two negroes, one of them mine, who was called Sebastian, & the other one of Melchior Perez, the son of the licentiate La Torre. This negro was married and had his wife and children. I also recall that several Indians remained behind in the Quivira region, besides a Tarascan belonging to my company, who was named Andrew. Friar Juan de Padilla preferred to return to Quivira, and persuaded them to give him those Indians who I said we had brought as guides. They gave him these, and he also took a Portuguese and a free Spanish-speaking Indian, who was the interpreter, and who passed as a Franciscan friar, and a half-blood and two Indians from Capottan (*or* Capotean)[32] or thereabouts, I believe. He had brought these up and took them in the habits of friars, and he took some sheep and mules and a horse and ornaments & other trifles. I do not know whether it was for the sake of these or for what reason, but it seems that they killed him, & those who did it were the lay servants, or these same Indians whom he took back from Tiguex, in return for the good deeds which he had done. When he was dead, the Portuguese whom I mentioned fled, and also one of the Indians that I said he took in the habits of friars, or both of them, I believe. I mention this because they came back to this country of New Spain by another way and a shorter route than the one of which I have told, and they came out in the valley of Panico.[33] I have given Gonzalo Solis de Meras and Isidoro de Solis an account of this, because it seemed to me important, according to what I say I have understood, that His Majesty ordered Your Lordship to find or discover a way so as to unite that land to this. It is perhaps also very likely that this Indian Sebastian, during the time he was in Quivira, learned about its territory and the country round about it, and also of the sea, and the road by which he came, & what there is to it, & how many days' journey before arriving there. So that I am sure that if Your Lordship acquires this Quivira on this account, I am certain that he can confidently bring many people from Spain to settle it according to the appearance and the character of the land.

REPORT OF
HERNANDO DE ALVARADO

Account of what Hernando de Alvarado and Fríar Juan de Padílla díscovered goíng ín search of the South Sea.[1]

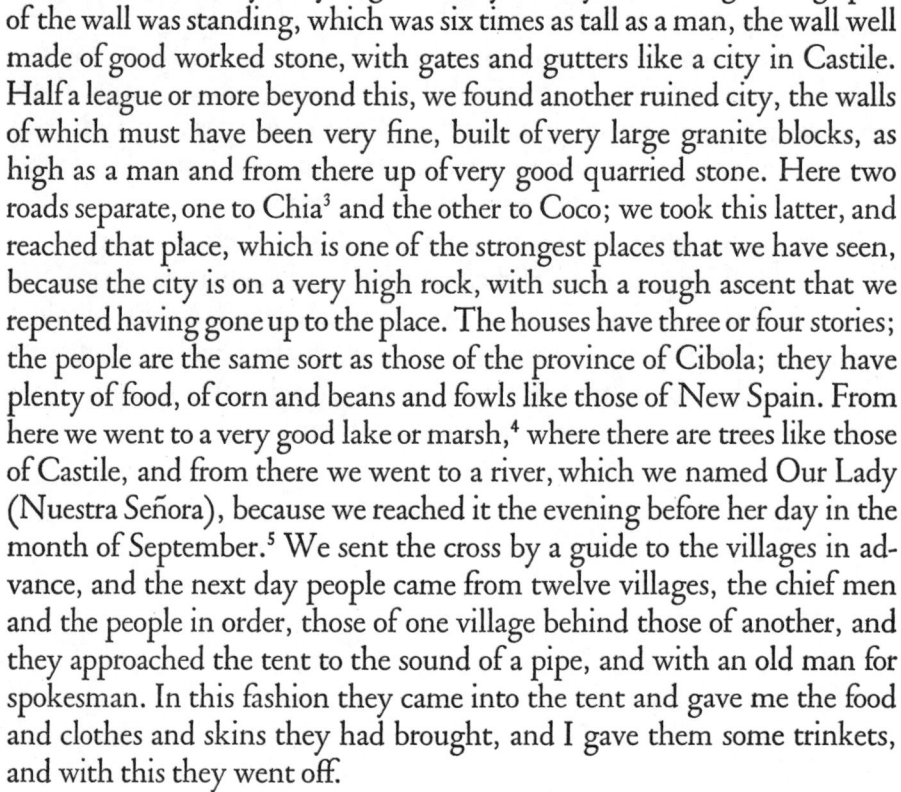

WE set out from Granada on Sunday, the day of the beheading of Saint John the Baptist, the 29th of August, in the year 1540, on the way to Coco.[2] After we had gone two leagues, we came to an ancient building like a fortress, & a league beyond this we found another, and yet another a little farther on, and beyond these we found an ancient city, very large, entirely destroyed, although a large part of the wall was standing, which was six times as tall as a man, the wall well made of good worked stone, with gates and gutters like a city in Castile. Half a league or more beyond this, we found another ruined city, the walls of which must have been very fine, built of very large granite blocks, as high as a man and from there up of very good quarried stone. Here two roads separate, one to Chia[3] and the other to Coco; we took this latter, and reached that place, which is one of the strongest places that we have seen, because the city is on a very high rock, with such a rough ascent that we repented having gone up to the place. The houses have three or four stories; the people are the same sort as those of the province of Cibola; they have plenty of food, of corn and beans and fowls like those of New Spain. From here we went to a very good lake or marsh,[4] where there are trees like those of Castile, and from there we went to a river, which we named Our Lady (Nuestra Señora), because we reached it the evening before her day in the month of September.[5] We sent the cross by a guide to the villages in advance, and the next day people came from twelve villages, the chief men and the people in order, those of one village behind those of another, and they approached the tent to the sound of a pipe, and with an old man for spokesman. In this fashion they came into the tent and gave me the food and clothes and skins they had brought, and I gave them some trinkets, and with this they went off.

This river of Our Lady flows through a very wide open plain sowed with corn plants; there are several groves, and there are twelve villages.[6] The houses are of earth, two stories high; the people have a good appearance, more like laborers than a warlike race; they have a large food supply of corn, beans, melons and fowl in great plenty; they clothe themselves with cotton and the skins of cows and dresses of the feathers of the fowls; they wear their hair short. Those who have the most authority among them are the old men; we regarded them as witches, because they say that they go up into the sky and other things of the same sort.[7] In this province there are seven other villages, depopulated & destroyed by those Indians who paint their eyes, of whom the guides will tell Your Grace; they say that these live in the same region as the cows, & that they have corn and houses of straw.[8]

Here the people from the outlying provinces came to make peace with me, and as Your Grace may see in this memorandum, there are 80 villages there of the same sort as I have described, and among them one which is situated on some streams; it is divided into twenty divisions which is something remarkable; the houses have three stories of mud walls and three others made of small wooden boards, and on the outside of the three stories with the mud wall they have three balconies; it seemed to us that there were nearly 15,000 persons in this village.[9] The country is very cold; they do not raise fowls nor cotton; they worship the sun and water. We found mounds of dirt outside of the place, where they are buried.

In the places where crosses were raised, we saw them worship these. They made offerings to these of their powder[10] and feathers, and some left the blankets they had on. They showed so much zeal that some climbed up on the others to grasp the arms of the cross, to place feathers & flowers there; and others bringing ladders, while some held them, went up to tie strings, so as to fasten the flowers and the feathers.

TESTIMONY
CONCERNING THOSE WHO WENT
ON THE EXPEDITION WITH
FRANCISCO VAZQUEZ
DE CORONADO[1]

AT Compostela, on February 21, 1540, Coronado presented a petition to the viceroy Mendoza, declaring that he had observed that certain persons who were not well disposed toward the expedition which was about to start for the newly discovered country had said that many of the inhabitants of the City of Mexico and of the other cities and towns of New Spain, and also of Compostela and other places in this province of New Galicia were going on the expedition at his request or because of inducements offered by him, as a result of which the City of Mexico and New Spain were left deserted, or almost so. Therefore, he asked the viceroy to order that information be obtained, in order that the truth might be known about the citizens of New Spain and of this province who were going to accompany him. He declared that there were very few of these, and that they were not going on account of any attraction or inducement offered by him, but of their own free will, and as there were few of them, there would not be any lack of people in New Spain. And as Gonzalo de Salazar, the factor or royal agent, and Pero Almidez Cherino, the veedor or royal inspector of His Majesty for New Spain, and other citizens of Mexico who knew all the facts and had the necessary information, were present there, Coronado asked His Grace to provide and order that which would best serve His Majesty's interests and the welfare and security of New Spain.

The viceroy instructed the licentiate Maldonado, oidor of the royal audiencia,[2] to procure this information. To facilitate the hearing he provided that the said factor and veedor and the regidores, and others who were there, should attend the review of the army, which was to be held on the following day. Nine of the desired witnesses were also commanded by Maldonado to attend the review & observe those whom they knew in the army.

On February 26³ the licentiate Maldonado took the oaths of the witnesses in proper form, and they testified to the following effect:

Hernand Perez de Bocanegra, a citizen of Mexico, stated that he had been present on the preceding Sunday, at the review of the force which the viceroy was sending for the pacification of the country recently discovered by the father provincial, Fray Marcos de Niza, and that he had taken note of the force as the men passed before him; and at his request he had also been allowed to see the list of names of those who were enrolled in the army; and he declared that in all the said force he did not recognize any other citizens of Mexico who were going except Domingo Martin, a married man, whom he had sometimes seen living in Mexico, & provided him with messengers; and one Alonso Sanchez, who was going with his wife and a son, and who was formerly a shoemaker; and a young man, son of the *bachiller* Alonso Perez, who had come only a few days before from Salamanca, and who had been sent to the war by his father on account of his restlessness; and two or three other workmen or tradespeople whom he had seen at work in Mexico, although he did not know whether they were citizens there; and on his oath he did not see in the whole army anyone else who was a citizen of Mexico, although for about fourteen years he had been a citizen and inhabitant of that city, unless it was the captain-general, Francisco Vazquez de Coronado, & Lopez de Samaniego the army-master; and, moreover, he declared that he felt certain that those above mentioned were going of their own free will, like all the rest.

Antonio Serrano de Cardona, one of the magistrates of Mexico, who was present from beginning to end of the review of the preceding Sunday, testified in similar form. He said that Alonso Sanchez had formerly been a citizen of Mexico, but that for a long time his house had been empty & he had traveled as a trader, and that he was going in search of something to live on; and one Domingo Martin was also going, who formerly lived in Mexico, and whose residence he had not known likewise for a long time, nor did he think that he had one, because he had not seen him living in Mexico. He did not think it would have been possible for any citizens of Mexico to have been there whom he did not know, because he had lived in Mexico during the twenty years since he came to Mexico, and ever since the city was established by Christians, and besides, he had been a magistrate for fifteen years. And besides, all those whom he did see who were going, were the most contented of any men he had ever seen in this country starting off for conquests. After the force left the City of Mexico, he had been there, and had noticed that it was full of people and that there did not seem to be any scarcity on account of those who had started on this expedition.

Gonzalo de Salazar, His Majesty's factor for New Spain, & also a magistrate of the City of Mexico, declared that the only person on the expedition who possessed a repartimiento or estate in New Spain was the captain-general, Vazquez de Coronado, and that he had noticed one other citizen who did not have a repartimiento. He had not seen any other citizen of Mexico, nor of New Spain, although one of the greatest benefits that could have been done New Spain would have been to draw off the young and vicious people who were in that city and all over New Spain.

Pedro Almidez Cherino, His Majesty's veedor in New Spain, had, among other things, noted the horses and arms of those who were going, during the review. He had noticed Coronado and Samaniego, and Alonso Sanchez and his wife, whom he did not know to be a citizen, and Domingo Martin, who was away from Mexico during most of the year. All the rest of the force were people without settled residences, who had recently come to the country in search of a living. It seemed to him that it was a very fortunate thing for Mexico that the people who were going were about to do so because they had been injuring the citizens there. They had been for the most part vicious young gentlemen, who did not have anything to do in the city nor in the country. They were all going of their own free will, and were very ready to help pacify the new country, & it seemed to him that if the said country had not been discovered, almost all of these people would have gone back to Castile, or would have gone to Peru or other places in search of a living.

Servan Bejarano, who had been in business among the inhabitants of Mexico ever since he came to that city, added the information that he knew Alonso Sanchez to be a provision dealer, buying at wholesale and selling at retail, and that he was in very great need, having nothing on which to live, and that he was going to that country in search of a living. He was also very sure that it was a great advantage to Mexico and to its citizens to have many of the unmarried men go away, because they had no occupation there and were bad characters, and were for the most part gentlemen and persons who did not hold any property, nor any repartimientos of Indians, without any income, and lazy, and who would have been obliged to go to Peru or some other region.

Cristobal de Oñate had been in the country about sixteen years, a trifle more or less, and was now His Majesty's veedor for New Galicia. He knew the citizens of Mexico, and also declared that not a citizen of Compostela was going on the expedition. Two citizens of Guadalajara were going, one of whom was married to an Indian, and the other was single. As for the many young gentlemen and the others who were going, who lived in Mexico and in other parts of New Spain, it seemed to him that their departure was a benefit rather than a disadvantage, because they were leading vicious lives and had nothing with which to support themselves.

When these statements and depositions had all been duly received, signed and attested, and had been shown to his most illustrious lordship, the viceroy, he ordered an authorized copy to be taken, which was made by Joan de Leon, clerk of Their Majesties' court and of the royal audiencia of New Spain, the 27th of February, 1540, witnessed by the secretary, Antonio de Almaguer, and sent to His Majesty, to be laid before the lords of the council, that they might provide and order that which should be most serviceable to their interests.

THE END

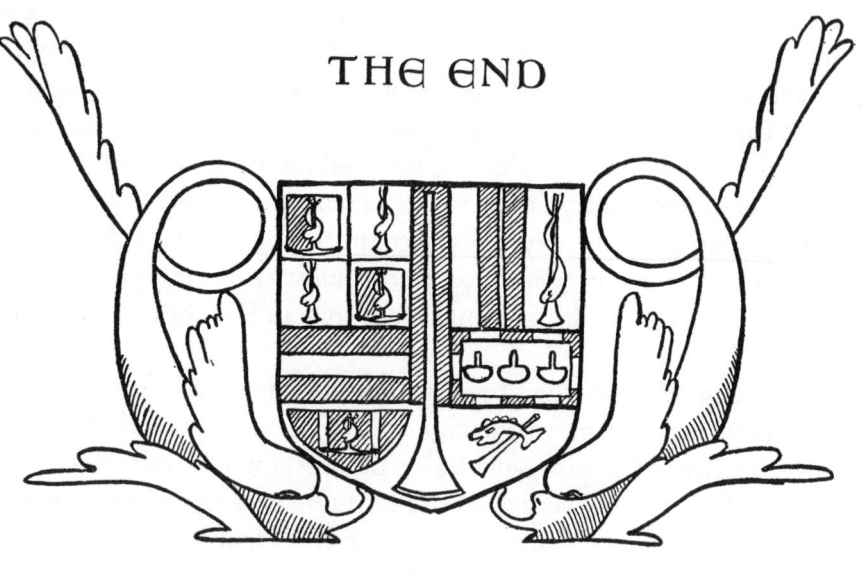

NOTES

The initials following the respective notes signify George Parker Winship (W.) and Frederick Webb Hodge (H.).

Castañeda's Narrative:
Preface

1. Mendoza was named viceroy and governor of New Spain and president of the Audiencia (the administrative and judicial board which governed the province) in 1535. After a rule of fifteen years he was transferred to Peru, dying at Lima, July 21, 1552. See Arthur S. Aiton, "Antonio de Mendoza, First Viceroy of New Spain," Durham, N. C., 1927. (W., H.)

First Part: Chapter i

1. Marqués del Valle de Oaxaca y Capitan General de la Nueva España y de la Costa del Sur. (W.)
2. Guzmán had presided over the trial of Cortés, who was in Spain at the time, for the murder of his first wife in October, 1522. See Zaragoza's edition of Suarez de Peralta's "Tratato," p. 315. (W.)
3. The name was changed in 1540. (W.)
4. For the story of the Seven Caves and the Seven Cities see Bandelier, "Contributions to the History of the Southwestern Portion of the United States," Cambridge, Mass., 1890; Woodbury Lowery, "Spanish Settlements within the Present Limits of the United States, 1513-1561," New York, 1901; William H. Babcock, "Legendary Islands of the Atlantic," New York, 1922. (W., H.)

First Part: Chapter ii

1. A judge appointed to investigate the accounts and administration of a royal official. (W)
2. A full account of the licentiate de la Torre and his administration is given by Matias de la Mota Padilla, "Historia de la Conquista de la Provincia de la Nueva-Galicia, escrita en 1742," Mexico, 1870, pp. 103-106. Torre was appointed *juez,* March 17, 1536, and died during 1538. (W.)
3. They appeared in New Spain in April, 1536, before Coronado's appointment. Castañeda may be right in the rest of the statement. (W.) The narrative of Cabeza de Vaca was first published at Zamora in 1542 under the title, "La Relacion que dio Aluar Nuñez Cabeça de Vaca de lo acaescido (etc.)." and was reprinted at Valladolid in 1555, and at various times elsewhere. An English translation by Buckingham Smith was published at Washington in 1851, reprinted New York 1871, and again reprinted with introduction and notes by F. W. Hodge in *Spanish Explorations in the Southern United States,* New York, 1907. Another translation, by Fanny R. Bandelier, was published in New York in 1905. (H.)

First Part: Chapter iv

1. A. F. Bandelier ("Contributions," *op. cit.,* 104) says this was Topia, in Durango, a locality since noted for its rich mines. (W.)

First Part: Chapter v

1. See Mendoza's letter to the King, page 81, regarding Samaniego's position. (W.)
2. In a statement made by Don Tristán de Luna y Arellano in Mexico, March 7, 1575, he asserted that his grandparents, Don Tristán de Luna y Arellano and his wife Doña Isabel de Roxas, were among the first settlers and conquerors of New Spain and that the grandfather for more than forty years continuously served His Majesty in every way that offered, and with great zeal, especially in the expedition to Cibola, in which he was appointed *maestro de campo* and where he rendered many and important services; as likewise in the expedition to Florida. See C. W. Hackett, ed., "Documents, etc.," *op. cit.,* i, 48-49, Washington, 1923. (H.)
3. A *repartimiento* of Indians was granted to Diego López by *cédula* and *encomienda* by Francisco Vásquez de Coronado, consisting of various towns in the valley of Culiacan. Gonzálo, son of Diego, succeeded to the *encomienda.* See Hackett "Documents, etc.," i. 94-101, Washington, 1923. (H.)
4. In a declaration made evidently in 1549, Alvarado stated that he was a native of *La Montaña,* in the Province of Santander and that he was the legitimate son of Juan Sánchez de Alvarado and Doña Mencia de Salazar. He went to New Spain with Cortés "nineteen years ago [1530] and has spent those years in the service of His Majesty in the first discovery of the South Sea [1536], on the expedition which the said Marqués [Cortés] made, and on the expedition to Cibola. . . . On all these expeditions he served as captain at his own expense with many horses and servants, receiving no salary from His Majesty nor from any other person, and he has not been remunerated; hence he lives in necessity." Hackett, *op cit.,* 39. For Alvarado's report see page 129. (H.)

First Part: Chapter vi

1. The correct date is 1540. Castañeda carries the error throughout the narrative. (W.)
2. See the instructions given by the viceroy Mendoza to Alarcon in Buckingham Smith, "Coleccion de Varios Documentos para la Historia de la Florida," Madrid 1857, pp. 1-6. (W.)
3. The present Patzcuaro. (H.)
4. See Fray Antonio Tello, "Fragmentos de una Historia de la Nueva Galicia," in Icazbalceta's *Mexico,* ii, 343-438, Mexico, 1866; Mota Padilla, *op. cit.;* Beatrice Quijada Cornish, "The Ancestry and Family of Juan de Oñate," in *The Pacific Ocean in History,* edited by H. Morse Stephens and Herbert E. Bolton, New York, 1917, pp. 452-464. (W., H.) Much of the early prosperity of New Galicia— what there was of it—seems to have been due to Oñate's skillful management. (W.)

First Part: Chapter vii

1. The report of Diaz is incorporated in the letter from Mendoza to the King, translated herein. This letter seems to imply that Diaz stayed at Chichilticalli; but if such was his intention when writing the report to Mendoza, he must have changed his mind and returned with Saldívar as far as Chiametla. (W.)

First Part: Chapter ix

1. This was a ruin, evidently more or less similar to the present Casa Grande, in the Gila valley, Graham County, Arizona. The name Chichilticalli signified "red house" in the Aztec language. (H.)
2. This was the Zuñi River. The "Río Vermejo" of Jaramillo's narrative (p. 119) was the Little Colorado. (H.)
3. Mota Padilla (op. cit., p. 113): "They reached Tzibala, which was a village divided into two parts, which were encircled in such a way as to make the village round, and the houses adjoining three and four stories high, with doors opening in a great court or plaza, leaving one or two doors in the wall, so as to go in and out. In the middle of the plaza there is a hatchway or trapdoor, by which they go down to a subterranean hall [a kiva, or ceremonial chamber], the roof of which was of large pine beams, and a little hearth in the floor, and the walls plastered. The Indian men stayed there days and nights playing (or gaming) and the women brought them food; and this was the way the Indians of the neighboring villages lived." For the identification of this first pueblo with the Zuñi village of Hawikuh, see the Introduction. (H.)
4. The war cry or "loud invocation addressed to Saint James before engaging in battle with the infidels."—Captain John Steven's "Dictionary." (W.)
5. Compare the translation of the "Traslado de las Nuevas" herein. There are some striking resemblances between that account and Castañeda's narrative. (W.)
6. The persistent use of the form "Señora" (Madame), for the place "Sonora" may be due to the copyists. (W.)
7. This Indian was probably a Seri of Tiburon Island or the adjacent coast of the Gulf of California. To this day the Seri are noted for their tallness. (H.)
8. This should be September. (W.)

First Part: Chapter x

1. These were the Yuma Indians of the lower reaches of the Rio Colorado. There are other stories of Indians who showed remarkable strength. For example, while on the California coast in 1579, Sir Francis Drake met Indians who were "exceedingly swift of foot, and strong enough to carry what two or three Englishmen could hardly bear." See Henry R. Wagner, "Sir Francis Drake's Voyage Around the World," San Francisco, 1926, p. 146. (W.)
2. Father Sedelmair, in his "Relacion," mentions this custom of the Indians. See A. F. Bandelier, "Final Report," i. p. 108, Cambridge, Mass., 1890. (W.)

3. Cortés. (W.)
4. And yet California often appeared as an island on later maps for a long period. (H.)
5. This was the province, in all likelihood, in which the settlement called Vacapa by Fray Marcos de Niza was situated. See the Introduction. The Zuñi Indians make a similar preserves from the fruit of the tuna cactus and the yucca. (H.)

First Part: Chapter xi

1. Compare Chapter 13. These two groups of pueblos were not the same. Castañeda confused Tutahaco with Tusayan (the Hopi country of Arizona). (W., H.)
2. Compare the lines which the Hopi still mark with sacred corn meal during certain ceremonials, as described by J. Walter Fewkes in Journal of American Ethnology and Archaeology, ii, Boston and New York, 1892. (W.)
3. See "The Expedition into New Mexico made by Antonio de Espejo in 1582-1583 as Revealed in the Journal of Diego Pérez de Luxán," translated by George P. Hammond and Agapito Rey, Quivira Society Publications, Vol. i, Los Angeles, 1929, pp. 95-96. Luxán says "We halted in the province of Moje [Moqui or Hopi], at a pueblo that had been attacked and destroyed by Coronado because they had killed five of the nine men he had sent to discover this province of Mojose while he remained in the province of Sumi [Zuñi]. When Coronado heard the news he fell upon it with his men and devastated and destroyed it. It was and is situated a league from the pueblo of Aguato [Awatobi]." The pueblo referred to as having been destroyed was doubtless Kawaioku, the archaeology of which shows comparatively recent occupancy. (H.)
4. Castañeda was in error. The Hopi were noted throughout the pueblo region for the cotton they cultivated and wove into garments. When Espejo visited them in 1583 the Hopi presented him and his companions with a great number of cotton fabrics. (H.)
5. The river was the Colorado, and the large people were the Yuma. See Chapter X, Note 1.
6. "From rim to rim that portion of the canyon within the park varies from 4 to 18 miles in width; it is more than a mile deep measured from the north rim, which averages nearly a thousand feet higher than the south rim."—"General Information Regarding Grand Canyon National Park, Arizona." National Park Service, Washington, 1933. (H.)
7. So far as known this report no longer exists. (H.)
8. Although both the Tovar-Padilla and the Cárdenas parties passed through the Navaho country, no mention is made that the Navaho or any other Indians resided between the Zuñi pueblos and the Hopi province. Indeed there is no evidence that the Navaho and Apache lived in present Arizona at that time. (H.)

First Part: Chapter xii

1. The pueblo of Pecos on the Rio Pecos. It was the easternmost of the settlements in New Mexico

in historic times and was abandoned, in 1838, to seventeen survivors settling at Jemez where their descendants now live. Important archeological excavations of the Pecos ruins have been conducted over a period of years by Dr. A. V. Kidder in behalf of Phillips Academy, Andover, Mass. (H.)
2. The report of Alvarado, translated herein, is probably the official account of what he accomplished. (W.)
3. This was the pueblo of Ácoma, then, as now, on the summit of a mesa, 357 feet high, eleven miles southeast of McCarthy station on the Atchison, Topeka and Santa Fe railroad. The name comes from *Akóme*, "people of the white rock," the native name of the pueblo being Áko. The Coronado chroniclers, of course, first heard the Zuñi form of the name of the tribe and pueblo, Hákukme ("Ácoma people") and Hakukia, respectively. Alvarado was the first white man to visit the spot. Ácoma suffered severely in 1599 when attacked by Vincente de Zaldívar of Oñate's army of colonists in revenge for the killing of his brother Juan a short time before. The population in 1930 was 1,025, including that of its outlying villages. Ácoma is the oldest continuously occupied settlement in the United States. (H.)
4. An error for Tiguex, a group of Tigua pueblos in the Rio Grande valley about the present Bernalillo. The Tigua now occupy the pueblos of Taos and Picuris in the north, and Sandia and Isleta in the south. (H.)
5. The "Turk," a Pawnee from the present Nebraska, was probably so called from the early custom of the Pawnee of wearing a kind of turban. (H.) Supplementary information regarding this Indian is noted by Mota Padilla, *op. cit.*, cap. xxxii, 5, p. 161, and by Gomara, "Indies," cap. ccxiiii. (W.)

First Part: Chapter xiii

1. This province has always been a historical puzzle. Coronado probably reached the Rio Grande about Isleta, and it is also likely that the pueblos in this vicinity formed the province of Tutahaco, for Castañeda speaks of other pueblos down the Rio Grande, which evidently were the Piro settlements. On the other hand, Tutahaco may have included the Tigua and Piro pueblos east of the Rio Grande, which were inhabited until the seventh decade of the 17th century, when the Apache forced their abandonment. (H.)
2. Needless to say, there was not a word of truth in anything the "Turk" said, except the name for gold, *acochis*, a corruption of *hakwichis*, signifying "metal." None of these Indians knew anything whatsoever about gold. (H.)

First Part: Chapter xiv

1. This was Matsaki, near the northwestern base of Towayalane, or Corn Mountain, a great sandstone mesa, nearly a thousand feet high, about three miles northeast of present Zuñi. Matsaki was the last of the Zuñi villages reached by one traveling eastward from Hawikuh. It was abandoned at the time of the Pueblo Rebellion of 1680. (H.)

2. The route was by way of Matsaki, up the Zuñi River, past the present summer village of Piscado (Heshotatsinakwin) to El Morro or Inscription Rock, where later explorers carved their names, across the pine-clad Zuñi mountains, through Guadalupe or Zuñi Pass to El Gallo, where the town of San Rafael now is and where the first Fort Wingate was established, thence to the site of McCarthy station and Ácoma. (H.)

First Part: Chapter xv

1. It should be borne in mind that the Pueblo Indians had no real chiefs or "governors" at that time, for they were purely theocratic, as Castañeda states in regard to the natives of Cibola (Zuñi). Bigotes (whiskers) and the old man were doubtless priests. (H.)
2. Juan Aleman, a resident of Pueblo de Los Angeles, Mexico (founded 1532), was born in Hozenploce, Germany, legitimate son of Hans Gelique and Margarita Bergrier. After various exploits as a soldier, he went to Florida in search of the men whom Narváez took thither, and later to New Spain. He married the former wife of Francisco de Quevedo who had held in *encomienda* the town of Xilotepec, but which was taken from him by Cortés and given to Juan de Jaramillo, who accompanied Cortés to New Spain. By royal *cédula* the viceroy appointed Aleman to a *corregimiento*. See Hackett, ed., "Documents, etc.," *op. cit.*, i, 32-33. (H.)
3. The instructions which Mendoza gave to Alarcon, printed in Buckingham Smith's "Florida," show how carefully the viceroy tried to guard against any such trouble with the natives. (W.)
4. Evidently the underground, or partly underground, *kivas* or ceremonial chambers. (W.)
5. In the fight at Tiguex by Coronado's men, one Francisco de Santillana, a veterinary and blacksmith, was wounded in the shoulder by an arrow, from which his right arm was permanently maimed. See Hackett, "Documents," *op. cit.*, i, 51-53, Washington, 1923. In 1583 Antonio de Espejo attacked the large Tigua pueblo of Puala in the same vicinity and because the Indians mocked the Spaniards when they asked for food, the latter laid siege to the village, imprisoned captives in a *kiva* where others had taken refuge, and set fire to the pueblo. Sixteen of the captives were taken out two at a time, lined up against some cottonwoods, and killed. This pueblo was the scene of the murder of Fray Augustín Rodríguez and Fray Francisco Lopez in 1581. See Luxán, "Journal of the Espejo Expedition," *Quivira Society Publication*, i, Los Angeles, 1929. (H.)

First Part: Chapter xvi

1. Wooden war clubs, probably shaped like old fashioned potato mashers. (W.)
2. The year was 1541.

First Part: Chapter xvii

1. An error for Alcaraz. (W.)

First Part: Chapter xviii

1. The Keres pueblo of Sia, or Tsïa, on the Rio Jemez 16 miles northwest of Bernalillo, the present population is 177.
2. This was the Queres, or Keres, group of pueblos which, in addition to Sia, now consists of Santo Domingo, San Felipe, Cochiti, and Santa Ana. Ácoma and Laguna form the western group of the stock, but the latter village was not established until 1699. (H.)
3. These have been identified as the Pawnee and the Kansa, or Kansas, tribes respectively. (H.)
4. Or Cervantes. (W.)
5. Coronado says in his letter of October 20 that he started April 23. (W.)

First Part: Chapter xix

1. This was the Rio Pecos, on which the Pueblo of Pecos, or Cicuye, was situated. (W.)
2. The Querechos were the Apache of the plains who transported their belongings by means of the *travois*. All references to "cows" of course mean the bison. The army was now on the Staked Plains of the present northwestern Texas. (H.)
3. This Indian was a Wichita of the Province of Quivira. The tattooing (*pintado*, or tattooed, in the Spanish text) referred to is characteristic of the Wichita, whose tribal name is *Ki'dï ḳi desh*, signifying "Raccoon Eyes," on account of the former practice of tattooing circles about the eyes, covering both lids. The French called the Wichita "Pani Piques" by reason of the custom. (H.)
4. The reference is clearly to the district of Colima in western Mexico, where one of the earliest Spanish settlements was made. (W.)

First Part: Chapter xx

1. *A manera de alixares.* The margin reads *Alexeres.* The word means threshing floor. (W.)
2. "Among the tribes of eastern Texas the word *texas (texias, thecas?, techan, teysas, techas?*, etc., pronounced, there is reason to suspect, as indicated by the last spelling) had wide currency before the coming of the Spaniards. Its usual meaning there was 'friends,' or, more technically, 'allies,' and it was used, by the Hasinai at least (to whom the word later became fastened as a name), to designate a large group of tribes, both Caddoan and others...." H. E. Bolton in "Handbook of American Indians," pt. 2, p. 738, Washington, 1910. (H.)
3. Capt. John Stevens's "New Dictionary" says the *sanbenito* was "the badge put upon converted Jews brought out by the Inquisition, being in the nature of a scapula or broad piece of cloth hanging before and behind, with a large Saint Andrew's cross on it, red and yellow. The name corrupted from Saco Benito, answerable to the sackcloth worn by penitents in the primitive church." (W.)
4. The Tiguex country is often referred to as the region where the settlements were. (W.)

First Part: Chapter xxi

1. These, of course, were prairie dogs. (H.)
2. The Mississippi is referred to. (H.)

First Part: Chapter xxii

1. Castañeda's date, is, as usual, a year later than the actual one. (W.)
2. The present Jemez pueblos, on the Jemez River. There were at least seven pueblos of Jemez before the Pueblo Rebellion of 1680-92. (H.)
3. This was the Tewa pueblo of Yunggĕoⁿwïnggĕ on the site of the hamlet of Chamita at the confluence of the Chama and the Rio Grande, opposite San Juan pueblo, New Mexico. Don Juan de Oñate moved his capital from San Juan (de los Caballeros) to the site of "Yuqueyunque," naming the new place San Gabriel, or San Gabriel de los Españoles, before December, 1600. The second village, on the opposite side of the river, was apparently San Juan. (H.)
4. Braba, probably referring to a kind of net or snare, was applied by the Spaniards, for some unknown reason, to the Tigua pueblo of Taos, which then, as now, consisted of two villages, commonly known as North Town and South Town, separated by the Rio de Taos. The population in 1930 was 694. The name Valladolid was probably given because of a fancied resemblance of Taos to the city of that name in Spain. (H.)
5. This rendering, doubtless correct, is due to Ternaux-Compans. The Guadiana, however, reappears above ground some time before it begins to mark the boundary of the Spanish province of Estremadura. The Castañeda family had its seat in quite the other end of the peninsula. (W.) This reference affords some information respecting the identification of Tutahaco with the Tigua pueblos about the present Isleta, for the only pueblos on the Rio Grande south of that group of settlements were those of the Piro, above the Jornada del Muerto, where "the river sank into the earth." (H.)

Second Part

1. Spelled in the original Naxara, for Nájera. (W.)
2. The Newfoundland region. (W.) The name *Bacallaos* signifies codfish. (H.)

Second Part: Chapter i

1. See Chapter I, page 5.
2. The Tahus (Tahue), as well as the Pacaxees (Pacasa) and the Acaxee, later mentioned, were languages formerly spoken in Sinaloa. (H.)
3. The snake cult entered into the religious practices of many Indian tribes. In the United States it still survives in the so-called Snake Dance of the Hopi Indians of Arizona. (H.)
4. For information on these "men-women" among the Zuñi, see Elsie Clews Parsons, "The Zuñi Hlámana," *American Anthropologist,* vol. 18, no. 4, pp. 521-528, Lancaster, Pa., Oct.-Dec. 1916. (H.)
5. The Rio Colorado. (H.)
6. The reference is to the Indians of Lower California.

Second Part: Chapter ii

1. The tribes occupying the valleys of the streams of this region, which flow into the Gulf of California, belong to the Piman linguistic stock, mem-

bers of which extended as far north as southern Arizona, where Pima and Papago still reside. The dwellings of these people were made of mats, as Castañeda says—"petates" as they are commonly called, from Aztec *petatl*. Winship quotes Bandelier ("Final Report," i, p. 58, Cambridge, 1890) as saying that he found the Opata Indians of the valley of the Rio Sonora living in houses made with "a slight foundation of cobble-stones which supported a framework of posts standing on a thin wall of rough stones and mud, while a slanting roof of yucca or palm leaves covered the whole." (H.)

2. The *Opuntia tuna* or prickly pear. (W.)

3. *Prosopis juliflora*. (W.) The word mesquite, from Aztec *mesquitl*, is often mispronounced mĕs'-kĕt, even by the dictionaries. (H.)

4. *Cereus thurberii*. (W.)

5. The Rio Petlatlan, or Petatlan, was the present Rio Sinaloa; Castañeda's Sinoloa is the Fuerte of today. If mentioned in their order, going northward, the Boyomo and Teocomo respectively were the Rio Mayo and the Rio Cocoraqui; the Yaquimí is readily identified with the Yaqui, and the Señora with the Sonora. (H.)

6. The inhabitants of the valley of the Rio Sonora were the Opata, now largely Mexicanized. (H.)

7. The valley of Cuya was really the upper part of the Sonora valley, not a valley drained by another stream. The town of San Hieronimo, at or near the present Ures, was established at Los Corazones, where Cabeza de Vaca and his companions were given the hearts of deer. (H.)

8. The beans of the mesquite were ground into meal and made into a nutritious bread. (H.)

9. These were doubtless cantaloupes. The Southwestern Indians still slice and dry them in a manner similar to that here described. (W.) Pumpkins and squashes are similarly treated. (H.)

10. The Pueblo Indians, particularly the Zuñi and Hopi, keep eagles for their feathers, which are highly prized because of their reputed sacred character. (W.)

Second Part: Chapter iii

1. This structure, evidently similar to the present Casa Grande, was situated in the Gila valley, probably in the vicinity of Old Camp Goodwin. (H.)

2. The animals were evidently the mountain lion and the wildcat, respectively. (W.) The *barbels* and *picones* may have been Gila trout and catfish. (H.)

3. The origin of "Cibola" (in the form *cibolo* later applied to the bison), is not known, although attempts have been made to correlate it with *Shiwina*, the name by which the Zuñi call themselves. The name was first employed by Fray Marcos de Niza, who heard of its use by an Indian of Sonora during his journey northward in 1539, but it seems to have suffered from misunderstanding or corruption. That the term applies to the Zuñi pueblos of the period there is no question whatsoever. (H.)

4. This was Matsaki, the ruins of which lie near the northwestern base of Towayalane, or Corn Mountain, about three miles from the present Zuñi. (H.)

5. Cotton was extensively cultivated, especially by the Hopi Indians, who traded it in the form of woven garments to other Pueblo tribes. Clothing ornamented with feathers has been preserved in cliff dwellings in the Southwest. Robes made of twisted strips of rabbit-skin were made by the sedentary Indians of the Southwest, and of California until very recent times. (H.)

6. It was the custom of Hopi maidens to wear their hair in a whorl at each side of the head until the time of marriage, but the practice recently fell into disuse when Government schools compelled children to cut the hair short. It will be noted that, according to Castañeda, the same custom was in vogue among the Zuñi. (H.)

7. The character of the Zuñi valley, bounded by great sandstone mesas, is well described, as also is the Zuñi method of cultivating corn, which still persists. See F. H. Cushing, "Zuñi Breadstuff," New York, 1920. (H.)

8. Turquoise was obtained by the Zuñi through trade with pueblos of the Rio Grande, who mined it at Los Cerrillos, near Santa Fé. (H.)

9. The term *pápa* in Zuñi signifies "elder brother" and may apply either to relationship or to ceremonial rank. (H.)

10. This reference still applies in the main to the custom of the Sun Priest, or *pékwin*, of Zuñi, who prays to the rising sun. (H.)

11. In his "Few Summer Ceremonials at Tusayan," p. 6, Dr. Fewkes says that "with the exception of their own dances, women do not take part in the secret kibva [estufa] ceremonials; but it can not be said that they are debarred as assistants in making the paraphernalia of the dances, or when they are called upon to represent dramatizations of traditions in which women figure." (W.)

12. Excavations at Hawikuh, one of the Zuñi pueblos of the time of Coronado, who named it Granada, reveal that both cremation and interment were practised by the Zuñi in the 16th century. (H.)

13. The pueblos of the Hopi in the present Arizona. (H.)

14. This would make a total population for the Zuñi and Hopi pueblos of about 10,500 to 14,000, whereas the two peoples probably did not number more than half that estimate. (H.)

Second Part: Chapter iv

1. As before stated, Tiguex was the province of the Tigua group of pueblos (exclusive of the related villages of Taos and Picuris), now represented by Sandia and Isleta. The river, of course, is the Rio Grande; the mountains to the eastward are the Sandias. (H.)

2. Quirix is synonymous with Queres or Keres (see p. 36). Hemes, *i. e.,* Jemez, is only twenty miles northwest (not northeast) of the former Tiguex, but in 1540 there were Jemez pueblos about 35 miles northwest, not 40 leagues (106 miles). (H.)

3. Acha is Picuris pueblo, which was and is about 80 miles northeast of Tiguex province in an airline. (H.)

4. See page 20.

5. That is, the Pueblo Indians were governed by bodies of priests; there were no chiefs as in many other tribes, and the present civil officials were unknown before 1591. (H.)

6. Adobes were not molded in wooden forms by the Pueblos until taught to do so by the Spaniards; indeed the houses were usually built of stones laid in adobe mortar such as Castañeda describes. The "thyme" referred to was sagebrush. (H.)

7. The kivas with the large wooden pillars were seen at Taos, as previously described. Castañeda's general description would have applied almost perfectly to a kiva uncovered by excavation at Hawikuh, which is very likely the typical one he had in mind. (H.)

8. This is not true of Zuñi today. There is no such volunteer crop of corn as the author describes. In the years of productiveness the crop is usually sufficient to last for two seasons' food supply. (H.)

9. The American turkey cock. (W.)

10. A custom still general at Zuñi until a few years ago, when, at the instance of missionaries, Indian Bureau officials compelled its abandonment, after which time the entire village became a public latrine. Urine was formerly used as a mordant in dyeing. (H.)

11. For food and its preparation by the Zuñi, see F. H. Cushing, "Zuñi Breadstuff," New York, 1920. (H.)

12. For Pueblo pottery and its manufacture, see Carl E. Guthe, "Pueblo Pottery Making," New Haven, 1925; Ruth Bunzel, "The Pueblo Potter," New York, 1929.

Second Part: Chapter v

1. For the recent literature of Pecos (Cicuye), see A. V. Kidder, "An Introduction to the Study of Southwestern Archaeology with a Preliminary Account of the Excavation at Pecos," New Haven, 1924; *Ibid.,* "The Pottery of Pecos," vol. I, New Haven, 1931; *Ibid.,* "The Artifacts of Pecos," New Haven, 1932; E. A. Hooton, "The Indians of Pecos Pueblo," New Haven, 1930. (The above works are Haven, 1931; *Ibid.,* "The Artifacts of Pecos," New the product of the Department of Archaeology, Phillips Academy, Andover, Mass.) For earlier references consult F. W. Hodge, *ed.,* "Handbook of American Indians," pt. 2, Washington, 1910, and authorities therein cited. (H.)

2. In "A Visit to the Aboriginal Ruins in the Valley of the Rio Pecos" (*Archaeological Institute Papers,* i, pt. 2, Boston, 1881). Bandelier stated that the spring was "still trickling out beneath a massive ledge of rocks on the west sill" in 1880. (W.)

3. The former Tano pueblo of Galisteo about 22 miles south of Santa Fé. In the Pueblo Revolt of 1680 its inhabitants killed the resident priest and removed to Santa Fé, after the Spaniards had been driven from the country. In 1692 they were expelled by Vargas; in 1706 their pueblo was reëstablished, but it remained an inconsiderable village until between 1782 and 1794, when it was abandoned. (H.)

4. This pueblo, apparently occupied by Tano, was

called Coquite by Mota Padilla, "Historia de la Conquista de la Nueva-Galicia," 1742, p. 164, repr. 1870. (W.)

5. A warlike tribe of the Texas plains previously mentioned. They were not the Comanche, who did not make their appearance in New Mexico until about 1700. (H.)

6. The term *Chichimecas* was applied to any warlike predatory Indians of Mexico. (H.)

Second Part: Chapter vi

1. Bandelier ("Final Report," pt. 1, p. 34, Boston, 1890) says: "with the exception of Ácoma, there is not a single pueblo standing where it was at the time of Coronado, or even sixty years later, when Juan de Oñate accomplished the peaceable reduction of the New Mexican village Indians." (W.)

2. The Spaniards had become so obsessed with the idea that there were *seven* pueblos of Cibola, from the ancient myth of the Seven Islands on which seven bishops built seven cities, that when they reached the Zuñi country the number seven had become firmly fixed in their minds. In fact there were only six pueblos — Hawikuh, Kechipauan, Halona, Kwakina, Kaikima, and Matsaki. The ruins of these are all well known. (H.)

3. These groups of pueblos, with few exceptions, have already been noted. "Aguas Calientes" no doubt refers to those Jemez pueblos situated in the San Diego cañon of Jemez valley about 14 miles above the present Jemez. (H.)

4. Castañeda is not consistent here in his total nor always in the number of villages comprising the various groups of settlements previously noted. (H.)

5. The trend of the river in the section of the old pueblo settlements is really westward. (W.)

6. The Spaniards. (W.)

7. See the "Carta escrita por Santisteban á Mendoza," which tells nearly everything that is known of the voyage of Villalobos. We can only surmise what Castañeda may have known about it. (W.)

8. Compare page 26 and 112.

Second Part: Chapter vii

1. More than once Castañeda seems to be addressing those about him where he is writing in Culiacan. (W.)

2. The well known *travois* of the Plains Indians. (W.)

3. Pemmican. (W.)

Second Part: Chapter viii

1. The ravines to which Castañeda alludes were certainly in northwestern Texas, among the "breaks" of the western part of the Staked Plain. Quivira therefore was situated north of the ravines, not west of it, as the description of the journey to Quivira will indicate. (H.) And Mr. Savage in *The Transaction of the Nebraska Historical Society,* vol. i., p. 198, shows how closely the descriptions of Castañeda, Jaramillo, and the others of the expedition, harmonize with the flora and fauna of his State. (W.)

2. One of the evidences that Quivira was the terri-

tory occupied by the Wichita Indians of the Arkansas River valley in Kansas is the typical grass houses (not the roofs alone) of those people. For illustrations see E. S. Curtis, "The North American Indian," vol. xix, Norwood, Mass., 1930; Paul A. Jones, "Quivira," Wichita, Kans., 1929. (H.)
3. The Mississippi and Missouri rivers. (W.)
4. Arache, or Harahey, is derived from *Awáhi*, the Wichita name for the Skidi Pawnee. See Hodge (after Murie) in *American Anthropologist*, 17: 216, Lancaster, Pa., 1915. (H.)
5. This is probably a reminiscence of Cabeza de Vaca's narrative. (W.)
6. Mota Padilla (*op. cit.,* cap. xxxiii, 4, p. 166) gives the reasons for the failure of the expedition: "It was most likely the chastisement of God that riches were not found on this expedition, because, when this should have been the secondary object of the expedition, and the conversion of all those heathen their first aim, they bartered with fate and struggled after the secondary; and thus the misfortune is not so much that all those labors were without fruit, but the worst is that such a number of souls have remained in their blindness." (W.)

Third Part: Chapter iii

1. As we have seen, San Hieronimo, or Corazones, had been established at or near the site of the present Ures on the Rio Sonora, but was later moved some miles upstream. Suya, the new settlement, was in another stretch of the Sonora valley, probably about the present Bacuachi. This was the territory of the Teguima Opata, a generally peaceful people, who however were now compelled to contend with the slave-hunting brute Diego de Alcaraz, fit companion of the notorious Nuño de Guzmán, to whom both Cabeza de Vaca and Castañedo pay their respects. For the arrow poison, compare Jaramillo's statement and see also Rudo Ensayo (1762); Guiteras translation, p. 161, Phila., 1894, which says: "Mago, in the Opata language, is a small tree, very green, luxuriant, and beautiful to the eye; but it contains a deadly juice which flows upon making a slight incision in the bark. The natives rub their arrows with it, and for this reason they call it arrow grass; but at present they use very little." On the route, see F. W. Hodge, "Coronado's March to Quivira," in J. V. Brower, "Harakey," *Memoirs of Explorations in the Basin of the Mississippi,* ii, p. 37, St. Paul, 1899; Carl Sauer, "The Road to Cibola," *Ibero-Americana,* 3, Berkeley, 1932. For Alcaraz, see "Relation that Alvar Nuñez Cabeca de Vaca Gave, etc.," printed from the Buckingham Smith translation of 1871 by The Grabhorn Press, San Francisco, 1929. (H.)

Third Part: Chapter iv

1. The correct date is, of course, 1542. (W.)
2. A Franciscan. He was a "frayle de misa." (W.) For further information see A. F. Bandelier, "Fray Juan de Padilla, the First Catholic Missionary Martyr in Eastern Kansas," *American Catholic Quarterly Review,* xv, no. 59, pp. 551-565, Phila., 1890. (H.)
3. Gen. W. W. H. Davis, in his "Spanish Conquest

of New Mexico," p. 231, gives the following extract, translated from an old Spanish MS. at Santa Fé: "When Coronado returned to Mexico, he left behind him, among the Indians of Cibola, the father fray Francisco Juan de Padilla, the father fray Juan de la Cruz, and a Portuguese named Andrés del Campo. Soon after the Spaniards departed, Padilla and the Portuguese set off in search of the country of the Grand Quivira, where the former understood there were innumerable souls to be saved. After travelling several days, they reached a large settlement in the Quivira country. The Indians came out to receive them in battle array, when the friar, knowing their intentions, told the Portuguese and his attendants to take to flight, while he would await their coming, in order that they might vent their fury on him as they ran. The former took to flight, and, placing themselves on a height within view, saw what happened to the friar. Padilla awaited their coming upon his knees, and when they arrived where he was they immediately put him to death. The same happened to Juan de la Cruz, who was left behind at Cibola [Cicuye] which people killed him. The Portuguese and his attendants made their escape, and ultimately arrived safely in Mexico, where he told what had occurred." In reply to a request for further information regarding this manuscript, General Davis stated that when he revisited Santa Fé, a few years ago, he learned that one of his successors in the post of governor of the territory, having despaired of disposing of the immense mass of old documents and records deposited in his office, by the slow process of using them to kindle fires, had sold the entire lot—an invaluable collection of material bearing on the history of the Southwest and its early European and native inhabitants—as junk. [This was an exaggeration on the part of General Davis—(H.).] (W.) When Antonio de Espejo visited Zuñi in 1583, he found crosses erected near the pueblos; "and here we found three Christian Indians, who said their names were Andrés of Cuyuacan [Coyoacán], Gaspar of Mexico, and Anton of Guadalajara, and stated that they had come with said governor Francisco Vasquez [de Coronado]. We instructed them again in the Mexican tongue, which they had almost forgotten." (Espejo's narrative in H. E. Bolton, "Spanish Exploration in the Southwest," 1542-1706, p. 184, New York, 1930.) Espejo's statement is confirmed by Diego Pérez de Luxán, a member of the party, who wrote: "We found very well built †† in all these pueblos, because Coronado had been in this land. ... Here we found Mexican Indians and also some from Guadalajara, of those that Coronado had brought.... Here we found a book and a small old trunk left by Coronado." ("Luxán's Journal," in *Quivira Society Publications,* i, 89-90, Los Angeles, 1929.) Descendants of these Indians were found among the Zuñi by Juan de Oñate in 1598. (H.)

Third Part: Chapter v

1. There were two Opata settlements of this name, the one here evidently referred to being on the Rio Moctezuma, about 22 miles east of Ures, site of the

first Corazones. It became the seat of the Jesuit Mission of Santa María in 1620. If this is the Batuco mentioned by Castañeda, it would seem that instead of retracing his journey down the Rio Sonora, he followed the Rio Moctezuma evidently on account of the hostility of the Opata at Suya (Corazones) in the Sonora valley. (H.)

Third Part: Chapter vii

1. The letters of Mendoza during the early part of his administration in Mexico repeatedly call attention to the lack of arms and ammunition among the Spaniards in the New World. (W.)

Third Part: Chapter viii

1. The region referred to was evidently northwestern Texas. (H.)
2. The kersey or coarse woolen cloth out of which the habits of the Franciscan friars were made; hence the name grey friars. (W.)
3. The earliest description of the American buffalo by a European is in Cabeza de Vaca's Narrative, *op. cit.* (W.)
4. These were prayer offerings, the form of which, of course, had nothing to do with Christian belief or symbolism. (H.)

Third Part: Chapter ix

1. The northeastern province of New Spain. (W.)
2. The Mississippi. The conception of the great inland plain stretching between the great lakes at the head of the St. Lawrence and the Gulf of Mexico came to cosmographers very slowly. Almost all of the early maps show a disposition to carry the mountains which follow the Atlantic Coast along the Gulf Coast as far as Texas, a result, doubtless, of the fact that all the expeditions which started inland from Florida found mountains. Coronado's journey to Quivira added but little to the geographical knowledge of America. The name reached Europe, and it is found on the maps, along the fortieth parallel, almost everywhere from the Pacific Coast to the neighborhood of a western tributary to the St. Lawrence system. Castañeda could have aided them considerably, but the map makers did not know of his book. (W.)
3. Zacatecas was founded as a result of the discovery of mines thereabouts in 1548 by Cristobal de Oñate, Diego de Ibarra, Baltasar Treviño de Bañuelos; and Juan de Tolosa, who became the wealthiest men in America at that time. See Beatrice Quijada Cornish in Bolton and Marshall, "Pacific Ocean in History," pp. 457-458, New York, 1917; Gaspár Pérez de Villagra, "Historia de la Nueva Mexico," 1610, Quivira Society repr., Los Angeles, 1933, p. 75. (H.)
4. All subsequent expeditions to New Mexico in the 16th century went by way of the Conchos and Rio Grande—Rodríguez-Chamuscado, 1581; Espejo, 1582-83; Castaño de Sosa, 1590; Oñate, 1598. (H.)
5. Also Guachichile (the usual form) and Cuachichiles. A tribe, or group, which according to Orozco y Berra ("Geografía de las Lenguas," p. 285, Mex-

ico, 1864) occupied an immense area, embracing parts of the present states of Zacatecas, San Luis Potosí, Nueva León, and Coahuila. The missions established among them by the Franciscans were San Luis, Saltillo, Vanado, Charcas, Valle de Atotonilco, Pinos, Asunción Tlaxcalilla, and San Miguel Mezquitic. See Thomas and Swanton, "Indian Languages of Mexico and Central America," Washington, 1911. (H.)
6. Apparently the location of this island gradually drifted westward [like Antilia and Brazil] with the increase of geographical knowledge, until it was finally located in the Philippine group. (W.)

Letter from Mendoza to the King.

1. From the Spanish text in Pacheco y Cárdenas, "Documentos de Indias," ii, p. 256. The letter mentioned in the opening sentence is not known to exist. (W.)
2. Presumably the fortress of which Samaniego was warden. (W.)
3. Buckingham Smith's "Florida" gives many documents relating to the damage done by French brigantines to the Spanish West Indies during 1540-41. (W.)
4. That is, the doorless lower rooms were used for storage. Excavations at the Zuñi (Cibola) pueblo of Hawikuh revealed such loop-holes in the walls of many rooms. (H.)
5. The Indian informants of Melchior Diaz gave truthful information regarding the Zuñi weapons. The war clubs were shaped like old-fashioned wooden potato-mashers. The "other weapons made of sticks" were probably a kind of lances which were used in hand-to-hand encounters. The Zuñi were not consumers of human flesh. The fowls alluded to were turkey, of which the Pueblo Indians had many flocks. (H.)
6. It is not known what animals the Indians attempted to describe here. The native tribes had dogs, and the skins of rabbits served in making robes. It is evident that Melchior Diaz misunderstood his informants. (H.)
7. The typical headdress of Zuñi warriors was a skull cap, perforated for ventilation and having a tuft of feathers at the top. The only other headgear was a woven band worn around the head to confine the hair and a narrow woven band to tie the hair-knot at the back of the head. (H.)
8. These doubtless were quartz crystals, which are still employed by Zuñi medicine-men in their incantations. (H.)
9. The celebrated Zuñi Salt Lake, 42 miles south by east of Zuñi pueblo, the source of supply of the Zuñi and other Indians for centuries. See Villagrá, "Historia de la Nueva Mexico," 1610, pp. 168, 170, repr. 1933, and references therein. (H.)
10. For Zuñi ceremonies see M. C. Stevenson, "The Zuñi Indians," *23d Report Bureau of American Ethnology,* 1904. (H.)
11. Peaches, watermelons, cantaloupes, grapes, and apples were introduced about the middle of the 17th century by Franciscan missionaries. Before that time they depended on the fruit of cactus and yucca, wild berries and nuts, and the like. (H.)
12. There is some contradiction among the early

Spanish chroniclers as to whether the Zuñi Indians cultivated cotton, but be that as it may, there is no doubt that the Hopi were the great cotton farmers, as well as weavers, among the Pueblos, and that they continued to supply fabrics of native cotton until very recent times. When Espejo visited the Hopi villages in 1583, his party was given "six hundred widths of blankets small and large, white and painted." See Luxán, "Journal," in *Quivira Society Publications,* p. 98, 1929. (H.)

13. Probably the pueblo of Marata mentioned by Fray Marcos de Niza, who was informed during his journey northward that it had been destroyed by the people of Cibola some years before. (W., H.)

Letter of Coronado to Mendoza

1. Translated from the Italian version in Ramusio's "Viaggi," vol. iii, fol. 359 (ed. 1556). There is another English translation in "Hakluyt's Voyages," iii, p. 373 (ed. 1600). Hakluyt's translation is printed in *Old South Leaflet,* general series, No. 20. The proper names, excepting such as are properly translated, as spelled as in the Italian text. (W.)
2. This statement is probably not correct. It may be due to a blunder by Ramusio in translating from the original text. Eighty days would be nearly the time which Coronado probably spent on the journey from Culiacan to Cibola and this interpretation would render the rest of the sentence much more intelligible. (W.)
3. The valley into which Friar Marcos did not dare to enter. (W.) Compare what Castañeda says of Melchior Diaz's journey, Part I, chapter vii.
4. Doubtless the Yaquimi or Yaqui River. (W.)
5. See previous notes on these and other localities. (W.)
6. These were doubtless the Seri who occupied, and still occupy, a strip of the Gulf Coast between latitude 28° and 29° and the Island of Tiburon. The Seri had a reputation for ferocity, but in recent years they have become greatly modified by civilization. See W. J. McGee, "The Seri Indians," *17th Ann. Rep. Bur. Amer. Ethnology,* 1st, p. 1, Washington, 1898; A. L. Kroeber, "The Seri," *Southwest Museum Papers,* no. 6, Los Angeles, 1931. (W., H.)
7. As Indian news goes, there is no reason why this may not have been one of Ulloa's ships, which sailed along this coast during the previous summer. It can hardly have been a ship of Alarcon's fleet. (W.)
8. The coast of Sonora of course trends northwestward throughout its length. The latitude of Chichilticale (or Chichilticalli) would have been about 33°. The early Spaniards were usually about two degrees wrong in their calculations of latitude. (H.)
9. Probably the Colorado Chiquito. (H.)
10. It is possible that this is a blunder, in Ramusio's text, for "His Majesty." The Marquis, in New Spain, is always Cortés, for whom neither Mendoza nor Coronado had any special regard. (W.)
11. This was the Zuñi pueblo of Hawikuh, 12 miles southwest of the present Zuñi, New Mexico. (H.)
12. Don García López de Cárdenas. (H.)

13. The kivas or ceremonial chambers. Compare Castañeda, Part II, chapter iv. (H.)
14. There were only six Zuñi pueblos in Coronado's time. See note 2, chapter vi, Second Part, Castañeda's Narrative. The subject is discussed by F. W. Hodge, "The Six Cities of Cibola," *New Mexico Historical Review,* Santa Fé, Oct. 1926. (H.)
15. Many garnets are found on the ant-hills throughout the region, especially in the Navaho country. (W.)
16. While turkeys were kept for their feathers, from the numbers of turkey-bones found in the excavations of the refuse-heaps of Hawikuh, they must have been used also for food. In one of these refuse-heaps was the burial of a turkey with a food bowl near by.
17. It should be noted that Coronado clearly distinguishes between hills or mesas and mountains. Zuñi valley is hemmed in by heights ranging from 500 to 1000 feet. (W.)
18. This accords perfectly with the condition of the vegetation in the Zuñi valley at the present time. (W.) The pasturage referred to was in the Ojo Caliente valley, only two or three miles from Hawikuh, where Coronado was writing. Grass is still abundant there. (H.)
19. Doubtless a slip of Ramusio's pen for cows, *i.e.,* buffalos. (W.)
20. Coronado doubtless misinterpreted what the natives intended to communicate. The "hot lake" was in all probability the salt lake above alluded to. Totonteac was Tusayan, "Tucano," the Hopi pueblos. (W.) In all probability Marata was the result of misunderstanding on the part of Fray Marcos. Attempts to identify it with ruins in the Zuñi country have met with only questionable success. Acus; from the report of Fray Marcos, is, as Coronado states, identified with Acucu, from the Zuñi name of Ácoma, *i.e.,* Hákukia. (H.)
21. Compare Castañeda, Part II, chap. iii.
22. It is true that many of the Pueblo Indian ceremonies are designed to bring rain. (H.)
23. The earrings and the combs were made of wood inlaid with small squares of turquoise. See F. W. Hodge, "Turquoise Work of Hawikuh," *Leaflets of the Museum of the American Indian,* no. 2, New York, 1921. (H.)
24. The identical custom is followed by Zuñi women today. (H.)
25. The "hammers" were short war-clubs of the form of old-fashioned wooden potato-mashers. Bone arrowpoints were found in the excavation of Hawikuh. (H.)
26. The conquerors, in the literature of New Spain, are almost always those who shared with Cortés in the labors and the glory of the Spanish Conquest of Mexico. (W.)
27. References to the "painting" of garments in all probability are intended to mean embroidery. (H.)

Translado de las Nuevas

1. Translated from Pacheco y Cárdenas, *Documentos de Indias,* xix, p. 529. This document is anonymous but it is evidently a copy of a letter from

some trusted companion, written from Granada (Hawikuh), about the time of Coronado's letter of August 3, 1540. In the title to the document as printed, the date is given as 1531, but there can be no doubt that it is an account of Coronado's journey. (W.) It may be suggested that the author of the report was no other than Don García López de Cárdenas, for the reason that no mention is made of the gallant behavior of the army-master in aiding in the rescue of the wounded Coronado in the attack on Hawikuh, whereas the incident is especially noted by Castañeda, by Coronado himself, and by the author of the *Relación del Suceso.* Cárdenas returned to New Spain, on receiving news of the death of his brother, before Coronado left New Mexico with his army. (H.)

2. A part of Granada near the Alhambra. There is a curious similarity in the names Albaicin and Hawikuh, the latter being the Zuñi name of Coronado's Granada. (W.)

3. Uttering the war-cry of Santiago. (W.)

4. The printed manuscript is V. M., which signifies Your Majesty. (W.)

5. The rock was Tawayalene, or Corn Mountain, the refuge of the Zuñi in times of trouble, as during the Pueblo Revolt of 1680-92. (H.)

6. From a manuscript in possession of the family of the late Sr. D. Joaquin García Icazbalceta, of the City of Mexico. This appears to be a transcript from letters written, probably from Tiguex, on the Rio Grande, during the late summer or early fall of 1541. (W.)

7. The houses of Cibola were of stone, but plastered inside and out with adobe mortar, giving them the appearance of being built of "dirt and mud." (H.)

8. The maguey does not grow in the Zuñi country. The yucca is meant. (H.)

9. The pueblo of Pecos. (H.)

10. This is probably the most comprehensive account of the dependence of the Plains Indians on the buffalo ever recorded. The Indians here especially alluded to were the Querechos, or Apache, of the Texas plains. (H.)

11. An excellent description of the method of employing the *travois* by the Plains Indians. (H.)

Relación del Suceso

1. The Spanish text of this document is printed in Buckingham Smith's "Florida," p. 147, from a copy made by Muñoz, and also in Pacheco y Cárdenas, *Documentos de Indias,* xiv, p. 318, from a copy found in the Archives of the Indies at Seville. No date is given in the document, but there can be no doubt that it refers to Coronado's expedition. In the heading of the document in the Pacheco y Cárdenas *Colección,* the date is given as 1531, and it is placed under that year in the chronologic index of the *Colección.* (W.)

2. An error for yucca. (H.)

3. The prayer-sticks which the Zuñi still plant at springs and in fields and shrines. The "yellow powder" was in all probability pollen. (H.)

4. The latitude is overestimated by two degrees as usual. (H.)

5. The Tusayan of other chroniclers, the Hopi country of today. (H.)

6. See note 7.

7. See Coronado's letter of August 3, 1540. (W.)

8. The Ácoma people call their pueblo Áko, while the name for themselves is Akómě, "people of the white rock." The Zuñi name of Ácoma, as previously stated, is Hákukia; of the Ácoma people, Hákukwe. Hakus was applied by Fray Marcos de Niza to Hawikuh, not Ácoma. (H.)

9. The Rio Grande—the Rio Tiguex of other chroniclers. (W.)

10. This was the pueblo of Taos, the native name of which is Tuatá, the Picuris name being Tuopá. (H.)

11. The population here given is many times exaggerated. (H.)

12. Identical with Castañeda's Cicuye, or Cicuyc. (W.)

13. Taos is only about eight miles east of the Rio Grande in an air line. (H.)

14. Compare Castañeda's account of the siege of Tiguex. (H.)

15. That is Harahey, identified with the Pawnee of Nebraska. (H.)

16. Southeast in Buckingham Smith's Muñoz copy. (W.)

17. The river was the Arkansas in central Kansas. The Quivira Indians were the Wichita. (H.)

18. Tareque (Tuxeque, in the Muñoz copy—W) has not been identified, but from the statement that its houses were made of straw, it would seem to have been a Wichita settlement. Arae is evidently synonymous with Harahey, the Pawnee "province." The typical dwelling of the Pawnee, however, was the earth lodge, but they used skin tipis when hunting. (H.)

19. Or mines, as Muñoz guesses. (W.) If the Pawnee possessed copper, as is quite probable, it was obtained by trade, no doubt, from the Indians of the Lake Superior region, though not directly. (H.)

20. It is evident that, on his return journey from Quivira to the Rio Grande, Coronado followed a trade route which approximated the later Santa Fé Trail. (H.)

21. Traveling northward from the Texas plains the Spaniards doubtless reached the Arkansas River in the vicinity of Ford, Ford County, Kansas, in lat. 37° 40', whence they continued northeastward, downstream, to Greatbend, Barton County, in lat. 38° 20'. "The river" here referred to was evidently the Rio Grande in the vicinity of Tiguex in lat. 35° 20'. (H.)

22. For the *travois* see note 2, Chapter VII, Second Part.

23. "And jerked beef dried in the sun," in the Muñoz copy only. (W.)

Letter from Coronado to the King

1. The text of this letter is printed in Pacheco y Cárdenas, *Documentos de Indias,* iii, p. 363, from a copy made by Muñoz, and also in the same collection, xiii, p. 261, from a copy in the Archives of the Indies at Seville. (W.)

2. See note 8 to Letter of Coronado to Mendoza.

3. Coronado had apparently forgotten the atrocities committed by the Spaniards at Tiguex. (W.)

Jaramillo's Narrative

1. The text of this narrative is found in Buckingham Smith's "Florida," p. 154, from a copy made by Muñoz, and in Pacheco y Cárdenas, *Documentos de Indias,* xiv, p. 304, from a copy in the Archives of the Indies at Seville. (W.)
2. Petatlan River of the other narratives—the present Rio Sinaloa. (H.)
3. The Rio Fuerte. (H.)
4. The Rio Mayo. (H.)
5. The Rio Yaqui. (H.)
6. For Corazones and other features of the journey, see the previous notes. (H.)
7. See Bandelier's "Gilded Man," p. 175. This is Castañeda's "Guagarispa" as mistakenly interpreted by Ternaux-Compans, the present Arispe, or, in the Indian dialect, Huc-aritz-pa. The words "Ispa, que" are not in the Pacheco y Cárdenas copy. (W.)
8. The Rio San Pedro. (H.)
9. That is, the agave and the fruit of the saguaro cactus. (H.)
10. The deep and reedy river was no doubt the Gila in southern Arizona. (H.)
11. Apparently the Gila Bonito. (H.)
12. Identifiable with the Salado or Salt River. (H.)
13. The Spaniards seem to have here crossed an upper branch of the Colorado Chiquito. (H.)
14. Evidently the Colorado Chiquito proper. (H.)
15. The Rio Zuñi. (H.)
16. Jaramillo is the only chronicler of the expedition who gives the true number of the Cibola villages. (H.)
17. Doubtless the reference is to the alkali soil and vegetation. (W.)
18. This is quite true of the mesas bordering the Zuñi valley, the trees being piñon and juniper.
19. This observation alone places beyond all question that Cibola and Zuñi were identical. A few miles east of Zuñi the spring known as Ojo Pescado gives source to the Zuñi River, beyond which point is the Continental Divide. (W.)
20. This pueblo was Matsaki. (H.)
21. Jaramillo confused the name of Áko, or Ácoma, with the name Tutahaco, mentioned by Castañeda as that of another group of pueblos to the eastward. (H.)
22. These pueblos respectively were Sia, Taos, and Pecos. Uraba is the Yuraba of the Relación del Suceso and the Braba of Castañeda. (W.)
23. Tiguex is here doubtless referred to. (W.)
24. One of the villages whose names Jaramillo did not know was probably the Ximena (Galisteo) of Castañeda. (W.) The others were probably the pueblos known as San Cristóbal and San Marcos in later times. (H.)
25. The Rio Pecos, of course. Jaramillo errs when he says that "it seems to me that we went rather toward the northeast to reach this river where we crossed it"—an obvious slip for southeast; in other words, the army followed the Pecos downstream for four days before crossing it as Castañeda relates. (H.)

26. The blind Indian may have been an Juniano who had seen Cabeza de Vaca and his companions when they crossed the Rio Conchos in Chihuahua on their journey westward. (H.)
27. For the river and the place where the Spaniards reached it, see note 21, page 112. (H.)
28. The Turk was a Pawnee, Isopete a Wichita of Quivira. (H.)
29. In Buckingham Smith's copy occurs the phrase, *"que decian ellos para significarnoslo Teucarea."* This is not in Pacheco y Cárdenas. (W.)
30. The pueblos of the Rio Grande. (W.)
31. See note 21, page 112.
32. For Capotlan? (H.)
33. This is the spelling of Panuco in both texts. (W.)

Report of Hernando de Alvarado

1. The text of this report is printed in Buckingham Smith's "Florida," p. 65, from the Muñoz copy and in Pacheco y Cárdenas, *Documentos de Indias,* iii, p. 511. (W.)
2. Ácuco or Ácoma. The route taken by Alvarado from Granada (Hawikuh) was not the same as that followed by Coronado, who went by way of Matsaki. Alvarado's course was the old Ácoma trail which led directly eastward from Hawikuh by way of the Ojo Caliente cañon. (W.)
3. The pueblo of Sia. (H.)
4. This was the "lake or marsh" from which the popular name of the present pueblo of Laguna, established in 1699, was derived. (H.)
5. Day of the Nativity·of the Blessed Virgin, September 8. This was the Rio Tiguex of the other chroniclers, the present Rio Grande. (H.)
6. The groves, no doubt, were of cottonwoods. The twelve villages were those of Tiguex, or the Tigua. (H.)
7. Compare what Castañeda says of the government of Cibola, or the Zuñi villages. Evidently Jaramillo misunderstood the old native priests in regard to their claim of the power of levitation. (H.)
8. The reference is obviously to the Quivira (Wichita) Indians; but the marauders were not the Wichita, but the warlike Teya of Texas. (H.)
9. The pueblo referred to was Taos. (H.)
10. Sacred corn-meal. (H.)

Testimony of Coronado's Companions

1. Translated freely and abridged from the depositions as printed in Pacheco y Cárdenas, *Documentos de Indias,* xiv, p. 373. The statements of the preceding witnesses are usually repeated, in effect, in the testimony of those who follow. (W.)
2. Judge of the highest court of the province. (W.)
3. Thursday. (W.)

A CATALOG OF SELECTED
DOVER BOOKS
IN ALL FIELDS OF INTEREST

A CATALOG OF SELECTED DOVER BOOKS IN ALL FIELDS OF INTEREST

DRAWINGS OF REMBRANDT, edited by Seymour Slive. Updated Lippmann, Hofstede de Groot edition, with definitive scholarly apparatus. All portraits, biblical sketches, landscapes, nudes. Oriental figures, classical studies, together with selection of work by followers. 550 illustrations. Total of 630pp. 9⅛ × 12¼.
21485-0, 21486-9 Pa., Two-vol. set $25.00

GHOST AND HORROR STORIES OF AMBROSE BIERCE, Ambrose Bierce. 24 tales vividly imagined, strangely prophetic, and decades ahead of their time in technical skill: "The Damned Thing," "An Inhabitant of Carcosa," "The Eyes of the Panther," "Moxon's Master," and 20 more. 199pp. 5⅜ × 8½. 20767-6 Pa. $3.95

ETHICAL WRITINGS OF MAIMONIDES, Maimonides. Most significant ethical works of great medieval sage, newly translated for utmost precision, readability. Laws Concerning Character Traits, Eight Chapters, more. 192pp. 5⅜ × 8½.
24522-5 Pa. $4.50

THE EXPLORATION OF THE COLORADO RIVER AND ITS CANYONS, J. W. Powell. Full text of Powell's 1,000-mile expedition down the fabled Colorado in 1869. Superb account of terrain, geology, vegetation, Indians, famine, mutiny, treacherous rapids, mighty canyons, during exploration of last unknown part of continental U.S. 400pp. 5⅜ × 8½. 20094-9 Pa. $6.95

HISTORY OF PHILOSOPHY, Julián Marías. Clearest one-volume history on the market. Every major philosopher and dozens of others, to Existentialism and later. 505pp. 5⅜ × 8½. 21739-6 Pa. $8.50

ALL ABOUT LIGHTNING, Martin A. Uman. Highly readable non-technical survey of nature and causes of lightning, thunderstorms, ball lightning, St. Elmo's Fire, much more. Illustrated. 192pp. 5⅜ × 8½. 25237-X Pa. $5.95

SAILING ALONE AROUND THE WORLD, Captain Joshua Slocum. First man to sail around the world, alone, in small boat. One of great feats of seamanship told in delightful manner. 67 illustrations. 294pp. 5⅜ × 8½. 20326-3 Pa. $4.95

LETTERS AND NOTES ON THE MANNERS, CUSTOMS AND CONDITIONS OF THE NORTH AMERICAN INDIANS, George Catlin. Classic account of life among Plains Indians: ceremonies, hunt, warfare, etc. 312 plates. 572pp. of text. 6⅛ × 9¼. 22118-0, 22119-9 Pa. Two-vol. set $15.90

ALASKA: The Harriman Expedition, 1899, John Burroughs, John Muir, et al. Informative, engrossing accounts of two-month, 9,000-mile expedition. Native peoples, wildlife, forests, geography, salmon industry, glaciers, more. Profusely illustrated. 240 black-and-white line drawings. 124 black-and-white photographs. 3 maps. Index. 576pp. 5⅜ × 8½. 25109-8 Pa. $11.95

THE BOOK OF BEASTS: Being a Translation from a Latin Bestiary of the Twelfth Century, T. H. White. Wonderful catalog real and fanciful beasts: manticore, griffin, phoenix, amphivius, jaculus, many more. White's witty erudite commentary on scientific, historical aspects. Fascinating glimpse of medieval mind. Illustrated. 296pp. 5⅜ × 8¼. (Available in U.S. only)   24609-4 Pa. $5.95

FRANK LLOYD WRIGHT: ARCHITECTURE AND NATURE With 160 Illustrations, Donald Hoffmann. Profusely illustrated study of influence of nature—especially prairie—on Wright's designs for Fallingwater, Robie House, Guggenheim Museum, other masterpieces. 96pp. 9¼ × 10¾.   25098-9 Pa. $7.95

FRANK LLOYD WRIGHT'S FALLINGWATER, Donald Hoffmann. Wright's famous waterfall house: planning and construction of organic idea. History of site, owners, Wright's personal involvement. Photographs of various stages of building. Preface by Edgar Kaufmann, Jr. 100 illustrations. 112pp. 9¼ × 10.
23671-4 Pa. $7.95

YEARS WITH FRANK LLOYD WRIGHT: Apprentice to Genius, Edgar Tafel. Insightful memoir by a former apprentice presents a revealing portrait of Wright the man, the inspired teacher, the greatest American architect. 372 black-and-white illustrations. Preface. Index. vi + 228pp. 8¼ × 11.   24801-1 Pa. $9.95

THE STORY OF KING ARTHUR AND HIS KNIGHTS, Howard Pyle. Enchanting version of King Arthur fable has delighted generations with imaginative narratives of exciting adventures and unforgettable illustrations by the author. 41 illustrations. xviii + 313pp. 6⅛ × 9¼.   21445-1 Pa. $5.95

THE GODS OF THE EGYPTIANS, E. A. Wallis Budge. Thorough coverage of numerous gods of ancient Egypt by foremost Egyptologist. Information on evolution of cults, rites and gods; the cult of Osiris; the Book of the Dead and its rites; the sacred animals and birds; Heaven and Hell; and more. 956pp. 6⅛ × 9¼.
22055-9, 22056-7 Pa., Two-vol. set $21.90

A THEOLOGICO-POLITICAL TREATISE, Benedict Spinoza. Also contains unfinished *Political Treatise*. Great classic on religious liberty, theory of government on common consent. R. Elwes translation. Total of 421pp. 5⅜ × 8½.
20249-6 Pa. $6.95

INCIDENTS OF TRAVEL IN CENTRAL AMERICA, CHIAPAS, AND YUCATAN, John L. Stephens. Almost single-handed discovery of Maya culture; exploration of ruined cities, monuments, temples; customs of Indians. 115 drawings. 892pp. 5⅜ × 8½.   22404-X, 22405-8 Pa., Two-vol. set $15.90

LOS CAPRICHOS, Francisco Goya. 80 plates of wild, grotesque monsters and caricatures. Prado manuscript included. 183pp. 6⅜ × 9⅜.   22384-1 Pa. $4.95

AUTOBIOGRAPHY: The Story of My Experiments with Truth, Mohandas K. Gandhi. Not hagiography, but Gandhi in his own words. Boyhood, legal studies, purification, the growth of the Satyagraha (nonviolent protest) movement. Critical, inspiring work of the man who freed India. 480pp. 5⅜ × 8½. (Available in U.S. only)
24593-4 Pa. $6.95

ILLUSTRATED DICTIONARY OF HISTORIC ARCHITECTURE, edited by Cyril M. Harris. Extraordinary compendium of clear, concise definitions for over 5,000 important architectural terms complemented by over 2,000 line drawings. Covers full spectrum of architecture from ancient ruins to 20th-century Modernism. Preface. 592pp. 7½ × 9⅝. 24444-X Pa. $14.95

THE NIGHT BEFORE CHRISTMAS, Clement Moore. Full text, and woodcuts from original 1848 book. Also critical, historical material. 19 illustrations. 40pp. 4⅝ × 6. 22797-9 Pa. $2.50

THE LESSON OF JAPANESE ARCHITECTURE: 165 Photographs, Jiro Harada. Memorable gallery of 165 photographs taken in the 1930's of exquisite Japanese homes of the well-to-do and historic buildings. 13 line diagrams. 192pp. 8⅝ × 11¼. 24778-3 Pa. $8.95

THE AUTOBIOGRAPHY OF CHARLES DARWIN AND SELECTED LETTERS, edited by Francis Darwin. The fascinating life of eccentric genius composed of an intimate memoir by Darwin (intended for his children); commentary by his son, Francis; hundreds of fragments from notebooks, journals, papers; and letters to and from Lyell, Hooker, Huxley, Wallace and Henslow. xi + 365pp. 5⅜ × 8. 20479-0 Pa. $5.95

WONDERS OF THE SKY: Observing Rainbows, Comets, Eclipses, the Stars and Other Phenomena, Fred Schaaf. Charming, easy-to-read poetic guide to all manner of celestial events visible to the naked eye. Mock suns, glories, Belt of Venus, more. Illustrated. 299pp. 5¼ × 8¼. 24402-4 Pa. $7.95

BURNHAM'S CELESTIAL HANDBOOK, Robert Burnham, Jr. Thorough guide to the stars beyond our solar system. Exhaustive treatment. Alphabetical by constellation: Andromeda to Cetus in Vol. 1; Chamaeleon to Orion in Vol. 2; and Pavo to Vulpecula in Vol. 3. Hundreds of illustrations. Index in Vol. 3. 2,000pp. 6⅛ × 9¼. 23567-X, 23568-8, 23673-0 Pa., Three-vol. set $37.85

STAR NAMES: Their Lore and Meaning, Richard Hinckley Allen. Fascinating history of names various cultures have given to constellations and literary and folkloristic uses that have been made of stars. Indexes to subjects. Arabic and Greek names. Biblical references. Bibliography. 563pp. 5⅜ × 8½. 21079-0 Pa. $7.95

THIRTY YEARS THAT SHOOK PHYSICS: The Story of Quantum Theory, George Gamow. Lucid, accessible introduction to influential theory of energy and matter. Careful explanations of Dirac's anti-particles, Bohr's model of the atom, much more. 12 plates. Numerous drawings. 240pp. 5⅜ × 8½. 24895-X Pa. $4.95

CHINESE DOMESTIC FURNITURE IN PHOTOGRAPHS AND MEASURED DRAWINGS, Gustav Ecke. A rare volume, now affordably priced for antique collectors, furniture buffs and art historians. Detailed review of styles ranging from early Shang to late Ming. Unabridged republication. 161 black-and-white drawings, photos. Total of 224pp. 8⅜ × 11¼. (Available in U.S. only) 25171-3 Pa. $12.95

VINCENT VAN GOGH: A Biography, Julius Meier-Graefe. Dynamic, penetrating study of artist's life, relationship with brother, Theo, painting techniques, travels, more. Readable, engrossing. 160pp. 5⅜ × 8½. (Available in U.S. only) 25253-1 Pa. $3.95

HOW TO WRITE, Gertrude Stein. Gertrude Stein claimed anyone could understand her unconventional writing—here are clues to help. Fascinating improvisations, language experiments, explanations illuminate Stein's craft and the art of writing. Total of 414pp. 4⅜ × 6⅜. 23144-5 Pa. $5.95

ADVENTURES AT SEA IN THE GREAT AGE OF SAIL: Five Firsthand Narratives, edited by Elliot Snow. Rare true accounts of exploration, whaling, shipwreck, fierce natives, trade, shipboard life, more. 33 illustrations. Introduction. 353pp. 5⅜ × 8½. 25177-2 Pa. $7.95

THE HERBAL OR GENERAL HISTORY OF PLANTS, John Gerard. Classic descriptions of about 2,850 plants—with over 2,700 illustrations—includes Latin and English names, physical descriptions, varieties, time and place of growth, more. 2,706 illustrations. xlv + 1,678pp. 8½ × 12¼. 23147-X Cloth. $75.00

DOROTHY AND THE WIZARD IN OZ, L. Frank Baum. Dorothy and the Wizard visit the center of the Earth, where people are vegetables, glass houses grow and Oz characters reappear. Classic sequel to *Wizard of Oz*. 256pp. 5⅜ × 8. 24714-7 Pa. $4.95

SONGS OF EXPERIENCE: Facsimile Reproduction with 26 Plates in Full Color, William Blake. This facsimile of Blake's original "Illuminated Book" reproduces 26 full-color plates from a rare 1826 edition. Includes "The Tyger," "London," "Holy Thursday," and other immortal poems. 26 color plates. Printed text of poems. 48pp. 5¼ × 7. 24636-1 Pa. $3.50

SONGS OF INNOCENCE, William Blake. The first and most popular of Blake's famous "Illuminated Books," in a facsimile edition reproducing all 31 brightly colored plates. Additional printed text of each poem. 64pp. 5¼ × 7. 22764-2 Pa. $3.50

PRECIOUS STONES, Max Bauer. Classic, thorough study of diamonds, rubies, emeralds, garnets, etc.: physical character, occurrence, properties, use, similar topics. 20 plates, 8 in color. 94 figures. 659pp. 6⅛ × 9¼. 21910-0, 21911-9 Pa., Two-vol. set $15.90

ENCYCLOPEDIA OF VICTORIAN NEEDLEWORK, S. F. A. Caulfeild and Blanche Saward. Full, precise descriptions of stitches, techniques for dozens of needlecrafts—most exhaustive reference of its kind. Over 800 figures. Total of 679pp. 8⅛ × 11. Two volumes. Vol. 1 22800-2 Pa. $11.95
Vol. 2 22801-0 Pa. $11.95

THE MARVELOUS LAND OF OZ, L. Frank Baum. Second Oz book, the Scarecrow and Tin Woodman are back with hero named Tip, Oz magic. 136 illustrations. 287pp. 5⅜ × 8½. 20692-0 Pa. $5.95

WILD FOWL DECOYS, Joel Barber. Basic book on the subject, by foremost authority and collector. Reveals history of decoy making and rigging, place in American culture, different kinds of decoys, how to make them, and how to use them. 140 plates. 156pp. 7⅞ × 10¾. 20011-6 Pa. $8.95

HISTORY OF LACE, Mrs. Bury Palliser. Definitive, profusely illustrated chronicle of lace from earliest times to late 19th century. Laces of Italy, Greece, England, France, Belgium, etc. Landmark of needlework scholarship. 266 illustrations. 672pp. 6⅛ × 9¼. 24742-2 Pa. $14.95

ILLUSTRATED GUIDE TO SHAKER FURNITURE, Robert Meader. All furniture and appurtenances, with much on unknown local styles. 235 photos. 146pp. 9 × 12. 22819-3 Pa. $7.95

WHALE SHIPS AND WHALING: A Pictorial Survey, George Francis Dow. Over 200 vintage engravings, drawings, photographs of barks, brigs, cutters, other vessels. Also harpoons, lances, whaling guns, many other artifacts. Comprehensive text by foremost authority. 207 black-and-white illustrations. 288pp. 6 × 9. 24808-9 Pa. $8.95

THE BERTRAMS, Anthony Trollope. Powerful portrayal of blind self-will and thwarted ambition includes one of Trollope's most heartrending love stories. 497pp. 5⅜ × 8½. 25119-5 Pa. $8.95

ADVENTURES WITH A HAND LENS, Richard Headstrom. Clearly written guide to observing and studying flowers and grasses, fish scales, moth and insect wings, egg cases, buds, feathers, seeds, leaf scars, moss, molds, ferns, common crystals, etc.—all with an ordinary, inexpensive magnifying glass. 209 exact line drawings aid in your discoveries. 220pp. 5⅜ × 8½. 23330-8 Pa. $4.50

RODIN ON ART AND ARTISTS, Auguste Rodin. Great sculptor's candid, wide-ranging comments on meaning of art; great artists; relation of sculpture to poetry, painting, music; philosophy of life, more. 76 superb black-and-white illustrations of Rodin's sculpture, drawings and prints. 119pp. 8⅜ × 11¼. 24487-3 Pa. $6.95

FIFTY CLASSIC FRENCH FILMS, 1912–1982: A Pictorial Record, Anthony Slide. Memorable stills from Grand Illusion, Beauty and the Beast, Hiroshima, Mon Amour, many more. Credits, plot synopses, reviews, etc. 160pp. 8¼ × 11. 25256-6 Pa. $11.95

THE PRINCIPLES OF PSYCHOLOGY, William James. Famous long course complete, unabridged. Stream of thought, time perception, memory, experimental methods; great work decades ahead of its time. 94 figures. 1,391pp. 5⅜ × 8½. 20381-6, 20382-4 Pa., Two-vol. set $19.90

BODIES IN A BOOKSHOP, R. T. Campbell. Challenging mystery of blackmail and murder with ingenious plot and superbly drawn characters. In the best tradition of British suspense fiction. 192pp. 5⅜ × 8½. 24720-1 Pa. $3.95

CALLAS: PORTRAIT OF A PRIMA DONNA, George Jellinek. Renowned commentator on the musical scene chronicles incredible career and life of the most controversial, fascinating, influential operatic personality of our time. 64 black-and-white photographs. 416pp. 5⅜ × 8¼. 25047-4 Pa. $7.95

GEOMETRY, RELATIVITY AND THE FOURTH DIMENSION, Rudolph Rucker. Exposition of fourth dimension, concepts of relativity as Flatland characters continue adventures. Popular, easily followed yet accurate, profound. 141 illustrations. 133pp. 5⅜ × 8½. 23400-2 Pa. $3.50

HOUSEHOLD STORIES BY THE BROTHERS GRIMM, with pictures by Walter Crane. 53 classic stories—Rumpelstiltskin, Rapunzel, Hansel and Gretel, the Fisherman and his Wife, Snow White, Tom Thumb, Sleeping Beauty, Cinderella, and so much more—lavishly illustrated with original 19th century drawings. 114 illustrations. x + 269pp. 5⅜ × 8½. 21080-4 Pa. $4.50

SUNDIALS, Albert Waugh. Far and away the best, most thorough coverage of ideas, mathematics concerned, types, construction, adjusting anywhere. Over 100 illustrations. 230pp. 5⅜ × 8½. 22947-5 Pa. $4.50

PICTURE HISTORY OF THE NORMANDIE: With 190 Illustrations, Frank O. Braynard. Full story of legendary French ocean liner: Art Deco interiors, design innovations, furnishings, celebrities, maiden voyage, tragic fire, much more. Extensive text. 144pp. 8⅜ × 11¾. 25257-4 Pa. $9.95

THE FIRST AMERICAN COOKBOOK: A Facsimile of "American Cookery," 1796, Amelia Simmons. Facsimile of the first American-written cookbook published in the United States contains authentic recipes for colonial favorites—pumpkin pudding, winter squash pudding, spruce beer, Indian slapjacks, and more. Introductory Essay and Glossary of colonial cooking terms. 80pp. 5⅜ × 8½. 24710-4 Pa. $3.50

101 PUZZLES IN THOUGHT AND LOGIC, C. R. Wylie, Jr. Solve murders and robberies, find out which fishermen are liars, how a blind man could possibly identify a color—purely by your own reasoning! 107pp. 5⅜ × 8½. 20367-0 Pa. $2.50

THE BOOK OF WORLD-FAMOUS MUSIC—CLASSICAL, POPULAR AND FOLK, James J. Fuld. Revised and enlarged republication of landmark work in musico-bibliography. Full information about nearly 1,000 songs and compositions including first lines of music and lyrics. New supplement. Index. 800pp. 5⅜ × 8¼. 24857-7 Pa. $14.95

ANTHROPOLOGY AND MODERN LIFE, Franz Boas. Great anthropologist's classic treatise on race and culture. Introduction by Ruth Bunzel. Only inexpensive paperback edition. 255pp. 5⅜ × 8½. 25245-0 Pa. $5.95

THE TALE OF PETER RABBIT, Beatrix Potter. The inimitable Peter's terrifying adventure in Mr. McGregor's garden, with all 27 wonderful, full-color Potter illustrations. 55pp. 4¼ × 5½. (Available in U.S. only) 22827-4 Pa. $1.75

THREE PROPHETIC SCIENCE FICTION NOVELS, H. G. Wells. *When the Sleeper Wakes, A Story of the Days to Come* and *The Time Machine* (full version). 335pp. 5⅜ × 8½. (Available in U.S. only) 20605-X Pa. $5.95

APICIUS COOKERY AND DINING IN IMPERIAL ROME, edited and translated by Joseph Dommers Vehling. Oldest known cookbook in existence offers readers a clear picture of what foods Romans ate, how they prepared them, etc. 49 illustrations. 301pp. 6⅛ × 9¼. 23563-7 Pa. $6.50

SHAKESPEARE LEXICON AND QUOTATION DICTIONARY, Alexander Schmidt. Full definitions, locations, shades of meaning of every word in plays and poems. More than 50,000 exact quotations. 1,485pp. 6½ × 9¼. 22726-X, 22727-8 Pa., Two-vol. set $27.90

THE WORLD'S GREAT SPEECHES, edited by Lewis Copeland and Lawrence W. Lamm. Vast collection of 278 speeches from Greeks to 1970. Powerful and effective models; unique look at history. 842pp. 5⅜ × 8½. 20468-5 Pa. $11.95

THE BLUE FAIRY BOOK, Andrew Lang. The first, most famous collection, with many familiar tales: Little Red Riding Hood, Aladdin and the Wonderful Lamp, Puss in Boots, Sleeping Beauty, Hansel and Gretel, Rumpelstiltskin; 37 in all. 138 illustrations. 390pp. 5⅜ × 8½. 21437-0 Pa. $5.95

THE STORY OF THE CHAMPIONS OF THE ROUND TABLE, Howard Pyle. Sir Launcelot, Sir Tristram and Sir Percival in spirited adventures of love and triumph retold in Pyle's inimitable style. 50 drawings, 31 full-page. xviii + 329pp. 6½ × 9¼. 21883-X Pa. $6.95

AUDUBON AND HIS JOURNALS, Maria Audubon. Unmatched two-volume portrait of the great artist, naturalist and author contains his journals, an excellent biography by his granddaughter, expert annotations by the noted ornithologist, Dr. Elliott Coues, and 37 superb illustrations. Total of 1,200pp. 5⅜ × 8.
Vol. I 25143-8 Pa. $8.95
Vol. II 25144-6 Pa. $8.95

GREAT DINOSAUR HUNTERS AND THEIR DISCOVERIES, Edwin H. Colbert. Fascinating, lavishly illustrated chronicle of dinosaur research, 1820's to 1960. Achievements of Cope, Marsh, Brown, Buckland, Mantell, Huxley, many others. 384pp. 5¼ × 8¼. 24701-5 Pa. $6.95

THE TASTEMAKERS, Russell Lynes. Informal, illustrated social history of American taste 1850's-1950's. First popularized categories Highbrow, Lowbrow, Middlebrow. 129 illustrations. New (1979) afterword. 384pp. 6 × 9.
23993-4 Pa. $6.95

DOUBLE CROSS PURPOSES, Ronald A. Knox. A treasure hunt in the Scottish Highlands, an old map, unidentified corpse, surprise discoveries keep reader guessing in this cleverly intricate tale of financial skullduggery. 2 black-and-white maps. 320pp. 5⅜ × 8½. (Available in U.S. only) 25032-6 Pa. $5.95

AUTHENTIC VICTORIAN DECORATION AND ORNAMENTATION IN FULL COLOR: 46 Plates from "Studies in Design," Christopher Dresser. Superb full-color lithographs reproduced from rare original portfolio of a major Victorian designer. 48pp. 9¼ × 12¼. 25083-0 Pa. $7.95

PRIMITIVE ART, Franz Boas. Remains the best text ever prepared on subject, thoroughly discussing Indian, African, Asian, Australian, and, especially, Northern American primitive art. Over 950 illustrations show ceramics, masks, totem poles, weapons, textiles, paintings, much more. 376pp. 5⅜ × 8. 20025-6 Pa. $6.95

SIDELIGHTS ON RELATIVITY, Albert Einstein. Unabridged republication of two lectures delivered by the great physicist in 1920-21. *Ether and Relativity* and *Geometry and Experience*. Elegant ideas in non-mathematical form, accessible to intelligent layman. vi + 56pp. 5⅜ × 8½. 24511-X Pa. $2.95

THE WIT AND HUMOR OF OSCAR WILDE, edited by Alvin Redman. More than 1,000 ripostes, paradoxes, wisecracks: Work is the curse of the drinking classes, I can resist everything except temptation, etc. 258pp. 5⅜ × 8½. 20602-5 Pa. $4.50

ADVENTURES WITH A MICROSCOPE, Richard Headstrom. 59 adventures with clothing fibers, protozoa, ferns and lichens, roots and leaves, much more. 142 illustrations. 232pp. 5⅜ × 8½. 23471-1 Pa. $3.95

CATALOG OF DOVER BOOKS

PLANTS OF THE BIBLE, Harold N. Moldenke and Alma L. Moldenke. Standard reference to all 230 plants mentioned in Scriptures. Latin name, biblical reference, uses, modern identity, much more. Unsurpassed encyclopedic resource for scholars, botanists, nature lovers, students of Bible. Bibliography. Indexes. 123 black-and-white illustrations. 384pp. 6 × 9. 25069-5 Pa. $8.95

FAMOUS AMERICAN WOMEN: A Biographical Dictionary from Colonial Times to the Present, Robert McHenry, ed. From Pocahontas to Rosa Parks, 1,035 distinguished American women documented in separate biographical entries. Accurate, up-to-date data, numerous categories, spans 400 years. Indices. 493pp. 6½ × 9¼. 24523-3 Pa. $9.95

THE FABULOUS INTERIORS OF THE GREAT OCEAN LINERS IN HISTORIC PHOTOGRAPHS, William H. Miller, Jr. Some 200 superb photographs capture exquisite interiors of world's great "floating palaces"—1890's to 1980's: *Titanic, Ile de France, Queen Elizabeth, United States, Europa,* more. Approx. 200 black-and-white photographs. Captions. Text. Introduction. 160pp. 8⅞ × 11¾. 24756-2 Pa. $9.95

THE GREAT LUXURY LINERS, 1927–1954: A Photographic Record, William H. Miller, Jr. Nostalgic tribute to heyday of ocean liners. 186 photos of Ile de France, Normandie, Leviathan, Queen Elizabeth, United States, many others. Interior and exterior views. Introduction. Captions. 160pp. 9 × 12. 24056-8 Pa. $9.95

A NATURAL HISTORY OF THE DUCKS, John Charles Phillips. Great landmark of ornithology offers complete detailed coverage of nearly 200 species and subspecies of ducks: gadwall, sheldrake, merganser, pintail, many more. 74 full-color plates, 102 black-and-white. Bibliography. Total of 1,920pp. 8⅝ × 11¼. 25141-1, 25142-X Cloth. Two-vol. set $100.00

THE SEAWEED HANDBOOK: An Illustrated Guide to Seaweeds from North Carolina to Canada, Thomas F. Lee. Concise reference covers 78 species. Scientific and common names, habitat, distribution, more. Finding keys for easy identification. 224pp. 5⅜ × 8½. 25215-9 Pa. $5.95

THE TEN BOOKS OF ARCHITECTURE: The 1755 Leoni Edition, Leon Battista Alberti. Rare classic helped introduce the glories of ancient architecture to the Renaissance. 68 black-and-white plates. 336pp. 8⅜ × 11¼. 25239-6 Pa. $14.95

MISS MACKENZIE, Anthony Trollope. Minor masterpieces by Victorian master unmasks many truths about life in 19th-century England. First inexpensive edition in years. 392pp. 5⅜ × 8½. 25201-9 Pa. $7.95

THE RIME OF THE ANCIENT MARINER, Gustave Doré, Samuel Taylor Coleridge. Dramatic engravings considered by many to be his greatest work. The terrifying space of the open sea, the storms and whirlpools of an unknown ocean, the ice of Antarctica, more—all rendered in a powerful, chilling manner. Full text. 38 plates. 77pp. 9¼ × 12. 22305-1 Pa. $4.95

THE EXPEDITIONS OF ZEBULON MONTGOMERY PIKE, Zebulon Montgomery Pike. Fascinating first-hand accounts (1805–6) of exploration of Mississippi River, Indian wars, capture by Spanish dragoons, much more. 1,088pp. 5⅜ × 8½. 25254-X, 25255-8 Pa. Two-vol. set $23.90

CATALOG OF DOVER BOOKS

A CONCISE HISTORY OF PHOTOGRAPHY: Third Revised Edition, Helmut Gernsheim. Best one-volume history—camera obscura, photochemistry, daguerreotypes, evolution of cameras, film, more. Also artistic aspects—landscape, portraits, fine art, etc. 281 black-and-white photographs. 26 in color. 176pp. 8⅜ × 11¼.   25128-4 Pa. $12.95

THE DORÉ BIBLE ILLUSTRATIONS, Gustave Doré. 241 detailed plates from the Bible: the Creation scenes, Adam and Eve, Flood, Babylon, battle sequences, life of Jesus, etc. Each plate is accompanied by the verses from the King James version of the Bible. 241pp. 9 × 12.   23004-X Pa. $8.95

HUGGER-MUGGER IN THE LOUVRE, Elliot Paul. Second Homer Evans mystery-comedy. Theft at the Louvre involves sleuth in hilarious, madcap caper. "A knockout."—Books. 336pp. 5⅜ × 8½.   25185-3 Pa. $5.95

FLATLAND, E. A. Abbott. Intriguing and enormously popular science-fiction classic explores the complexities of trying to survive as a two-dimensional being in a three-dimensional world. Amusingly illustrated by the author. 16 illustrations. 103pp. 5⅜ × 8½.   20001-9 Pa. $2.25

THE HISTORY OF THE LEWIS AND CLARK EXPEDITION, Meriwether Lewis and William Clark, edited by Elliott Coues. Classic edition of Lewis and Clark's day-by-day journals that later became the basis for U.S. claims to Oregon and the West. Accurate and invaluable geographical, botanical, biological, meteorological and anthropological material. Total of 1,508pp. 5⅜ × 8½.
21268-8, 21269-6, 21270-X Pa. Three-vol. set $25.50

LANGUAGE, TRUTH AND LOGIC, Alfred J. Ayer. Famous, clear introduction to Vienna, Cambridge schools of Logical Positivism. Role of philosophy, elimination of metaphysics, nature of analysis, etc. 160pp. 5⅜ × 8½. (Available in U.S. and Canada only)   20010-8 Pa. $2.95

MATHEMATICS FOR THE NONMATHEMATICIAN, Morris Kline. Detailed, college-level treatment of mathematics in cultural and historical context, with numerous exercises. For liberal arts students. Preface. Recommended Reading Lists. Tables. Index. Numerous black-and-white figures. xvi + 641pp. 5⅜ × 8½.
24823-2 Pa. $11.95

28 SCIENCE FICTION STORIES, H. G. Wells. Novels, *Star Begotten* and *Men Like Gods*, plus 26 short stories: "Empire of the Ants," "A Story of the Stone Age," "The Stolen Bacillus," "In the Abyss," etc. 915pp. 5⅜ × 8½. (Available in U.S. only)
20265-8 Cloth. $10.95

HANDBOOK OF PICTORIAL SYMBOLS, Rudolph Modley. 3,250 signs and symbols, many systems in full; official or heavy commercial use. Arranged by subject. Most in Pictorial Archive series. 143pp. 8⅜ × 11.   23357-X Pa. $5.95

INCIDENTS OF TRAVEL IN YUCATAN, John L. Stephens. Classic (1843) exploration of jungles of Yucatan, looking for evidences of Maya civilization. Travel adventures, Mexican and Indian culture, etc. Total of 669pp. 5⅜ × 8½.
20926-1, 20927-X Pa., Two-vol. set $9.90

DEGAS: An Intimate Portrait, Ambroise Vollard. Charming, anecdotal memoir by famous art dealer of one of the greatest 19th-century French painters. 14 black-and-white illustrations. Introduction by Harold L. Van Doren. 96pp. 5⅜ × 8½.
25131-4 Pa. $3.95

PERSONAL NARRATIVE OF A PILGRIMAGE TO ALMANDINAH AND MECCAH, Richard Burton. Great travel classic by remarkably colorful personality. Burton, disguised as a Moroccan, visited sacred shrines of Islam, narrowly escaping death. 47 illustrations. 959pp. 5⅜ × 8½. 21217-3, 21218-1 Pa., Two-vol. set $17.90

PHRASE AND WORD ORIGINS, A. H. Holt. Entertaining, reliable, modern study of more than 1,200 colorful words, phrases, origins and histories. Much unexpected information. 254pp. 5⅜ × 8½. 20758-7 Pa. $5.95

THE RED THUMB MARK, R. Austin Freeman. In this first Dr. Thorndyke case, the great scientific detective draws fascinating conclusions from the nature of a single fingerprint. Exciting story, authentic science. 320pp. 5⅜ × 8½. (Available in U.S. only) 25210-8 Pa. $5.95

AN EGYPTIAN HIEROGLYPHIC DICTIONARY, E. A. Wallis Budge. Monumental work containing about 25,000 words or terms that occur in texts ranging from 3000 B.C. to 600 A.D. Each entry consists of a transliteration of the word, the word in hieroglyphs, and the meaning in English. 1,314pp. 6⅜ × 10. 23615-3, 23616-1 Pa., Two-vol. set $27.90

THE COMPLEAT STRATEGYST: Being a Primer on the Theory of Games of Strategy, J. D. Williams. Highly entertaining classic describes, with many illustrated examples, how to select best strategies in conflict situations. Prefaces. Appendices. xvi + 268pp. 5⅜ × 8½. 25101-2 Pa. $5.95

THE ROAD TO OZ, L. Frank Baum. Dorothy meets the Shaggy Man, little Button-Bright and the Rainbow's beautiful daughter in this delightful trip to the magical Land of Oz. 272pp. 5⅜ × 8. 25208-6 Pa. $4.95

POINT AND LINE TO PLANE, Wassily Kandinsky. Seminal exposition of role of point, line, other elements in non-objective painting. Essential to understanding 20th-century art. 127 illustrations. 192pp. 6½ × 9¼. 23808-3 Pa. $4.50

LADY ANNA, Anthony Trollope. Moving chronicle of Countess Lovel's bitter struggle to win for herself and daughter Anna their rightful rank and fortune—perhaps at cost of sanity itself. 384pp. 5⅜ × 8½. 24669-8 Pa. $6.95

EGYPTIAN MAGIC, E. A. Wallis Budge. Sums up all that is known about magic in Ancient Egypt: the role of magic in controlling the gods, powerful amulets that warded off evil spirits, scarabs of immortality, use of wax images, formulas and spells, the secret name, much more. 253pp. 5⅜ × 8½. 22681-6 Pa. $4.50

THE DANCE OF SIVA, Ananda Coomaraswamy. Preeminent authority unfolds the vast metaphysic of India: the revelation of her art, conception of the universe, social organization, etc. 27 reproductions of art masterpieces. 192pp. 5⅜ × 8½.
24817-8 Pa. $5.95

CHRISTMAS CUSTOMS AND TRADITIONS, Clement A. Miles. Origin, evolution, significance of religious, secular practices. Caroling, gifts, yule logs, much more. Full, scholarly yet fascinating; non-sectarian. 400pp. 5⅜ × 8½.
23354-5 Pa. $6.50

THE HUMAN FIGURE IN MOTION, Eadweard Muybridge. More than 4,500 stopped-action photos, in action series, showing undraped men, women, children jumping, lying down, throwing, sitting, wrestling, carrying, etc. 390pp. 7⅞ × 10⅝.
20204-6 Cloth. $19.95

THE MAN WHO WAS THURSDAY, Gilbert Keith Chesterton. Witty, fast-paced novel about a club of anarchists in turn-of-the-century London. Brilliant social, religious, philosophical speculations. 128pp. 5⅜ × 8½. 25121-7 Pa. $3.95

A CEZANNE SKETCHBOOK: Figures, Portraits, Landscapes and Still Lifes, Paul Cezanne. Great artist experiments with tonal effects, light, mass, other qualities in over 100 drawings. A revealing view of developing master painter, precursor of Cubism. 102 black-and-white illustrations. 144pp. 8¾ × 6⅜. 24790-2 Pa. $5.95

AN ENCYCLOPEDIA OF BATTLES: Accounts of Over 1,560 Battles from 1479 B.C. to the Present, David Eggenberger. Presents essential details of every major battle in recorded history, from the first battle of Megiddo in 1479 B.C. to Grenada in 1984. List of Battle Maps. New Appendix covering the years 1967–1984. Index. 99 illustrations. 544pp. 6½ × 9¼. 24913-1 Pa. $14.95

AN ETYMOLOGICAL DICTIONARY OF MODERN ENGLISH, Ernest Weekley. Richest, fullest work, by foremost British lexicographer. Detailed word histories. Inexhaustible. Total of 856pp. 6½ × 9¼.
21873-2, 21874-0 Pa., Two-vol. set $17.00

WEBSTER'S AMERICAN MILITARY BIOGRAPHIES, edited by Robert McHenry. Over 1,000 figures who shaped 3 centuries of American military history. Detailed biographies of Nathan Hale, Douglas MacArthur, Mary Hallaren, others. Chronologies of engagements, more. Introduction. Addenda. 1,033 entries in alphabetical order. xi + 548pp. 6½ × 9¼. (Available in U.S. only)
24758-9 Pa. $11.95

LIFE IN ANCIENT EGYPT, Adolf Erman. Detailed older account, with much not in more recent books: domestic life, religion, magic, medicine, commerce, and whatever else needed for complete picture. Many illustrations. 597pp. 5⅜ × 8½.
22632-8 Pa. $8.95

HISTORIC COSTUME IN PICTURES, Braun & Schneider. Over 1,450 costumed figures shown, covering a wide variety of peoples: kings, emperors, nobles, priests, servants, soldiers, scholars, townsfolk, peasants, merchants, courtiers, cavaliers, and more. 256pp. 8⅜ × 11¼. 23150-X Pa. $7.95

THE NOTEBOOKS OF LEONARDO DA VINCI, edited by J. P. Richter. Extracts from manuscripts reveal great genius; on painting, sculpture, anatomy, sciences, geography, etc. Both Italian and English. 186 ms. pages reproduced, plus 500 additional drawings, including studies for *Last Supper, Sforza* monument, etc. 860pp. 7⅞ × 10¾. (Available in U.S. only) 22572-0, 22573-9 Pa., Two-vol. set $25.90

THE ART NOUVEAU STYLE BOOK OF ALPHONSE MUCHA: All 72 Plates from "Documents Decoratifs" in Original Color, Alphonse Mucha. Rare copyright-free design portfolio by high priest of Art Nouveau. Jewelry, wallpaper, stained glass, furniture, figure studies, plant and animal motifs, etc. Only complete one-volume edition. 80pp. 9⅜ × 12¼. 24044-4 Pa. $8.95

ANIMALS: 1,419 COPYRIGHT-FREE ILLUSTRATIONS OF MAMMALS, BIRDS, FISH, INSECTS, ETC., edited by Jim Harter. Clear wood engravings present, in extremely lifelike poses, over 1,000 species of animals. One of the most extensive pictorial sourcebooks of its kind. Captions. Index. 284pp. 9 × 12.
23766-4 Pa. $9.95

OBELISTS FLY HIGH, C. Daly King. Masterpiece of American detective fiction, long out of print, involves murder on a 1935 transcontinental flight—"a very thrilling story"—NY Times. Unabridged and unaltered republication of the edition published by William Collins Sons & Co. Ltd., London, 1935. 288pp. 5⅜ × 8½. (Available in U.S. only) 25036-9 Pa. $4.95

VICTORIAN AND EDWARDIAN FASHION: A Photographic Survey, Alison Gernsheim. First fashion history completely illustrated by contemporary photographs. Full text plus 235 photos, 1840–1914, in which many celebrities appear. 240pp. 6½ × 9¼. 24205-6 Pa. $6.00

THE ART OF THE FRENCH ILLUSTRATED BOOK, 1700–1914, Gordon N. Ray. Over 630 superb book illustrations by Fragonard, Delacroix, Daumier, Doré, Grandville, Manet, Mucha, Steinlen, Toulouse-Lautrec and many others. Preface. Introduction. 633 halftones. Indices of artists, authors & titles, binders and provenances. Appendices. Bibliography. 608pp. 8⅜ × 11¼. 25086-5 Pa. $24.95

THE WONDERFUL WIZARD OF OZ, L. Frank Baum. Facsimile in full color of America's finest children's classic. 143 illustrations by W. W. Denslow. 267pp. 5⅜ × 8½. 20691-2 Pa. $5.95

FRONTIERS OF MODERN PHYSICS: New Perspectives on Cosmology, Relativity, Black Holes and Extraterrestrial Intelligence, Tony Rothman, et al. For the intelligent layman. Subjects include: cosmological models of the universe; black holes; the neutrino; the search for extraterrestrial intelligence. Introduction. 46 black-and-white illustrations. 192pp. 5⅜ × 8½. 24587-X Pa. $6.95

THE FRIENDLY STARS, Martha Evans Martin & Donald Howard Menzel. Classic text marshalls the stars together in an engaging, non-technical survey, presenting them as sources of beauty in night sky. 23 illustrations. Foreword. 2 star charts. Index. 147pp. 5⅜ × 8½. 21099-5 Pa. $3.50

FADS AND FALLACIES IN THE NAME OF SCIENCE, Martin Gardner. Fair, witty appraisal of cranks, quacks, and quackeries of science and pseudoscience: hollow earth, Velikovsky, orgone energy, Dianetics, flying saucers, Bridey Murphy, food and medical fads, etc. Revised, expanded In the Name of Science. "A very able and even-tempered presentation."—The New Yorker. 363pp. 5⅜ × 8.
20394-8 Pa. $6.50

ANCIENT EGYPT: ITS CULTURE AND HISTORY, J. E Manchip White. From pre-dynastics through Ptolemies: society, history, political structure, religion, daily life, literature, cultural heritage. 48 plates. 217pp. 5⅜ × 8½. 22548-8 Pa. $4.95

SIR HARRY HOTSPUR OF HUMBLETHWAITE, Anthony Trollope. Incisive, unconventional psychological study of a conflict between a wealthy baronet, his idealistic daughter, and their scapegrace cousin. The 1870 novel in its first inexpensive edition in years. 250pp. 5⅜ × 8½. 24953-0 Pa. $5.95

LASERS AND HOLOGRAPHY, Winston E. Kock. Sound introduction to burgeoning field, expanded (1981) for second edition. Wave patterns, coherence, lasers, diffraction, zone plates, properties of holograms, recent advances. 84 illustrations. 160pp. 5⅜ × 8¼. (Except in United Kingdom) 24041-X Pa. $3.50

INTRODUCTION TO ARTIFICIAL INTELLIGENCE: SECOND, EN-LARGED EDITION, Philip C. Jackson, Jr. Comprehensive survey of artificial intelligence—the study of how machines (computers) can be made to act intelligently. Includes introductory and advanced material. Extensive notes updating the main text. 132 black-and-white illustrations. 512pp. 5⅜ × 8½. 24864-X Pa. $8.95

HISTORY OF INDIAN AND INDONESIAN ART, Ananda K. Coomaraswamy. Over 400 illustrations illuminate classic study of Indian art from earliest Harappa finds to early 20th century. Provides philosophical, religious and social insights. 304pp. 6⅛ × 9⅜. 25005-9 Pa. $8.95

THE GOLEM, Gustav Meyrink. Most famous supernatural novel in modern European literature, set in Ghetto of Old Prague around 1890. Compelling story of mystical experiences, strange transformations, profound terror. 13 black-and-white illustrations. 224pp. 5⅜ × 8½. (Available in U.S. only) 25025-3 Pa. $5.95

ARMADALE, Wilkie Collins. Third great mystery novel by the author of *The Woman in White* and *The Moonstone*. Original magazine version with 40 illustrations. 597pp. 5⅜ × 8½. 23429-0 Pa. $9.95

PICTORIAL ENCYCLOPEDIA OF HISTORIC ARCHITECTURAL PLANS, DETAILS AND ELEMENTS: With 1,880 Line Drawings of Arches, Domes, Doorways, Facades, Gables, Windows, etc., John Theodore Haneman. Sourcebook of inspiration for architects, designers, others. Bibliography. Captions. 141pp. 9 × 12. 24605-1 Pa. $6.95

BENCHLEY LOST AND FOUND, Robert Benchley. Finest humor from early 30's, about pet peeves, child psychologists, post office and others. Mostly unavailable elsewhere. 73 illustrations by Peter Arno and others. 183pp. 5⅜ × 8½. 22410-4 Pa. $3.95

ERTÉ GRAPHICS, Erté. Collection of striking color graphics: *Seasons, Alphabet, Numerals, Aces* and *Precious Stones*. 50 plates, including 4 on covers. 48pp. 9⅜ × 12¼. 23580-7 Pa. $6.95

THE JOURNAL OF HENRY D. THOREAU, edited by Bradford Torrey, F. H. Allen. Complete reprinting of 14 volumes, 1837–61, over two million words; the sourcebooks for *Walden*, etc. Definitive. All original sketches, plus 75 photographs. 1,804pp. 8½ × 12¼. 20312-3, 20313-1 Cloth., Two-vol. set $80.00

CASTLES: THEIR CONSTRUCTION AND HISTORY, Sidney Toy. Traces castle development from ancient roots. Nearly 200 photographs and drawings illustrate moats, keeps, baileys, many other features. Caernarvon, Dover Castles, Hadrian's Wall, Tower of London, dozens more. 256pp. 5⅜ × 8¼. 24898-4 Pa. $5.95

AMERICAN CLIPPER SHIPS: 1833–1858, Octavius T. Howe & Frederick C. Matthews. Fully-illustrated, encyclopedic review of 352 clipper ships from the period of America's greatest maritime supremacy. Introduction. 109 halftones. 5 black-and-white line illustrations. Index. Total of 928pp. 5⅜ × 8½.
25115-2, 25116-0 Pa., Two-vol. set $17.90

TOWARDS A NEW ARCHITECTURE, Le Corbusier. Pioneering manifesto by great architect, near legendary founder of "International School." Technical and aesthetic theories, views on industry, economics, relation of form to function, "mass-production spirit," much more. Profusely illustrated. Unabridged translation of 13th French edition. Introduction by Frederick Etchells. 320pp. 6⅛ × 9¼. (Available in U.S. only)
25023-7 Pa. $8.95

THE BOOK OF KELLS, edited by Blanche Cirker. Inexpensive collection of 32 full-color, full-page plates from the greatest illuminated manuscript of the Middle Ages, painstakingly reproduced from rare facsimile edition. Publisher's Note. Captions. 32pp. 9⅜ × 12¼.
24345-1 Pa. $4.95

BEST SCIENCE FICTION STORIES OF H. G. WELLS, H. G. Wells. Full novel *The Invisible Man,* plus 17 short stories: "The Crystal Egg," "Aepyornis Island," "The Strange Orchid," etc. 303pp. 5⅜ × 8½. (Available in U.S. only)
21531-8 Pa. $4.95

AMERICAN SAILING SHIPS: Their Plans and History, Charles G. Davis. Photos, construction details of schooners, frigates, clippers, other sailcraft of 18th to early 20th centuries—plus entertaining discourse on design, rigging, nautical lore, much more. 137 black-and-white illustrations. 240pp. 6⅛ × 9¼.
24658-2 Pa. $5.95

ENTERTAINING MATHEMATICAL PUZZLES, Martin Gardner. Selection of author's favorite conundrums involving arithmetic, money, speed, etc., with lively commentary. Complete solutions. 112pp. 5⅜ × 8½. 25211-6 Pa. $2.95

THE WILL TO BELIEVE, HUMAN IMMORTALITY, William James. Two books bound together. Effect of irrational on logical, and arguments for human immortality. 402pp. 5⅜ × 8½. 20291-7 Pa. $7.50

THE HAUNTED MONASTERY and THE CHINESE MAZE MURDERS, Robert Van Gulik. 2 full novels by Van Gulik continue adventures of Judge Dee and his companions. An evil Taoist monastery, seemingly supernatural events; overgrown topiary maze that hides strange crimes. Set in 7th-century China. 27 illustrations. 328pp. 5⅜ × 8½. 23502-5 Pa. $5.95

CELEBRATED CASES OF JUDGE DEE (DEE GOONG AN), translated by Robert Van Gulik. Authentic 18th-century Chinese detective novel; Dee and associates solve three interlocked cases. Led to Van Gulik's own stories with same characters. Extensive introduction. 9 illustrations. 237pp. 5⅜ × 8½.
23337-5 Pa. $4.95

Prices subject to change without notice.
Available at your book dealer or write for free catalog to Dept. GI, Dover Publications, Inc., 31 East 2nd St., Mineola, N.Y. 11501. Dover publishes more than 175 books each year on science, elementary and advanced mathematics, biology, music, art, literary history, social sciences and other areas.